SIEGFRIED'S JOURNEY
1916–1920

also by Siegfried Sassoon

★

MEMOIRS OF A FOX-HUNTING MAN
MEMOIRS OF AN INFANTRY OFFICER
SHERSTON'S PROGRESS
THE OLD CENTURY
THE WEALD OF YOUTH

SIEGFRIED SASSOON
(from the portrait by Glyn Philpot, R.A.)

SIEGFRIED'S JOURNEY
1916-1920

by

SIEGFRIED SASSOON

FABER AND FABER
AND THE BOOK SOCIETY

THIS EDITION ISSUED ON FIRST PUBLICATION
BY THE BOOK SOCIETY LTD. IN ASSOCIATION
WITH FABER AND FABER LIMITED
DECEMBER 1945

TO
RALPH HODGSON

ALL RIGHTS RESERVED
PRINTED IN GREAT BRITAIN
BY PURNELL AND SONS LTD.
PAULTON (SOMERSET) AND LONDON

I

At the beginning of August 1916 I found myself deposited at No. 3 General Service Hospital, which was in Somerville College, Oxford. My nine months in France with a Regular Battalion in the famous Seventh Division had been ended by some sort of gastric fever, just severe enough to get me sent across to England. Much though I had regretted forsaking my battalion, it was impossible not to feel intensely thankful that I was absolved from taking any further part in the Battle of the Somme, which had provided me with quite an adequate dose of war experience. I knew that I could have been fit to go back to my company in a month; but fate had been kind to me, and I felt that I had earned a holiday. To be lying in a little white-walled room, looking through the open window on to a College lawn, was for the first few days very much like Paradise. I happen to remember that I was reading *Evelina*, which anyhow proves that I had chosen the right sort of reading for my escapeful circumstances. A lively glimpse of the fashionable world in the time of George III took one well away from thoughts of the Fricourt trenches and the war to end war which appeared likely to go on indefinitely.

Better still, however, was the assurance that I should now be able to work off some of the poetry bottled up in me, which I should now have a chance to pour out in tranquil surroundings. At the Front I had managed to keep my mind alive under difficulties, and had done some writing when we were away from the line. But it wasn't easy to be a poet and a platoon commander at the same time, and I was overflowing with stored-up impressions and emotional reactions to the extraordinary things I had observed and undergone.

I got off the mark at once with some lines called *Stretcher-Case* in which I used my journey to Oxford in the Red Cross train for an objective and mildly satirical description of a wounded soldier's sensations. Recovering consciousness, he 'remembered that his name was Brown', and gazed with thanksgiving on the railwayside advertisements of 'Lung Tonic, Mustard, Liver Pills, and Beer'.

Siegfried's Journey, 1916–1920

After a week in hospital I was well enough to be allowed out for an hour or two after lunch. It was pleasant to stroll along to the bookshops or sit in the picture galleries of the Ashmolean, but I wanted someone to talk to, and so far nobody had been to see me. There weren't many people whom I could expect to see, and most of them were too busy to be able to get to Oxford, so I was very glad when my friend Robbie Ross telegraphed from London that he was coming down for an afternoon. I had first met him at the Gosses' in 1915, and although I had not seen him often since then I had written to him frequently while at the Front. When on leave in the previous February and June I had spent a few evenings with him. From the first I had found him one of the most attractive and amusing men I had ever met, and his spontaneous liking for me had been combined with an active interest in my poetic career.

Although seventeen years my senior, his intuitively sympathetic understanding of youth made him seem a benevolent and impulsive bachelor uncle with whom one could feel on easy terms of equality, while consenting to be guided by his astute and experienced advice.

Anyhow there he was, coming across the college lawn where I had been awaiting him under a tree—a small man in a light grey suit, wearing his soft black hat at a jaunty angle and carrying the ebony stick which somehow suggested his profession of art critic. My heart went out to his careworn face, lit up by pleasure at seeing me home from the war in an undamaged condition. My heart went out to him, as it always did, and as it does now; for he was one whose memory lives on through his gaiety and courage and the friendship which never failed those who benefited by it.

Expecting to find me a recumbent invalid, he had been, he explained, ready with his best bedside manner. As it was, my more than convalescent condition liberated us from the college lawn, where there were a good many wounded officers on beds or in wheeled chairs. So, after monopolizing the conversation for about ten minutes with a torrent of talk about myself, I suggested that we ought to go somewhere more amusing. Where to go on such a warm afternoon might have been a little difficult to decide, but I —as afterwards transpired—solved the problem by saying, 'Oh,

6

by the way, who is Lady Ottoline Morrell?'—a query which
caused him to exclaim—with that uplifting of the eyes which expressed astonished amusement—'How refreshing of you not to
know! But why do you ask?' I explained that I had received a
letter from her about six months before, adding that what had
made me ask about her was that she had written from an address
near Oxford. I went on to give him fuller details in some such
words as these. 'You remember that poem I wrote in January and
sent to Gosse in a letter, and how he managed to get it into *The
Times* with my initials underneath and "by a private soldier at
the Front" at the top. . . . Well, this Lady Ottoline wrote me
rather a nice high-flown letter about it, and wanted to know what
else I'd written. So when I was on leave I sent her my last Chis-
wick Press pamphlet and got another epistle, more enthusiastic
than ever.' I was quite taken aback when he told me that my unknown correspondent was 'frightfully well known in the literary
and artistic world', apart from being a half-sister of the Duke of
Portland and the wife of a Liberal M.P. who had made himself
rather conspicuous by taking an extreme pacifist line about the
War. My imagination had pictured her as a romantic-minded
young lady living in the depths of the country, and this notion
had been supported not only by her handwriting—which was an
arabesque of dots and flourishes—but by the way she expressed
herself. I had received the letter when we were starting on a
three days' march from rest billets up to the Somme trenches, and
Lady Ottoline's large sheet of beautiful hand-made notepaper had
seemed like something from another world. And for the time
being the lumbering organization of the battalion transport, for
which I was temporarily responsible, had allowed me little opportunity for meditating on the fact that someone in a manor house
in England had been thrilled by my poem in *The Times*, had
found in it 'that infinite quality which haunts one', and was telling me that 'it was such a delight to find—in these dark prison-
like days—a sympathetic desire to fly out beyond into the beauty
and colour and freedom that one so longs for'. 'It was only
through Poetry and wild days in the country that one could
escape,' she concluded. While helping to keep the mules and
draught horses on their legs, it hadn't occurred to me that I

should ever meet her, and I decided that she was a bit too intense.
The poem itself was a much more conventional and unrealistic
production than most of my subsequent efforts as a war poet, and
it must be admitted that I had rather 'asked for it' from my soul-
ful admirer by announcing in my invocation 'To Victory' that I
wanted 'to fill my gaze with blue and silver' and longed for 'hours
that move like a glitter of dancers'—sentiments which had found
no gratification while I was serving with the Seventh Division on
the Somme. Meanwhile Robbie, after briefly explaining that he
had known Lady Ottoline for a good many years and that she was
quite delightful, hastened to the telephone with the intention of
suggesting that he should bring me to see her that afternoon.
Undeterred by finding that she wasn't in the telephone directory,
he assumed that she was almost certain to be at home, and before
long we had disturbed the siesta of a solitary taxi-driver by the
Martyrs' Memorial in St. Giles's and were on our way out to
Garsington. During the six-mile drive we had so much to talk
about that he found no time to tell me what sort of a person we
were going to see. He did however say that the Morrells lived in
an enchanting house, and I fully agreed with him when we drew
up outside the tall iron gates and stood for a moment in the shadow of some lofty elms. Within the gates was a green forecourt, walled on either side by high yew hedges. Across the court a
paved path led to the manor house. Viewed in the buzzing mid-
afternoon stillness, the severe aloofness of the centuried grey
stone front made our rattling taxi-cab seem a vulgar intrusion.
Robbie remarked that he always felt an impostor when he arrived
at a place like this. My only words for it were the obvious ones—
'an absolute dream of beauty'. It was surely no wonder that Lady
Ottoline felt romantic and poetical in such surroundings! Having
discreetly jangled the bell, we were greeted by distant barkings,
and when the ancient oak door was opened an officious little pug
bustled out to give us a noisy greeting. The maid, who had the air
of being 'an old friend of the family', seemed glad to see 'Mr.
Ross', and informed us that her ladyship was out in the studio.
Thither she conducted us, and we found ourselves at the foot of a
ladder leading to a sort of trap-door, for the studio was in a barn-
like outbuilding, the lower part of which was used for storing

garden implements. Robbie having hailed Lady Ottoline by name, he was answered in tones of pleased surprise and our hostess came down to us. Let me say at once that for more than twenty years afterwards Lady Ottoline was one of my best friends. I have been indebted to her for innumerable acts of generosity and affection. But it must be confessed that my first view of her was somewhat disconcerting. Always original in her style of dress—which was often extremely beautiful—she happened on this occasion to be wearing voluminous pale-pink Turkish trousers; and these garments, as she descended the ladder backwards, were—unavoidably—the first part of her that I beheld. She was very tall, so it seemed a long time before her head became visible. I have never been very forthcoming about staring people full in the face, and during my first visit to Garsington I gave hers no more than a few shy glances, which were, however, enough to convince me that I had seldom seen anyone quite so extraordinary. In fact I must admit that it wasn't until about a year later that I began to feel at all comfortable with her. The reason for this was that in spite of her being so consistently nice to me I was embarrassed by her appearance, which seemed to have been artificially imposed on the rest of her personality. She had immense dignity and distinction, and could also be charmingly gay and unaffected; she drew me out sympathetically and made me feel that my ideas and emotions were intensely interesting and important to her. Why then did she insist on trying to make her fine features suggest that she was a sort of modern Messalina? In later years she allowed herself to become a beautiful woman again, but at that period the paint and powder and purple hair were a definite impediment to my understanding and appreciation of her splendid qualities. I wasn't accustomed to that sort of thing, and it made me nervous and prone to be priggishly critical of her. It would have made all the difference to me if she had managed to look a bit more like Rossetti's Blessed Damozel.

She now invited us to follow her up the ladder to the studio. We had arrived while she was sitting for her portrait, and this, I supposed, was the explanation of her being so oddly dressed. The young lady who was engaged on the almost life-size painting also took a bit of getting used to. She had bobbed hair which hung over

9

her eyes, and was wearing corduroy trousers—a thing I hadn't seen any young lady do before—and this one actually turned out to be an Honourable! The portrait suggested that she was still feeling her way towards knowing how to do it—so much so that she had found it necessary to add two strips of canvas to its original longitude. Did Lady Ottoline really look such a basilisk as this laboriously contrived picture, I wondered. Robbie did his best to proffer the kindly criticism of an expert, while the artist stared speechlessly at him through hanks of brown hair. Lady Ottoline's only comment was that she really didn't know how they would get it down the ladder if it kept on growing. Unable to resist making one of his 'mots', Robbie remarked that anyhow it wasn't every portrait that went into a second addition. The witticism evoked no response from the artist, whose odd air of remoteness was, as I soon discovered, due to deafness.

After that we all went out into the garden, and I found myself pacing to and fro with Lady Ottoline on a grass walk above the swimming pool, which was shadowed by an enormous ilex. Bemused with shyness I replied to her questions about my recent battle experiences, what I thought about the war, and whether I had written any more poetry lately. She did it in a gracious and sympathetic way, making me feel that I was a bit of a hero and that my visit was an event of exceptional significance for her. And I was able to think to myself—as we halted under the ilex to admire the charming view—that my present surroundings really were the greatest possible contrast to the trees I had been among about a month before—those trees which harboured German snipers. Somehow I succeeded in remarking that the thought of ever being in such a place as this again had been almost unbelievable when I was mixed up in the Somme attacks. I might have added that I had seldom been in such a perfect place before, and that to be hobnobbing about my poetry—however clumsily —with the sister of a Derby-winning Duke was one of the last things I had ever expected to do. Lady Ottoline received my remark with evident emotion. But she passed it off by speaking of Robbie and of how much she admired his chivalrous character. I began to feel that I liked her, and she put me still more at my ease by telling me how he had once jumped into the swimming-pool with all his clothes on, to rescue a girl who had decided that she was drowning in four feet of water. He had come out from Sutton Courtenay with Mr. Asquith, and some sort of outdoor fête for the villagers had happened to be in progress. 'He's always jumping into the water to pull people out, isn't he?' she said, with that curious slow enunciation which seemed to come from half-closed lips.

During tea he kept the conversation going with his usual gay adroitness, while I made intermittent efforts to communicate with the deaf young lady, who had an auxiliary apparatus attached to her. Soon afterwards we departed, as he had to catch a train to London. On the way back to the hospital he informed me that I had been a huge success, and urged me to be very nice to Lady Ottoline as she could be of the greatest help to me when my poems were published. This I was fully prepared to do, since I had taken a liking to her, and had also been rather provincially impressed by the whole thing. 'But you really must try not to look so like a shy and offended deer-hound next time you are talking to her,' he remarked. I excused myself by saying that the Turkish trousers had been a bit too much for me, and that I hoped she wouldn't wear them when she came into Oxford to go round the Ashmolean Museum with me, as had been arranged. He assured me that it was much more probable that she would be wearing brown velvet and a Gainsborough hat. 'Her sensibilities,' he explained, 'are over-elaborate and not always sensible, but she has exquisite taste in decoration and a genuine flair for spotting original artists.' He added that he himself was deeply indebted to her generous friendship in his times of trouble.

*   *   *

By the middle of the month it had become obvious that there was nothing wrong with my health, and I was waiting for the doctor to give me a permit to depart on sick leave. Most of my afternoons were spent in a canoe, and a person who was able to paddle himself as far as Water Eaton on the war-time weed-choked Cherwell could scarcely claim to be an invalid. I was even allowed a whole day's absence from the hospital, for the special purpose of going to see my Uncle Hamo, who was taking a holiday from sculpture at Burford. It was the sort of expedition which would have been enjoyable at any time, but for one who was liberated from the strain of sixteen months' military service— more than half of it at the front—what could be better than a dilatory train journey from Oxford to Shipton on a hot August day, followed by a drive in the Burford bus drawn by a sleepy old horse and steered by one of the oldest inhabitants, with one's Uncle Hamo waiting at the Bull Inn to be quietly proud of one for having done well enough to acquire a Military Cross? Burford itself was like a welcome home from the war as I came to it through the ripened harvest landscape, and crossed the stone bridge over the little Windrush at the lower end of the steep street of grey houses. It was the first time I had fully realized what it meant to be well away from the war, and its serenity seemed well worth preserving by such obscure personal efforts as one had managed to make. The tall poles of the wireless station on some high ground a few miles away were the only visible sign of the changes which had come over the world since Uncle Hamo was elected a Royal Academician. I had been about two years old then. Meanwhile I found him looking very much the countryman that he was by nature, sunburnt from the harvesting work he had been doing, proud of having already earned twenty-five shillings by piling corn-stooks on the local uplands, and equally pleased at having caught a half-pound trout in the Windrush. To be with him was a tranquillizing experience. His presence—for the time being—lent me a sense of proportion about the war and the mental disturbances which my grim contact with it had aroused in me. Courage, thoroughness, and a becoming reticence in the performance of duty were the qualities he valued, and I found it a relief to be walking about Burford with him in the role of a modest and undemonstrative nephew who had done quite decently at the Front. Later on in the war he was forced to disagree with my point of view, though he tried to tolerate it as a mere exhibition of youthful rebelliousness. But on that August afternoon I was mainly conscious of his rather touching satisfaction in showing me to a few of his local acquaintances. I remember that we conversed with the Burford saddler, a man of fine full-flavoured appearance and demeanour who might—as my uncle remarked afterwards—have figured in one of Hardy's novels. Since the war began I had taken to reading Hardy and he was now my main admiration among living writers, so I was greatly impressed when Uncle Hamo told me that he had been trying to persuade him to come to the Bull Inn for a few days. I knew that Hardy had sat to him for a bust in 1915, but I had not realized that they had known one another for more than thirty years, and I was still young enough to find it difficult to connect one of my near relatives with a writer whom I had independently 'discovered' and placed on a pinnacle. It seemed almost incredible that—after carrying a couple of the Wessex novels about with me during the Somme battle—I might have arrived at Burford to spend an afternoon in the presence of the great man himself! As it was, Uncle Hamo spoke of Hardy in a reserved and almost reverential way, but I learnt that he and my Aunt Agatha had stayed at Max Gate and had done quite a lot of bicycling in Dorset with Hardy. (Years afterwards, I discovered that he had my aunt's face in mind when describing 'Tess'.)

Meanwhile we were progressing comfortably along an afternoon of dozy sunshine. Burford was a wonderfully peaceful place. I had been shown the noble monuments in the church and had followed my uncle's architectural eye over the spandrelled doorways and mullioned windows of several quaint old houses. I was now being taken a little way up the hill to have tea with Mr. Horniman at the Priory. Mr. Horniman was a quietly distinguished man who had travelled a good deal and had been a member of Parliament. His lovely old house was museum-like in its accumulation of beautiful and interesting objects, which included what must have been an almost unique collection of clocks. While we were solemnly inspecting an elaborately-constructed water-clock, dated 1635, Mr. Horniman remarked that it was a perfect piece of mechanism, adding that nothing was more satisfactory than a thing well and truly accomplished. 'Yes. My nephew found that when he won his Cross,' my uncle replied in his quiet voice—rather irrelevantly, perhaps, but with a simple pride and generosity which it moves me to record. But what struck me at the time was a thought of the curious incongruity between this wonderful old water-clock and its ideally civilized surroundings, and the memory of myself crawling about in a mine-crater to bring in wounded men after a raid on the German trenches less than three months ago. The contrast between the war the infantry knew and having tea with Mr. Horniman—could the two things be mentally digested and rationalized by a kindly pat on the back from one's elders?

Mr. Horniman was showing me, with charming courtesy, an exquisite lacquer screen which he had bought in China. It was the best he could do for me, but—much though I appreciated its refinements in reds and greens—it couldn't alter the fact that I should be back in the trenches before I was many months older. The men I had been serving with were there now, and what they were going through didn't bear thinking about. Water-clocks dated 1635 were no use to them at zero hour of an attack. . . .

While the uncommunicative old busman was driving me to the station we passed what I assumed to be Uncle Hamo's harvest field. The corn-stooks had a somewhat amateurish look and a good few of them had collapsed. The widespread evening landscape seemed strangely quiet when one compared it with the gun-rumbled regions where I'd spent most of the summer. One listened, almost expecting to hear the muffled bang of a big gun somewhere along the horizon. At the station my train was a long time coming. I sat watching the remains of sunset, tranquil below a dove-grey cope of cloud. The day had been ideally pleasant; but there were vague stirrings of perplexity in my mind. How had Uncle Hamo and Mr. Horniman managed, I wondered, to make the war seem so different from what it really was? It wasn't possible to imagine oneself even hinting to them, that the Somme Battle was—to put it mildly—an inhuman and beastly business. One had to behave nicely about it to them, keeping up a polite pretence that to have taken part in it was a glorious and acceptable adventure. They must know what it was costing in lives of course; the casualty lists had told them that. But when Uncle Hamo's well-meant remark had reminded me of our battalion raid in the Fricourt sector I had felt that no explanation of mine could ever reach my elders—that they weren't capable of wanting to know the truth. Their attitude was to insist that it was splendid to be in the front-line. So it was—if one came out of it safely. But I resented their patriotic suppression of those aspects of war which never got into the newspapers. One didn't feel like that with Robbie Ross, who was almost recklessly outspoken about the mistakes and shortcomings of our military mandarins. He saw the thing from the front-line soldier's point of view and refused to turn his back on the ugly realities. He had encouraged me to write candidly about it; and I began to feel that, although I didn't want to upset Uncle Hamo, I should like to give some of the comfortable civilians a few shocks, even if they were to accuse me of being wrong-headed and ungentlemanly. Needless to say, a good many of them did.

II

By the last week of August I was back at Weirleigh, having been awarded a provisional period of sick leave which would take me to the beginning of October. I was moderately hopeful that my leave might then be extended for another month, but four weeks out of uniform were good enough to go on with, and the question was how to make full use of them. Life at Weirleigh was dull, and a bit depressing at times. My mother was feeling the oppression of the war, and was still overshadowed by the loss of my younger brother at Gallipoli twelve months before. The stables were empty and neglected; the two tennis-courts were a tangle of uncut hay; local cricket matches were a thing of the past; and the whole place felt less than half alive. No-one knew this better than my mother, who unselfishly urged me to go away and see as many of my friends as I could. But I was in the mood for writing, so for a couple of weeks it suited me to combine this with playing the piano and doing nothing particular in the garden. And when my mind refused to be restful I could always compare my comfortable existence with what it would be if I was still with my battalion or, as I was soon to hear, with the little that was left of it after a ghastly 'holding attack' which had been foredoomed to failure from the start. The war had taught me one useful lesson—that on the whole it was very nice to be alive at all; and I had also acquired the habit of observing things with more receptiveness and accuracy than I had ever attempted to do in my undisciplined past.

One morning when I had been at home a few days I was sitting in the ground-floor room which my mother called the smoking-room, though no-one ever smoked there except me and—when the wind was in a certain quarter—the chimney. My recent manuscripts were arranged on the table, for I had taken to using this room in preference to the studio, which felt memory-haunted, and was too silent and shadowy when I sat there at night with my two candles. The little smoking-room was more friendly, though rather dark, since its bow-window faced the high bank of the rock garden. The walls were hung with large photographs of my departed horses, and there was also a fox's mask which I had acquired after a long hunt with the Southdown. I had adopted the room for reading and writing at the beginning of 1915, when I had been at home for a couple of months with a badly broken arm which joined up very slowly—the result of a heavy fall over a blind hedge when out on a training scheme as a trooper in the Sussex Yeomanry. During this period of inactivity I had experienced a continuous poetic afflatus, of which I took the fullest advantage, regarding it—not unnaturally—as my final chance of being visited by the Muse. This productiveness had indeed been almost like a recovery of the vernal raptures of my juvenilia, but I had been conscious of a newly-acquired technical control, while pervaded by an exultant sense of verbal freshness. My main performance had been a poem of nearly two hundred blank verse lines, vigorously impersonating an old huntsman remembering better days; but I had been happiest in a dozen war-oblivious lyrical pieces which had arrived spontaneous and unexpected. It had been something of an ordeal when April recalled me to the Army as an officer in the Royal Welch Fusiliers.

While learning to be a second-lieutenant I was unable to write anything at all, with the exception of a short poem called 'Absolution', manifestly influenced by Rupert Brooke's famous sonnet-sequence. The significance of my too nobly worded lines was that they expressed the typical self-glorifying feelings of a young man about to go to the Front for the first time. The poem subsequently found favour with middle-aged reviewers, but the more I saw of the war the less noble-minded I felt about it. This gradual process began, in the first months of 1916, with a few genuine trench poems, dictated by my resolve to record my surroundings, and usually based on the notes I was making whenever I could do so with detachment. These poems aimed at impersonal description of front-line conditions, and could at least claim to be the first things of their kind. The only one which anticipated my later successes in condensed satire was 'Good Friday Morning', a jaunty scrap of doggerel versified from a rough note in my diary. Here I broke into realism by introducing my Muse to the word 'frowst'. Six years later, the reprinting of these lines in a New Zealand Socialist paper caused the editor to be prosecuted for blasphemous libel. After several days of law-court proceedings the editor was discharged—the jury adding a rider 'that similar publications of such literature be discouraged'. Nevertheless it summarized the feelings of thousands of other platoon commanders, and I consider it one of the most effective of my war productions. Meanwhile that Muse of mine could still bring me the relief of idyllic and melodious utterance, in which I indulged freely while at the Fourth Army School on a month's course. I went there towards the end of April—to Flixécourt—a pleasant little town half-way between Amiens and Abbeville. Splendid weather, beechwoods in their virginal green, and a quiet little billet where I could be alone in the evenings—these, combined with a springtime sense of escape from the trenches, enabled me to celebrate yet another farewell to poetry—authentic enough this time, since the Great Advance was already in the air. We were told that the attack was to be on a really grand scale this time, and we believed that the results would be proportionately progressive. At Flixécourt, however, I refused to allow myself to worry about the future. The world around me was luminous and lovely; I was filled with physical gratitude for it; and I strove to express that vision with spiritual exaltation. My dreams were mine, and even the rigorous routine of infantry warfare instruction could not dispel them. Alone with my Concise Oxford Dictionary when the long day's work was done, I became as much a poet as I have ever been in my life, though how I had the vitality to do it is now one of the mysteries associated with the superabundant energy of youth.

At Flixécourt my mind and imagination had been my own. During the next three months my existence had been so completely identified with the battalion and those nearest to me in it that I had lived very little with my private self. My diary shows me making diligent efforts to be a selfless spectator, and I often felt like a student historian of those tragic, vivid, and profoundly moving scenes in the Somme country. On certain occasions where initiative was needed I had indeed been able—somewhat recklessly —to rise above my plodding self, thereby earning the much-valued respect of my companions. All this had changed my emotional outlook on the war, but it had, of course, been impossible to do any independent thinking about it.

Siegfried's Journey, 1916–1920

Sitting at my table on that September morning, I had before me the carefully-revised manuscript of a decent-sized volume of verse. But it now seemed tame and conventional compared with the material of recent experience which I was carrying about in my head, and the lively notions whereby I intended to convert some of that experience into a vehicle for candid and ironic comment. Already I had scribbled a couple of notes which read as follows. *Badly-wounded soldier feeling glad about being safely out of the war—a citizen of life again—thinks 'Thank God they had to amputate'. Brother officer giving white-haired mother fictitious account of her cold-footed son's death at the front. 'He'd told the poor old dear some gallant lies which she would nourish all her days, no doubt.'* The notes were soon afterwards developed into *The One-Legged Man* and *The Hero*, with a strong sense of satisfaction that I was providing a thoroughly caddish antidote to the glorification of 'the supreme sacrifice' and such-like prevalent phrases. These performances had the quality of satirical drawings. They were deliberately devised to disturb complacency. While at Oxford I had written another short poem—*Died of Wounds*—which was on a higher plane of effectiveness. In *Died of Wounds* I had hit on a laconic anecdotal method of writing which astonished me by the way it indirectly expressed my passionate feeling about the agonizing episode described. At the time, however, I did not realize the irony of my exulting in having done a fine piece of work, when I owed the opportunity for it to the death of a pathetically youthful officer in the ward of the hospital at Amiens where I had happened to be. Nor was I aware that, while it could be argued against the other two poems that they were merely a display of dexterous sarcasm, the graphic sincerity of *Died of Wounds* was unanswerable. In the meantime there I was with my accumulated poems on the table, preparing to arrange them in some sort of sequence so that Robbie Ross could submit them to the influential publisher on whom he had resolved to exercise his powers of persuasion. He had looked through my pre-war pamphlets, but had advised against including more than a few of the poems in a published collection. 'They rather remind me of the delicious teas of thirty years ago,' he had remarked, quoting the well-known 'Mazawattee' advertisement. The sequence having been settled, I was about to begin transcribing my works in a manuscript book which Lady Ottoline had given me. Beautifully bound in orange-vermilion vellum, with end papers of a brocade-like Italian pattern of blue and marigold entwined on a dim-gilt background, its hundred leaves of hand-made paper seemed almost too exquisite even for my most careful handwriting. Lady Ottoline had also invited me to stay at Garsington, and my fair-copying would keep me pleasantly occupied until I went there in the middle of September.

*   *   *

It is interesting—though sometimes saddening—to recall and re-enact one's first appearance among people with whom one afterwards became intimate. During the next ten years or more I stayed a great deal at Garsington; in fact it was one of the few houses where I could feel unembarrassed and at liberty to do as I pleased. During the week I spent there in September 1916 I was probably less my natural self than on any subsequent occasion. As might be expected, I was self-conscious about the effect I was making in these new and delightful surroundings, and my lively enjoyment was intermittently impeded by an uncomfortable feeling that Lady Ottoline's elevated notion of me as a romantic young poet needed a lot of living up to. I was anxious to be what was expected of me, but the level of intensity demanded was too high, and I sometimes wished that I wasn't obliged to answer quite so many questions about myself and my attitude to life. My main help in behaving naturally was my dog Topper, whom I had brought with me. Topper was a handsome fox-terrier with engaging manners who took everything as it came to him, and showed no awareness of incurring any extra strain on his sensibilities while staying with the Duke of Portland's half-sister and being patted on the head by extreme pacifists who had 'accepted war work' on Mr. Morrell's farm, and who came in of an evening to puff churchwarden pipes by the fire and talk cleverly in cultured and earnest tones about significant form in the Arts and the misdeeds of the Militarists, while Lady Ottoline, in a Velasquez-like gown of rich brocade, stitched away at her embroidery frame, desisting occasionally to ignite aromatic substances on a metal plate. Always willing to be pleased, Topper sniffed the aroma with apparent appreciation, unregardful of the fact that Lady Ottoline's pug Socrates, who rightly regarded him as an outrageous intruder, was yapping indignantly from behind the door of the boudoir upstairs. Topper, anyhow, afforded me intervals of relief from cerebral exertion, and when I found myself out of my depth in a conversation I could always distract attention by making him do something amusing.

The panelled room in which we sat after dinner was painted a rich lacquer red and contained some fine old Italian furniture from which I absorbed a general impression of faded silks and velvets, and of dusky browns and purples and glints of tarnished gold from coffers and cabinets. There was a sort of sumptuous homeliness about it all, for everything in the manor house was arranged with instinctive tact and in harmony with its moderate proportions. Its interior structure was charmingly ancient and irregular and its character had been lovingly preserved. I had a pleasant feeling that its amenities had remained immune from interference by the war, and that—like me—if given a more liberal allowance of silence it would relapse into its natural self. Meanwhile the old house evidently had to overhear a sustained flow of discussion about the war, and it was a new experience for me to find it being criticized so unguardedly. Soldiers at the front were in the habit of grumbling at personal discomforts and the mismanagement of military operations, but it was their business to go on believing that the Germans must be finally defeated however badly things worked out for the troops. Nobody suggested that it was a wicked outrage on humanity which—for the benefit of all the belligerents —ought to be put a stop to at once. In 1916 it seemed as if it might go on for ever, and it was a case of 'theirs not to reason why'. At Garsington there was, it appeared, every reason for reasoning why at all hours of the day. The war was described as being waged for unworthy motives, and it was the duty of a courageous minority to stand out against the public opinion which supported its continuance and prolongation. I was impressed by Mr. Morrell's parliamentary connection, and listened to his judicially-expressed opinions with a feeling that I was at last learning the truth about what was happening behind the political scenes. It suited me to believe that the soldiers had cause for dissatisfaction, and the fact that I had taken part in the Battle of the Somme gave me a status of my own. For those at Garsington the war in France was all hearsay, while I was a scrap of living evidence to support their assumption that it was quite as bad as they had imagined. I gathered that the Germans had made tentative peace overtures through neutral channels and that the Prime Minister was in active disagreement with Lloyd George about it. That this should have an unsettling effect on my mind was not surprising. It was the beginning of a process of disillusionment which afterwards developed into a fomentation of confused and inflamed ideas. But I wasn't in the mood to be drawn out about my experience at the Front, and no-one pressed me to divulge harrowing details or indeed to describe the humanly rewarding aspects of war service. The Morrells showed a sympathetic understanding of my unwillingness to be reminded of what I had been through, while the conscientious objectors seemed to be living in a mental world of their own. They weren't unfriendly, but my being in uniform created a barrier between us.

Meanwhile Garsington offered plenty of agreeable distractions from brooding about the war. One morning a day or two after I arrived Lady Ottoline walked me down to the village and knocked on the door of a charming thatched cottage in which she had provided a temporary refuge for a distinguished 'enemy alien'. This was Jelly d'Aranyi, the violinist, whose fine playing I had already heard and admired. In the evening this high-spirited and beautiful young lady came up to the Manor House, dressed in her national costume, and we heard a magnificent performance of Bach's unaccompanied Chaconne. Watching her picturesque figure as she stood at the far end of the Red Room, I thought how insane it was that even musicians should be at war with one another. I was listening to the noblest violin music ever written. The composer had been a German; and it was being played by a great-niece of Joachim, a violinist who had been acclaimed and beloved as much in England as in Germany. The thought would be bewildering if I allowed my mind to dwell on it, so I prudently surrendered to the influence which made everything around me seem enriched and uplifted by emotion. Yet—O self-conscious youth—weren't you also a little over-aware that Lady Ottoline was watching you and being struck by the soul-transported expression of your face? I have already hinted that she had made me feel that her expectations of me were excessively high. During my visit we had long talks, and our exchanges of thought moved on a plane of lofty but vaguely-formulated ideas. She was in some ways an idealist, essentially generous but deficient in constructive comprehension of the problems which she contemplated with such intensity. At that period her idealism was still in the full flush of its immaturity. She had yet to learn that the writers and artists whom she befriended were capable of proving ungrateful. Undeterred by a not wholly successful intimacy with D. H. Lawrence, who had given evidence of biting the hand that fed him, she was planning to make Garsington a meeting-ground for the advanced spirits of the age. This aspiration was expressed in some touchingly amateurish pages of which she now gave me a manuscript copy. 'Come then,' she had written, 'gather here—all who have passion and who desire to create new conditions of life—new visions of art and literature and new magic worlds of poetry and music. If I could but feel that days at Garsington had strengthened your efforts to live the noble life: to live freely, recklessly, with clear Reason released from convention—no longer absorbed in small personal events but valuing personal affairs as part of a great whole—above all to live with passionate desire for Truth and Love and Understanding and Imagination.'

While perusing this invitation to the nobler existence, I wondered—smoking a pipe in my bedroom—whether, in so far as it applied to me, Lady Ottoline's aspirations were achievable. Obviously she couldn't expect these few days of my visit to produce any such results. The 'great whole' of which I was at present an ingredient would continue to be the Great War, and my main desire was to obtain another four weeks' extension of leave, getting as many days of October cub-hunting as I could, and working in some seaside golf as well. It was impossible for me to discard my absorption in these 'small personal events' when I was faced with the larger one of returning to the Front at the end of the year. The 'condition of life' I wanted was that Robbie Ross

should find a publisher for my poems, and the release of my
Reason from convention was restricted to an angry impulse to
compose scarifying verses against bloodthirsty civilians, profiteers,
and those who falsely glorified the war. It was nice of Lady Ottoline to welcome me to her flock of chosen spirits, but I felt that her
words were inappropriate to an infantry subaltern, even if he did
happen to be a fairly promising poet . . . 'To live freely, recklessly
. . .' My freedom was limited to a few weeks of absence from army
life, and I was more likely to die recklessly than to live in that
way! Nor was it any good denying that physical comfort mattered
more than intellectual idealism. Here I sat, in this perfect bedroom with its old mullioned windows looking across the green
forecourt to the tall wrought-iron gates. The moted sunlight of a
sweet September evening was touching the tops of the high yew
hedges; on the paved path below, the little Morrell girl was playing with the pug Socrates, and a peacock was parading with tail
outspread. I desired only to enjoy this comfort and security while
it lasted. On the table by the bed was a thin-paper copy of the
Oxford Book of Verse which Lady Ottoline had given me. The
bed was a creaky four-poster which looked antique and valuable
enough to be in a museum, and the book was delectably bound in
pale green vellum. But what counted with me was my thankfulness for having a bed to sleep on and a quiet room in which to let
my thoughts loiter idly along. Garsington was just about the
pleasantest house I had ever stayed in—so pleasant that it
wouldn't be safe to think about it when I was back at the Front.
In the meantime the maid had knocked at the door with my can
of hot water and I must get ready for another simple but delicious
dinner.

III

On a half-sheet of notepaper headed *Longthorpe, Peterborough*, which has achieved respectful preservation since 1916, I find the following paragraph of cub-hunting prose.

September 21st. Met at Orton Waterville, 6.30. Fine morning after slight frost. Found in the Long Covert and hunted one over the road and railway, through the osiers and along by the railway bridge; then back by the river and lost him beyond the ferry but picked one up in some seeds when going back to the osiers, where they afterwards killed a brace. Scent fair. Home 11.30. Rode Westmorland.

Four more notes of similar character complete my recording of a week in which I was out five mornings with the Fitzwilliam Hounds. I had put the sophisticated hospitalities of Garsington behind me, and was back in that pre-war personality which had flourished under the kindly tutelage of Norman Loder. Well supported by the M.C. ribbon on my tunic, I temporarily reverted to unthinkingness. Mounted on the hunt horses, I contrived to escape from the war atmosphere and to return to those sporting simplicities which I had provisionally rejected as a dead-end in the summer of 1914. At that time Norman had become joint-master of the Fitzwilliam, and soon after the outbreak of war he had married. But he had, of course, been prevented from hunting the hounds, and he was now out in France, while Mrs. Norman carried on gallantly as an amateur first and second whip in one, an activity for which she was well qualified by her brilliant and determined riding, though—as she said—she had some fairly murky moments while following the famous pack in that country of big woods and hairy-fenced ploughlands. She and I were very good friends, and as she was also an admirable pianist I was getting just what I needed to sustain my rather precarious peace of mind. Longthorpe was a pleasant little house about a mile from the kennels. While there I spent a non-hunting day in attending a far-distant meeting with a medical board which benevolently awarded me another month's leave, though how I managed to convince the medicos that there was anything the matter with me must remain a mystery. Meanwhile I asked nothing better than to be going out into the twilight of misty mornings, to climb on to a nice-mannered horse in the huge historic stable-yard at Milton, and jog away to draw some looming covert in a country I had long wanted to know. There was the grand cry of the famous dog-hounds, and the damp delicious smell of autumn woods. Of such things I had thought and dreamed when I was in musty front-line dug-outs and comfortless winter billets, drugging the ache of un-certainty whether I should ever experience them again. Out there, the physical sensation of starting for a day's hunting had been with me in memory more intensely than anything else at home. The war had brought me a deepened consciousness of peace-time values and enjoyments and a new determination to get the best out of life wherever I happened to be. I had learnt what it could mean to me—the smell of a soft southerly wind on a dark December morning when I had opened the window to look out at the clouded sky; and my imagination would fondly re-create the whole day, from the time when I was pulling on my boots by the light of a couple of candles to that last bit of hunting at the end of the afternoon when half the field had gone home and my zest for jumping was only mitigated by my horse being much more tired than I was. Anyhow, while staying at Longthorpe I had the com-fortable feeling that my efforts as an amateur infantry soldier had earned me this Fitzwilliam interlude. I could hold my head as high as I pleased, even when conversing respectfully with that great landed proprietor and sporting luminary Mr. Wentworth Fitzwilliam himself. All the same, while riding beside him among the Domesday oaks of his enormous deer park or sitting at his table during a somewhat unlively Sunday luncheon, I couldn't help wondering what emotions his large red baronial countenance would register in the improbable event of his ever perusing my out-spoken verses about the war. For he was nothing if not an up-holder of the feudal system; and the halls and corridors of Milton backed him up by being almost overstocked with noble suits of armour and obsolete weapons of war.

* * *

Siegfried's Journey, 1916-1920

After leaving Longthorpe I spent a week at home before going on to stay with a middle-aged friend who, as Acting Master, was keeping the Southdown Hunt on its legs until better times returned. Down in Sussex gloomy thoughts could be subdued; but at Weirleigh I hadn't much to occupy me actively except taking Topper for long walks which included a lot of whistling to persuade him away from his rabbit-hunting. Gloomy thoughts were caused by the news I'd received from my late Battalion, which had been very badly knocked about in a dud attack at a place called Ginchy. I could get no relief by discussing the war with my mother, whose way of looking at it differed from mine. For her, the British were St. George and the Germans were the Dragon; beyond that she had no more to say about it. The war had caused her so much suffering that she was incapable of thinking flexibly on the subject. And it was now making things worse by becoming a barrier between us, for I hadn't yet found out what it feels like to be an elderly civilian in a great war. However, when I had been at home two or three days a letter arrived which did much to produce cheerfulness about my own concerns. I had heard from Robbie, in one of his hasty and somewhat indecipherable notes, that he would be seeing his friend Heinemann and was intending to read some of my poems to him. I hadn't felt particularly hopeful about the result, so the letter which I now received was beyond my expectations. It was from the eminent publisher himself, and had the additional distinction of coming, non-typewritten, from his private address.

'Dear Mr. Sassoon,' he wrote, 'Ross gave me your poems a few days ago and I have just finished reading them with great pleasure and admiration. I shall be delighted to publish a selection from them, for they seem to me of varying interest and importance. Will you let me know if you will yourself make the selection, or if you prefer Ross to do so. I gather that you are soon going out again and I wonder if I shall have the opportunity of making your acquaintance before you start.' (At this point I paused, wondering how soon I *should* 'start' and whether he would ever see me again after I had done so.) 'I shall be in my office on Tuesday,' he concluded, 'and shall hope to hear from you. It will be a great pleasure to associate myself with your work and to do what I can to give it a wide circulation.' This was obviously the sort of letter one only gets once in a lifetime, and the prospect which it opened took my thoughts well away from that ghastly 'holding attack' at Ginchy in which I had so providentially escaped being involved. I lost no time in calling on Mr. Heinemann at his office, and though the details of the occasion have faded beyond recall the interview must have gone off smoothly, for a week later Robbie was writing to instruct me that the agreement was a fair one and suitable for me to sign. 'I suggest that you make the selection yourself,' he added. 'I will of course adopt *your* choice as mine in order to pacify the oracles. I expect I shall be more tolerant and inclusive than you yourself.' The oracles to whom he referred must have been Edmund Gosse and Eddie Marsh, both of whom had a preference for idealized soldier-poems when first-hand evidence was forthcoming from the Front. We were anticipating that Mr. Gosse's sensibilities would be antagonized by some of my war poems. 'Gosse', Robbie remarked, 'is in constant expectation that the Prussian Guard will arrive in Regent's Park. At the Reform Club the other day, he was *scolding* Hagberg Wright because the Russians are doing so badly!' (Dr. Hagberg Wright, the librarian of the London Library, was a leading authority on Russian Literature and had been partly educated in Russia.)

The collection which Mr. Heinemann had accepted contained very little that could offend sensitive opinion. Most of it was idyllic and graceful, and the war pieces were mainly descriptive. In a volume which ultimately made over a hundred pages there were less than a dozen poems in the satiric vein which Robbie was encouraging me to cultivate. These, of course, were the ones which drew public attention to the book, and caused Mr. Gosse to write of them as 'savage, disconcerting silhouettes drawn roughly against a lurid background', and of me as 'a young man who, finding the age out of joint, resents being called upon to mend it. His temper is not altogether to be applauded, for such sentiments must tend to relax the effort of the struggle.' He did, however, give me credit for 'honesty and courage', while doubting whether I had recorded my impressions with proper circumspection; for he was fond of me, and had been extremely kind on the several occasions when I had been to his house during the war. And one must

28

remember that in 1916 very few candid comments on the war had appeared in print, and that many people were genuinely shocked and startled by what I wrote. For me, the unexpected quality of these few pieces was that they revealed a hitherto unpredictable talent for satirical epigram. Nothing I had written before 1916 showed any symptom of this development. It was as if I had suddenly found myself to be an expert boxer without having undergone any training. I have never been able to ascertain that my method was modelled on any other writer, though the influence of Hardy's *Satires of Circumstance* is faintly perceptible in a few of the longer poems. I merely chanced on the device of composing two or three harsh, peremptory, and colloquial stanzas with a knock-out blow in the last line. And having brought off my effect once or twice, I was urged by Robbie to do it as often as I could. My verses appealed to his 'flair' for anything lively and enterprising in the arts, and were aimed at the type of person he most disliked, among whom were what he used to call 'the screaming scarlet Majors'. There was an element in his nature which delighted in provoking opposition; he hated the war, and was unable to be tolerant about it and those who accepted it with civilian bellicosity and self-defensive evasion of its realities. (In his 1917 Journal, Arnold Bennett noted that 'whenever Ross talks about the war his whole face changes'.)

In my forthcoming volume the poem which probably gave him fullest satisfaction was called *They*. And since it was the one most quoted by reviewers, both adverse and favourable, it may be of some interest to divulge its origin and the way I wrote it.

> ' *The Bishop tells us: When the boys come back*
> *They will not be the same.*'

Thus it begins, thereafter going its wicked way to the twelfth and last line where the Bishop remarks, when 'the boys' have answered him, that 'the ways of God are strange'. One evening toward the end of October, when I was staying with Robbie at his rooms in Half Moon Street, he had been exercising his wit rather freely at the expense of the Bishop of London, who—for some reason unknown to me at the time—was a frequent target of his. My own acquaintance with the Bishop had been restricted to a single occasion. I could claim to have met him, but only in the spiritual sense of the words. I had in fact been confirmed by him in St. Paul's Cathedral. The sequel, if sequel it can be called—since nothing in the poem implied that he was my source of inspiration —was totally unforeseeable by the mind of the surpliced boy whose head had received the Bishop's benediction thirteen years before. For the poem afforded me the opportunity of being—to the best of my knowledge—the first writer to bring the word 'syphilitic' into the realms of English verse.

On the evening I am describing, Robbie read me an extract from a speech or sermon reported in some newspaper, in which the Bishop had expressed his belief that those who were serving at the Front would return with their souls purged and purified by what they had experienced, or words to that effect. This sort of thing was often said at the time, by those beyond the age of active service. As an abstract idea there was nothing against it, and there may even have been a few cases where it really happened. But on the whole one was justified in resenting it as inappropriate though well-intentioned bunkum. Anyhow I went upstairs to bed after several hours of lively talk, feeling too tired to be bothering about the Bishop of London or anybody else. But while I lay there with the light out, not quite succeeding in falling asleep, the first few lines of *They* came into my head as though from nowhere. So I got up to scribble them in my note-book, and the rest of the poem was written then and there. That first draft is before me on my table now. On the next page is the slightly emended version which I made next morning. The peculiar thing about it was that while writing the first draft I was so drowsy that I could scarcely keep my eyes open, and was fast asleep a few minutes after finishing it. Such was the 'fine frenzy' with which I composed what subsequently proved to be the most publicly effective poem I had yet written.

Up to that time I had not been very often to Robbie's rooms, but they had already become—as they continued to be for the next two years—the pivot of my episodic doings in London. As he had done with so many of his friends, he made me feel that he was a central point in my existence. He was enlarging my London associations, and his rooms were an oasis in the confusion and un-certainty of the war. He had constituted himself my literary 'producer', and the circumstances were favourable for both of us. I was glad to accept his guidance, and he enjoyed devoting his ingenuity and experience to 'putting me on the map'. 'You must forgive me for being such an incorrigible chaperon,' he remarked, 'but making other people a success is my only real vocation.' This was an understatement. He had a genius for suggestion, and a prescient instinct for bringing together those who were likely to stimulate one another. At the risk of being thought a busybody, he would insist that certain people should meet, and by this agency he originated effects of which even those involved were only partially aware. Arnold Bennett, who valued him highly, once said to me, in his pauseful oracular manner, 'Our friend Robert is the most indirectly creative character I have known. He causes works of art and letters to occur.'

In his room on the first floor of 40 Half Moon Street I was absorbing more knowledge than I realized at the time, while, with charming and half-bantering affection, he modified some of my youthful crudities and misconceptions. Merely to enter that room was a discovery of finely matured artistic judgement, for everything in it gave a sense of ripened and sensitive selection. The objects which met one's eyes didn't appear to have been self-consciously collected by a dilettante. They were no more than the casual accumulations of an expert, but they seemed to have arrived there through a process of inevitable and decorative fitness. The tones of the room were mellow and subdued, half Italian and half Oriental, and yet essentially imbued by London homeliness. There was a richly-looming Roman landscape by Richard Wilson. A few small Chinese prints and pieces of faience, refined and delicate in colour, harmonized with the Persian carpet and the curtains of the tall windows which opened on a balcony where I liked to get a breath of night air and listen to the drone of the Piccadilly traffic when Robbie had been called to the telephone downstairs, or was engaged in a too specialized conversation with one of his Burlington Fine Arts Club cronies. In the large old glass-doored bookcase I could browse on an assortment of 'poetry and belles lettres'—an assortment which even then gave me clues to Robbie's prejudices and predilections among modern authors.

Along the middle of the room, parallel with the bookcase, was the table on which he did his writing; on the other side of it was the fireplace, before which he used to stand while talking to his friends. Behind his head, more than filling the length of wall above the mantelpiece, was a fifteenth-century Italian 'cassone front' which made a noble background with its patina of century-darkened bronze and gold that framed the panels containing missal-like figures representing episodes in the betrothal of a bride.

It is thus that he emerges in the mind-portrait of memory, his face—tired and old before its time—masking the sadness of wounding experience with a mood of witty reminiscence and word-play, while he bestowed on others the influence of his resolve to evoke gaiety and good sense in despite of the pervasive dullness and hostility of human affairs. There he would stand, in his loose grey alpaca jacket, wearing a black silk skull-cap and smoking his perpetual cigarette in its jade-green holder, emphasizing his lively pronouncements with controlled gestures of the left hand, on the third finger of which was a fair-sized scarab ring. (He more than once warned me that my own hands were somewhat over-illustrative, urging me to be less precipitate and inaudible; he added that this union of gesticulation and indistinctness was probably inherited from the paternal branch of my family.)

It must not be supposed that he was a monopolizer of conversation. He was at all times an admirable listener; but being by temperament an irrepressible entertainer, he frequently found himself compelled to take the lead and to sustain it, at the expense of his long-overtaxed vitality. And on such occasions as I am now remembering his audience usually consisted of one or two men who hadn't much to say for themselves and who needed to be explained to me afterwards.

On some such night, when I had been spending the earlier part of the evening elsewhere, I would return at about eleven o'clock to find him in his habitual position before the fire. With him would be those 'one or two men', middle-aged and rather war-weary, who had dropped in, not so much for a drink as for an infusion of his refreshing though sometimes intolerant talk, hoping also, perhaps, for a glimpse of one of his sprightly young friends. They would rise from their arm-chairs, and if I hadn't met them before he would introduce them with punctilious distinctness. They were usually connected with the art world; but Robbie's friends were a varied assortment, and I wondered at times how some of them could digest his unconventional opinions. There was Sir James Agg-Gardner for instance, who—as an extreme Conservative—had periodically represented Cheltenham in Parliament for more than forty years. This composed and courteous old gentleman was much addicted to acquiescent nods and museful monosyllables. When I asked Robbie whether he ever made a speech in the House he replied that dear old 'Aggie' was a born backbencher and restricted himself to one question in each session, though the question was always a pertinent one. Sir James brought a comfortable atmosphere of social solidity and club life conducted with a nice sense of order. Remembering the trenches and my own condition of being here to-day and gone to-morrow, I could almost envy his sedately septuagenarian existence. Had I been younger he would probably have tipped me a sovereign every time he saw me.

Another somewhat reticent figure in those evenings was Robbie's elder brother Alexander. In later years I knew him well and delighted in his company, but at Half Moon Street he chose to play an unobtrusive part, seldom contributing to the conversation unless his opinion was asked. In contrast to his more impulsive brother, whose admonitions were given with urgency and confidence, Alex offered his opinions temperately, making one feel that—the world being what it was—he didn't altogether expect his advice to be acted on. His utterance was slow and articulate, and his voice had a kind of burr in it which was, I think, caused by his being Canadian by birth. His sagaciously observant look, while listening to a discussion, was accentuated by his having only one eye. The closed eyelid and lashes of the absent one—combined with the kindly stoicism of his lip-compressed smile—gave him an oddly humorous expression, suggesting a fixed wink at the unreasonableness of humanity in general. His face, with its short, carefully-trimmed beard, resembled that of an old Greek philosopher, preferably Diogenes. Small and slightly bow-legged, he wore dark clothes which, like all else about him, had an air of

B   33

sober distinction. I remember being particularly impressed by his soft-fronted silk shirts and the ample cut of his cream-coloured waistcoat when he was 'in full fig' for a dinner party. As a young man he must have had leanings towards a literary career, for he once told me, quite casually, that he had at one time been a fairly regular contributor to the *Saturday Review*. I also heard him speak of 'poor old Besant' (with whom he had been associated in some editing work). I mention it because his intonation of that prolifically productive author's name had a sort of mournful resonance which remains in my mind as typical of his after-dinner deliberateness of utterance. I can see him lighting a cigar as he said it, after a perfectly designed dinner at his club. One of his admirable gifts was his taciturnity. He would plod the whole length of Pall Mall with his eyes on the pavement. Then, when we had crossed the road to go up St. James's Street, he would enunciate his brief and final comment on what had been in both our minds when we started. Robbie once remarked that, while he himself had been trying all his life to be brilliant, his brother's best epigrams were his silences. He was a famous connoisseur of vintages, and I have heard him speak with almost reverential respect of someone who, he affirmed, had the best palate in London for port. (Robbie took the subject less seriously, and had a preference for liqueurs.) In later years he had found his way to the City, where, as partner in a firm of stockbrokers, he had made a considerable fortune, from which he bestowed many quiet and circumspect benefactions. I always thought of him in connection with everything that was unassumingly excellent. He was the sort of man who knew exactly where to go for what he needed, whether it was a stick of sealing-wax or a fine prosaic piece of furniture which would be in his bachelor chambers for the rest of his life. For him there was no second-best. His requirements were moderate, but they had to satisfy a standard of soundness as irreducible as some classic aphorism from the Latin authors whom he could quote so aptly. The last time I saw him he was in a nursing home, after a severe operation. Clumsily sympathetic, I inquired whether he had suffered much—'Infandum, regina, jubes renovare dolorem, my dear Siegfried,' he sonorously murmured, his one good eye closed in philosophic resignation.

More Adey was another character whose presence was an inseparable feature of those evening hours. He was an old and intimate friend of Robbie's—so much so that he used to enter and make for his customary chair without expecting to receive a glance or nod of welcome. Often though I saw him, I find myself unable to remember his face distinctly, possibly because it was always so late at night when he shuffled in. I cannot even be certain about his beard; but I surmise that it was a black and curly one of the type that has been grown to avoid the trouble of shaving and then left to look after itself. I am, however, fairly sure that it looked a bit moth-eaten, since More was by no means spruce and not far removed from dingy. He was a sallow, moody little man with lustreless dark eyes, who smoked ceaseless cigarettes, totally unaware that two o'clock in the morning was the wrong hour for pursuing a subject to finality. Robbie, who slept badly owing to his attacks of asthma, used to sit up with him tolerantly; but by the time More had become fluent with his obliquely sardonic ramblings about Mr. Lloyd George and the conduct of the war, I had usually reached a state of suppressed yawns. He also had a way of being whimsically mysterious about himself, suggesting clandestine political activities of a subversive nature, and implying that the Government regarded him as dangerous—a sort of secret agent, in fact. And had he been less obviously ineffective, absentminded, and eccentric, he might almost have passed for one, with his cropped continental-looking hair and his peering, equivocal behaviour. I vaguely respected him as an authority on Art—was it Italian primitives he specialized in?—I have forgotten; but I imagined him scrutinizing the smoky canvases of old masters through a magnifying-glass, obsessedly desirous of discovering them to be fakes which fellow experts had failed to detect. His conversational mannerisms, when he became lively and communicative, resembled Robbie's, but they were a blurred reflection of the original. He could be humorous, and even playful, but there was a solitary and frustrated existence behind it all. After the War he retired to a fine old manor house in the west of England—a property which he had inherited as a young man. His oddity then became actively apparent, and for a while he was happy. Having got it into his head that the house contained hidden treasure, he employed a number of workmen to pull the place to pieces. Free cider flowed like water while More Adey gleefully superintended his party of demolitionists, walking about in a long black cloak, with a tame rook perched on his shoulder. No treasure was found, and the poor old lord of the manor was finally removed from the scene to live on for a few years as a certified case of mental derangement. Which accounts for the fact that even when I met him at Robbie's rooms I sometimes suspected him of being rather dotty.

IV

By the beginning of December I was back at the Regimental Depot. This was a training camp for several thousand men, accurately and unassumingly named 'The Huts, Litherland'. It was a few miles from Liverpool, and has already been fully described by Sherston as 'Clitherland Camp'. I had gone out to France about thirteen months before, resolved to put up as decent a performance as I could, though dubious of my practical abilities as an amateur soldier. Returning to the Depot, I had no cause to feel dissatisfied with what I had done, and was welcomed as one who had earned credit for himself and the Regiment.

Seen in perspective by the estimating eyes of my present self, I had gained much from that year of adventure and mental expansion. Apart from having acquired a purple and white ribbon and a name for performing foolhardy exploits, I had made unexpected progress as a poet, and was now well on the road towards reputation, with a notable impresario to assist me. Of all this, however, I was not coherently conscious. Conditions weren't favourable for retrospective self-congratulations. Meanwhile my military duties were unexacting and perfunctory. I was merely getting through the time until a medical board passed me for active service abroad. This I foresaw as by no means improbable at the end of December, and a stone-cold certainty four weeks later. An unusually severe winter had set in, making contemplation of trench life additionally gloomy and dispiriting when I was alone in my cheerless hut after dinner in the mess. Sitting up against the stove, with fog and snow outside, I was desolately divided from my long period of leave by the discontinuity of circumstances. It wasn't safe to think about it unless I had a couple of glasses of port inside me. There had been that week of golf early in November when I was staying in the Dormy House at Rye (breaking a strict rule of the club by bringing my dog Topper with me). The weather had been mild and dry, and most of my rounds were played with David Ayton, a retired professional who had been second in the Open Championship—which he still referred to as 'The Cham-

37

pion Belt'—about forty years before. He and his ancient wooden
putter, his pawky Scotch humour, and his habit of rising to the
occasion when partnering me in a foursome—all this had been
something snatched from a circumvention of the War, and doubly
delightful because of it. But it was behind me now, and I couldn't
imagine myself ever being there again to benefit by Ayton's
shrewd advice, which had produced a gratifying though ephemeral improvement in my game, both long and short. There had
been hunting in Sussex too, when I had been among friends who
had almost succeeded in making me forget there was a war on—
days when the past had been revived and the future ignored.
Outwardly I was now playing my part as a nicely-behaved subaltern who gained the approval of the senior officers on the permanent staff of the Depot by hunting with the Cheshire when
Saturday weather made it possible. Whenever I could get a free
afternoon I slipped away by the electric train for a solitary round
of golf at Formby. I was also to be seen dining at the luxurious
Adelphi Hotel in Liverpool, where my manner of ordering a
bottle of Chambertin and discussing the menu with the head
waiter caused me to be looked on by our youthful officers as quite
an expert in 'designing a dinner'. Inwardly, however, I was in a
state of spiritual discomfort. Being in the army had always worked
out as a sort of dual existence for me—a constant effort to combine
efficiency in my duties with a detached and active brain. And this
was made doubly difficult by the stupefyingly healthy life which
one led. More than ever now, I wanted to be alone and write
poetry—to read good literature and listen to good music. But even
at night it wasn't often possible to be by myself. Officers with
whom I had been at the Front came in for a talk, compelling me
to put aside my book, or interrupting the ideas I was attempting
to versify. When they had gone I lay awake watching the dull
glow of the stove and thinking that my spare time on earth
would probably be short enough without my having it wasted like
this. It was exasperating to be prevented from using my mind
properly just when I was at last having a bit of success. For my
war poems were getting themselves talked about. Thanks to the
efforts of Eddie Marsh and Robbie, a little crop of them had been
appearing in the literary journals. Editors had kept on the safe

side of their acceptances; but my friend Edward Dent had found a home for several outspoken ones in *The Cambridge Magazine*, and it seemed that they had caused quite a sensation among the readers of this refreshingly independent pacifist weekly. As evidence of their provocative effect, the editor had printed a letter of protest from an old Cambridge man who claimed to be 'an average Englishman, pained, not to say disgusted, that such a thing as the poem "The Hero" should appear in a magazine connected with the University of Cambridge'. This opinion would probably have been shared by a good many of the officers in my regiment, but with one or two trusted exceptions, none of them knew that I 'went in for writing'.

At the end of December I was given another month's home service, but this reprieve only prolonged my mental uneasiness. Waiting to be sent back to the War was in a way more uncomfortable than being out there. The idea of being killed was continually in one's mind. Once one was in the war zone it didn't seem to matter so much, and there was no time to worry. I could no longer indulge in fine feelings about being a hero, for although my period of active service had given me confidence in myself as a front-line officer I was ceasing to believe in the War itself. Like most of the infantry, I had expected too much of the Battle of the Somme. We had been told that it would be 'the Great Advance'. It was now obvious that it had been nothing of the kind, and disillusionment was inevitable. This feeling was intensified by the fact of the battalion I had served with having been rendered almost unrecognizable by heavy casualties, which naturally took a good deal of the heart out of me. The prospect of rejoining my former companions could have kept my fortitude up to the mark. But of those I'd liked best, very few remained, and those few must by now be much dispirited. My old friend the Quartermaster had written advising me to stay away as long as I could, until the worst of the winter was over. He said that after being up to their necks in mud in front of Beaumont-Hamel they had now got half the battalion being treated for frost-bitten feet. Of course all it boiled down to was that going out again was damned unpleasant. But I was too self-occupied in dramatizing my emotions to be capable of expressing it with such economy of thought. Also—as I noted in my diary—those four months away from the army had caused an evaporation of the slight sense of discipline I had managed to acquire. 'My absurd decoration', I added, 'is the only thing that gives me any sense of responsibility as a soldier.' Naturally, I did my best to be strong-minded about it. In this I had one compelling mental objective to support me. This was the need to obtain further material for war poems. My strength of mind thus consisted mainly in a ferocious and defiant resolve to tell the truth about the War in every possible way. For that purpose the more I could see of it the better my opportunities would be for discharging sardonic epigrams at those on 'the Home Front' whose behaviour was arousing my resentment.

I have already indicated that I had lost my belief in the War. It would be more accurate to say that during those two months at the Depot my loss of belief was shaping itself from a ferment of disturbing and disorderly ideas. My mental behaviour had become a typical case for the student of war psychology, made more interesting, perhaps, by the fact that disillusionment was combined with determination to employ my discontents as a subject for literary expression. While on leave I had avoided thinking seriously about it, though vaguely disturbed by the discussions I had listened to at Garsington. Robbie's rather unconstructive and petulant pacifism had also influenced me. Now, when my fate as an individual was about to be involved once again in the crass chancefulness of battle, I was all too ready to accuse the governing powers of injustice and improbity.

On New Year's Eve I was alone in my hut reading *Mr. Britling Sees It Through*, which was more of a revelation to me than anything I had met with, and seemed to light up the whole background of the War. Someone was speaking his mind fearlessly; and since it happened to be the mind of H. G. Wells I devoured his pages in a rapt surrender of attention. Finally I came to a startling passage that checked my rapid reading. For several minutes I sat staring at the words. Then I copied them carefully into the small note-book in which I recorded my nocturnal ruminations. I was in the panoramic and retrospective state of mind induced by New Year's Eve, and this was what one of England's most powerful imaginations told me.

Siegfried's Journey, 1916–1920

'It is a war now like any other of the mobbing, many-aimed cataclysms that have shattered empires and devastated the world; it is a war without point, a war that has lost its soul; it has become mere incoherent fighting and destruction, a demonstration in vast and tragic forms of the stupidity and ineffectiveness of our species. . . .'

The words are alone on the flimsy little page. I didn't venture to add my own commentary on them. But I am moderately sure that I remarked to myself, 'That's exactly what I'd been thinking, only I didn't know how to say it!' Nevertheless I had already written on a previous page, 'The War is settling down on everyone —a hopeless, never-shifting burden. There seems nothing left but to try and dodge through to the end—the victory that is more terrible than defeat—exhaustion, and blind men with medals, and people trying to clear up the mess that has been made of their lives.' Compared with most of my cogitations, this was quite explicit, though 'the victory that is more terrible than defeat' sounds too like a quotation to be convincing as a first-hand observation. The diary indeed discloses very little of my actual state of mind about the War. Some of its entries suggest that I was keeping my courage up by resorting to elevated feelings. My mental behaviour was still unconnected with any self-knowledge, and it was only when I was writing verse that I tried to concentrate and express my somewhat loose ideas. Moreover, those war diaries of mine were mostly written at the Front. My doings while in England didn't seem worth recording. At the War I did my best to describe what I observed and experienced. But when on the subject of himself, the young man was liable to regard his words as likely to be read after he'd been killed in action. It did not occur to him that the posterity which perused them would be merely himself. I now wish that my former self had allowed for the possibility of my some day writing a book about him! Meanwhile I find, here and there, a scrap of simple unaffected utterance.

'Now I've got a grip on the idea of life and describing it I hope I shan't get myself killed in 1917. There's such a lot to say.'

And there is nothing amiss with my laconic comment after a second medical board had passed me for General Service. 'As I went out into the grey street and the bitter east wind I felt as if a

41

load had been lifted from my heart. I'd been given another chance
to die a decent death—and a darned uncomfortable one, probably.'
For it really did bring a sense of relief when the paper was signed
and the door had closed behind me. Those weeks of suspense were
over; there was nothing to worry about now. But by the next
evening my mental apparatus had reverted to a more mystical
mood.

'I have lived and dreamed so immune since August that, without knowing it, I had forgotten the significance of 'going out
again' (although the thought of it has been in my head a thousand times—but only as a shadow—not the real storming tumult
of fiends and angels.)' (Do stop writing for effect like that, I now
exclaim.) 'The wings of doom are over me once more. And while
my body cries out against death, something within me lifts adoring
hands, something renews in me the desire for that benison and
promise of freedom. For I know that it will be mine again, that
sense of immolation to some vague aspiration, which I experienced last year—self-sacrifice, emotion at facing danger unafraid,
and that queer hankering for extinction which I can't explain.'
This was very much in the manner of Lady Ottoline, who had
written, when thanking me for some spiritually exalted poems I
had sent her—'I can only hold out to you with both hands a bowl-
ful of incense, which comes from my inner self, and which, if my
spirit could be a wind, would blow round you now and always . . .'
To redeem the dinginess of my surroundings she had knitted me
a large and lovely rug in brilliant coloured wools. I had given her
a description of the camp which must have been much the same
as the following extract from my diary. 'This is a dreary drab flat
place of fogs and bleary sunsets. At night there is the shuttered
smoky glare and muffled din of the explosive works a few hundred
yards away. One hears factory sirens hooting, and fog-horns out
on the mouth of the Mersey. The wind moans around the huts,
and the bugle blowing 'Lights out' sounds melancholy. These
noises make a picture of the disconsolate countryside—smoke-
drifted factories, meagre trees, sooty-looking farms and flat grey
fields disfigured by munition-making sheds. When the wind
blows the wrong way, the fumes from the T.N.T. works get in
one's throat, and the coke stove in my hut doesn't improve

matters.' Lady Ottoline had made a generous effort to counteract the atmosphere of Litherland by sprinkling a bottle of perfume on the rug. This rather embarrassed me, as my friends were continually coming in for a sniff of the superabundant aroma which pervaded my room, not without suggestions that it implied a romantic episode in my career.

Her letters had contributed to my uneasiness and disgruntlement about the War. My diary has preserved a typical example. 'The spirit and purpose of the war, that kept it fine and clean at first, dwindles and gets fainter, leaving it utterly ghastly. It is terrible to know that vast numbers of the fighting men simply loathe it and are kept there by the brutal fury of L.G. and politicians like him. It seems sheer insanity. Last week my hopes were high, for I heard from old Birrell, who came down here, that the Germans had made definite Peace proposals and he hoped they would come to something. It was this that caused the Cabinet row. But the possibility of Peace seems to make the devil leap up in people's hearts and to make them lust for more blood to be shed while there is yet time. The Spring offensive is pure devilry— when after all, peace could be made quite advantageously to the Allies. Another poor little harvest of village youths has been called up and has gone off to barracks. They do hate it, poor creatures.' She also quoted a patriotic lady who had said to her, 'I am quite content that the men should be sent to die; it does such wonderful things to the souls of their women; makes them selfless.' So this, I thought, was what the spirit and purpose of my own share in the War must contend with. And my next destination would be the Spring offensive! A few days later, however, I was finding consolation from the map of Cheshire while jotting down the details of a moderate day's hunting. 'Scent a bit catchy, but they ran quite nicely by Paradise and Hill's Gorse and over the railway at Wardle Bank,' etcetera, concluding my account with an uncustomary excursion into sporting sensibility. 'The wet watery green meadows and straggling bare hedges and grey winding lanes—the cry of hounds and thud of galloping hoofs—and then the ride home with the hunt servants in the chilly dusk—these are real things in this winter of unending war.' In contrast to this, my next January entry commemorates a concert in Liverpool at which I heard Elgar's Violin Concerto for the first time, an emotional experience which my afterthoughts impelled me to report in terms that had, it now seems, little relation to the music.

'In all the noblest passages of this glorious work I shut my eyes, seeing on the darkness a shape always the same—the suffering mortal figure on a cross. And around it a host of shadowy forms with upraised arms—the souls of men, agonized and aspiring, hungry for what they seek as God in vastness and confoundment.' This is followed by a poem which I now find just worth rescuing from the page where it has remained hidden since I scribbled it in a fine—and perhaps foolish—frenzy.

> *I have seen Christ when music wove*
> *Majestic vision. Storms of prayer*
> *Deep-voiced within me marched and strove.*
> *The sorrows of the world were there.*
>
> *A god for beauty shamed and wronged,*
> *A sign where faith and ruin meet*
> *In glooms of vanquished glory thronged*
> *By spirits blinded with defeat,*
> *His head for ever bowed in pain,*
> *I feel his presence plead above*
> *The violin that speaks in vain*
> *The crowned humility of love.*
>
> *O music undeterred by death*
> *And darkness closing on your flame,*
> *Christ whispers in your dying breath*
> *And haunts you with his tragic name.*

My present interpretation of this high-flown effusion is that, while attempting to express something universal, the motive behind it was my personal conviction that I should not live to hear the Elgar Concerto a second time. And it may be added that only by the fraction of an inch did this notion fail to be justified when —less than four months later—I was sniped above the collar-bone while indiscreetly looking out of a sap in the Hindenburg Trench. My diary makes no mention of the next entertainment I went to in Liverpool. This was a Revue at the Hippodrome, to which I was conducted by one of my fellow officers who in peace-time had worked in the organization known as 'Moss's Empires'. It is probable that I spent quite an amusing evening, since my companion was a pleasant and intelligent person (less fortunate than myself, for he was killed at Bullecourt in April 1917). The Hippodrome show, however, provided me with a bit of material for satire. A couple of days before my departure from the Depot for final leave, I wrote the afterwards well-known lines called *Blighters*, in which I asserted that I'd like to see a tank come down the stalls at a music-hall performance where—in my opinion—the jingoism of the jokes and songs appeared to 'mock the riddled corpses round Bapaume'. Perhaps I was intolerant, but I found a good many people—Thomas Hardy among them—who agreed with me. Anyhow it was my farewell to England, and as such it was the sort of thing I particularly wanted to say.

*   *   *

It is sufficiently obvious that, for those about to return to the firing-line, mental distractions were desirable. The grimness of the occasion had to be got over somehow, and the forced cheerfulness of one's dejected friends and relations made it no easier. The eight days of my final leave were about equally divided between Weirleigh and Half Moon Street. While staying with my mother I occupied myself with the revision of my book of poems, which had got itself into galley proofs, but I couldn't pretend that I felt festive, as was demonstrated by the final entry in my diary.

'*February* 7. At home again for the last time before going out to unmitigated hell—otherwise known as "The Big Push". A bright fire burning. Topper licking his paws in an arm-chair opposite me. Friendly books saying good-bye to me from their shelves and blue moonlight filtering through the white curtains from the dazzling white snow and starry night, while the wind makes a little crooning in the chimney and the grandfather clock in the hall strikes ten. This evening I was playing Elizabethan lute songs, so gay and full of tenderness. I have got to break it to poor mother that I'm going out again but haven't had the heart to do it yet. She was so pleased and unconscious of it when I arrived last night.'

In London I was able to keep on the move all the while. I see myself at Queen's Hall, hearing—was it Beethoven's Fifth Symphony?—breakfasting with Eddie Marsh in Gray's Inn on a Sunday morning and discussing my proofs—dining at the Gosses', where I was pained to hear that the Poet Laureate's house had been burnt to the ground a couple of days before, though his library had providentially escaped destruction. Returning to Half Moon Street I gave Robbie the news, which caused him to remark that he supposed the fire had been caused by dry rot—Bridges being one of those writers against whom he had a personal prejudice. (These prejudices could usually be traced to an unappreciative attitude towards the works of Wilde.) Robbie, who was much distressed by my going abroad again, made gallant efforts to keep our spirits up, and somehow managed to be in his wittiest form. We dined with Mr. Heinemann, whose table showed no sign of food restrictions. The fourth member of the party was Haddon Chambers, an agreeable playwright who had made his name with a comedy called *The Tyranny of Tears*. Heinemann told a lot of funny stories about Hall Caine and I drank some potent 'Kirsch' which made my laughter seem as though it belonged to someone else. It was just the sort of entertainment I needed—civilized and deliberately disregardful of the war, which my companions detested as much as I did.

Distraction of a different character was provided by Lady Ottoline, with whom I spent two whole afternoons which were by no means beneficial to my state of mind. Unlike my mother, who made the best of my departure by saying as little as possible about it, dear Lady Ottoline insisted on being intensely earnest and discursive. She was obsessed by what she felt to be the brutal stupidity and imbecile wastefulness of the War, and my own return to it had involved her in a crisis of emotional depression. This caused me to talk recklessly, with a sort of victimized bitterness. I should probably get killed, I said; but the main trouble was that I no longer knew what I was being killed for. 'One gets sent out again like a cabbage going to Covent Garden Market,' I exclaimed, adding that cabbages were better off, because they didn't claim to

have unconquerable souls, and weren't told that they were making a supreme sacrifice for the sake of unborn vegetables. These
discussions led neither of us anywhere; they were as undirected
and indeterminate as our wanderings about Bloomsbury. I can
remember her taking me across the Tower Bridge. It was a sombre-
skied afternoon, appropriate to the melancholy tone of our conversation. She was wearing some of her most unconventional and
vivid-coloured clothes, and an enormous feathered hat which made
her look very tall. Passers-by stopped to stare, but she appeared
unconscious of attracting attention as she stood, half-way across
the bridge, contemplating the broad iron-grey vista of the river
and saying that there was 'something so moving about it—so
mysterious and immense'. . . . To which I assented, while wishing
that she wouldn't go about looking quite so extraordinary, though
I realized that she was a noble and distinguished figure among the
drably-dressed nobodies who gaped at her so uncomprehendingly.
My own comprehension of her fine qualities did not begin until
some years later. The situation was too complex for the shy and
callow young man I was on that dreary February afternoon.

*   *   *

On February 15th I was at Waterloo for the noontide leave
train (or, to be exact, the leave train the wrong way round). My
mother was there to see the last of me, and Robbie had shepherded
me to the station. My one desire was to have no feelings about
anything. As we paced along the platform I remarked to Robbie
that the train was quite an old friend as this was the fourth time I
had travelled by it. When it at length began to move, their faces
kept up the usual forlorn pretence of looking bright. With the
egotism of youth I couldn't help wondering what they said to one
another about me after they had turned away from the vanishing
train. But I had no doubt that Robbie would rise to the occasion
and that my mother would appreciate the intuitive tactfulness
which never failed him where his heart was concerned.

47

V

About fifteen weeks after I went to France I found myself once again temporarily liberated from Army life. My bullet wound had healed quickly. A couple of weeks in a London hospital had been followed by a month's convalescence in perfect surroundings, for I was one of several officers who were staying with Lord and Lady Brassey at their beautiful home in Sussex. All possible kindness had been showered on me, every opportunity was there for healthy contentment and mental relaxation, and the fine early summer weather made the place an earthly paradise. But somehow or other I had only achieved superficial felicity, for the contrast between this luxurious and delightful existence and my lurid experiences on the Arras battlefield had been with me all the time. My mind had dwelt continually on the battalion with which I had been serving. Since I left it, ten officers had been killed and fourteen wounded. It wasn't surprising that this undermined my complacency about my own good fortune. There were moments when I felt irrationally hostile to the graciously-organized amenities of Chapelwood Manor which were providing such superlative compensation for my brief participation in the Spring Offensive. While in France, my anti-war ideas had been in abeyance. Out there one had been too busy to ask the reason why. One couldn't be 'above the battle' while engaged in it, and I had sometimes been able to resort to the emotional 'happy warrior' attitude which was so helpful in sustaining one's fortitude. My discontents were now simmering rebelliously and had acquired an added momentum. I went up to London resolved to write something more definitely antagonistic than satiric epigrams in *The Cambridge Magazine*, wherein I had recently made a lively appearance with the lines called *Base Details*. Four weeks of independence were ahead of me and I meant to make the most of them. I would go to Garsington and investigate the war situation by talking to the Morrells and Bertrand Russell, who was staying with them. Elsewhere I was being urged to take a home service job, and it seemed likely that I might be offered an instructorship with the

Officers' Training Corps at Cambridge. Meanwhile I was to be in London during most of the next two weeks. One reason for this was that Robbie had arranged with Glyn Philpot that he should do a drawing of me, and more than a single sitting would be needed. The price of this was to be fifty guineas, but when I presented myself at the studio in Tite Street I found that Philpot intended to paint a full-sized portrait. Knowing that he ought to receive five hundred pounds for this, I felt a bit uncomfortable. Without mentioning money, however, he indicated that he wanted to do it unprofessionally, as Robbie was a great friend of his and he thought me a good subject. Consequently, a good many of my afternoons were spent there, and very pleasant ones they were.

Glyn Philpot, who was never a strong man, had been invalided out of the army without having seen active service. We did not talk about the War at all, and his quiet studio was a perfect place in which to forget about it. His own existence was one that consisted largely in an ultra-refined appreciation of beautiful objects. He had what might be called a still-life temperament; his eyes delighted not so much in the living realities of nature as in the richness and elegance of things contrived by human handiwork. This was shown in his painting of silks, velvets, and brocades, and in anything which evoked his sensuous joy in surface qualities and harmonious arrangements of colour. Too subtle and fine to be accused of preciosity, his taste was superbly artificial. The interior environment he had devised for himself was a deliberately fastidious denial of war-time conditions, a delicate defence against the violence and ugly destruction which dominated the outside world. All this made sitting for my portrait a most tranquillizing occupation, slowing down my thoughts and soothing my sensibilities. I have always been fond of the smell of a studio, and this one—in the purposeful silences of those summer afternoons—was peculiarly pleasant. Musefully I sat there—a shade self-conscious about my appearance—while the artist unobtrusively observed me between his discreet and skilful brush-strokes. When I spoke my thoughts aloud he replied from only half his attention, and this created a sort of absent-minded atmosphere which made the place seem more peaceful than ever.

Siegfried's Journey, 1916–1920

After the sitting he produced a delicious tea, during which I did more than my share of the talking. Responsively impersonal, he encouraged my communicative questionings, receiving my exuberances with amused and gentle gravity. From the first I had found him a delightfully modest and likeable companion. A couple of years older than I, he was good-looking in a rather Italian way. To him I must have seemed a young person to whom the War was giving no immediate cause for dissatisfaction. The face shown in his portrait is almost scornfully severe and unspeculative, giving no indication of the conflict that was being enacted behind that mask of physical prosperity.

I must have been aware that—had I been willing to take the easiest road—the worst of my war experiences were behind me. Yet, during the fortnight when I was going to the Chelsea studio, I was otherwise engaged in formulating a course of action which not only asked for trouble but insisted on creating it for myself. With Philpot I was the young soldier poet whose book had been published less than a month and was already well on its way towards a second impression. I could tell him that Arnold Bennett had invited me to lunch. I might also have mentioned that he had sent me one of his books with an inscription 'To S.S. though it is only from A.B.', which was characteristic of his invariable generosity towards the younger writers. Thomas Hardy, to whom my book was dedicated, had written me a letter which I valued above anything else in my literary career. And Mr. Gosse had transmitted to me a message from the Poet Laureate, saying that I had more of the real stuff in me than almost any other of my generation. I had also met H. G. Wells, who had behaved as though my opinions were worth listening to, which seemed remarkable in one whose talk was so stimulating and humorous and full of ideas. But the main element in my advancement was the fact that I was alive when I might have been buried under a wooden cross in France. I could claim that I had 'done my bit', and everyone was being as nice as possible about it. When Arnold Bennett advised me to accept a home service job I agreed that it would probably be the best thing for me to do. Nevertheless I had already made up my mind that the only home service I could undertake must be getting sent to prison for refusing to perform any more military

50

duties! Such was my internal condition when, at the end of a
sitting, Philpot—putting away his palette and brushes—unobtrusively informed me that the portrait was completed. Inspecting
it for the first time (I had conscientiously avoided looking at it
before) I remarked that it was rather Byronic. 'You *are* rather,
aren't you?' he replied, gazing at me with dark, heavy-lidded
eyes which seemed courteously observant rather than keenly
scrutinizing. I assured him that I should very much like to be,
adding that there was no need to tell him how good I thought the
picture. While we were having tea I glanced at it occasionally with
a pleasant feeling that I had acquired a romantic, illustrative personality to preside over my published works. It was indeed an ideal
'posterity portrait'.

While walking away from Tite Street I regretfully realized that
there was no knowing when I should see Glyn again. The oppression of what lay ahead closed in upon me. Up to that time I had
been borne along by the impetus of my insurgent gesture. Bleaker
contemplations of its sickening results were now unavoidable,
when emotional excitement had abated and I had pledged myself
beyond possibility of withdrawal. Anyhow, it had never occurred
to me before that I was 'a bit Byronic', and the idea helped to
sustain my belief that I was about to do something spectacular and
heroic.

It was now the middle of June, and the short statement of my
reasons for protesting against the prolongation of the war had
been put on paper. Since my leave began I had been staying at
my club in St. James's Street. I had divulged my intention to no-
one except the Morrells, with whom I had spent a day at Garsington. Lady Ottoline had supported me with admiring enthusiasm,
but Philip Morrell had advised against the project. It would only
be a nine-days' wonder, he said, foreseeing the pathetic absurdity
of a solitary second-lieutenant raising his voice against the archi-
tects of a world conflict. Staring at the sunset as he leant on a farm
gate, he himself—in his wide-brimmed black hat—had looked
somehow defeated and ineffective, a compromising pacifist who
had lost hope of dissuading mankind from its madness. It was the
face of a man with fine aspirations, but his handsome features had
no potency behind them. Kind and magnanimous, he lacked

intellectual toughness. I returned to London undeterred from my resolve, with an introduction to Middleton Murry, whose opinions were much the same as mine, though he was at that time working in a Government Department of some sort. With him and Katherine Mansfield (of whose great talent as a story-writer I was still unaware) I spent a self-conscious sultry evening in a candle-lighted room in South Kensington. He was sympathetic and help-ful in clarifying my statement and reducing it to a more con-densed form. Katherine Mansfield was almost silent. The only thing I can remember her saying was 'Do you ever think about anything except the war?' Nothing now remained but to make a fair copy and take it to Bertrand Russell, who had undertaken to act as my impresario. With him I was going to see Mr. Lees-Smith, a pacifist M.P. (who afterwards achieved Cabinet rank as Postmaster-General in a Labour Government). He, it was hoped, would give the statement publicity by asking a question about it in the House of Commons. Such was the deadly procedure which I had contrived for myself. And in a few weeks its full effect would descend on my head when I broke the news to the Commanding Officer of the Royal Welch Fusiliers Depot at Litherland.

It thus happened that, about midnight on the day my portrait was finished, I sat alone in the club library with a fair copy of the 'statement' before me on the writing-table. The words were now solidified and unalterable. My brain was unable to scrutinize their meaning any more. They had become merely a sequence of declamatory sentences, designed to let me in for what appeared to be a moral equivalent of 'going over the top'; and, at the moment, the Hindenburg Line seemed preferable in retrospect. For the first time, I allowed myself to reflect upon the consequences of my action and to question my strength to endure them. Possibly what I disliked most was the prospect of being misunderstood and dis-approved of by my fellow officers. Some of them would regard my behaviour as a disgrace to the Regiment. Others would assume that I had gone a bit crazy. How many of them, I wondered, would give me credit for having done it for the sake of the troops who were at the Front? I had never heard any of them use the word pacifist except in a contemptuous and intolerant way, and in my dispirited mood I felt that my protest would have a pretty poor reception among them. Going to a window, I looked out at the searchlights probing the dark sky. Down below, the drone of London rumbled on. The streets were full of soldiers getting what enjoyment they could out of their leave. And there, on that sheet of paper under the green-shaded lamp, were the words I had just transcribed.

'I believe that this war, upon which I entered as a war of defence and liberation, has now become a war of aggression and conquest.'

To the soldiers it didn't matter, one way or the other. They all wanted it to stop, but most of them would say that the Boches had got to be beaten somehow, and the best thing to hope for was 'getting back to Blighty with a cushy wound'. Then I remembered that night, early in 1914, when I had been up in this room experiencing an emotional crisis in which I had felt that my life was being wasted on sport and minor poetry, and had imagined myself devoting my future to humanitarian services and nobly prophetic writings. On that occasion I had written some well-intentioned but too didactic lines, of which a fragment now recurred to me.

> *Destiny calls me home at last*
> *To strive for pity's sake;*
> *To watch with the lonely and outcast,*
> *And to endure their ache. . . .*

Much had happened since then. Realities beyond my radius had been brought under my observation by a European War, which had led me to this point of time and that sheet of paper on the table. Was this the fulfilment of that feeble and unforeseeing stanza? . . . And somehow the workings of my mind brought me a comprehensive memory of war experience in its intense and essential humanity. It seemed that my companions of the Somme and Arras battles were around me; helmeted faces returned and receded in vision; joking voices were overheard in fragments of dug-out and billet talk. These were the dead, to whom life had been desirable, and whose sacrifice must be justified, unless the War were to go down in history as yet another Moloch of murdered youth. Let indignant civilians and phrase-

coining politicians think what they chose. It was for the fighting
men that my appeal was made, for those whose loyalty and unthinkingness would have been betrayed, whatever acquisitions
the Peace might bring to the British Empire. I went back to the
statement on the table with fortified conviction that I was doing
right. Perhaps the dead were backing me up, I thought; for I was
a believer in the power of spiritual presences. . . .

> *Well, how are things in Heaven? I wish you'd say,*
> *Because I'd like to know that you're all right.*
> *Tell me, have you found everlasting day*
> *Or been sucked in by everlasting night?*

The words came into my head quite naturally. And by the time I
went to bed I had written a slangy, telephonic poem of forty lines.
I called it *To Any Dead Officer*, but it was addressed to one
whom I had known during both my periods of service in France.
Poignant though the subject was, I wrote it with a sense of
mastery and detachment, and when it was finished I felt that it
anyhow testified to the sincerity of my protest.

*   *   *

A few days afterwards I went home, to spend the remainder of
my leave waiting for the trouble to begin. Owing to the discomfort of deceiving him I had been avoiding Robbie lately; but on
my way to Charing Cross I called at the Reform Club on the
chance of seeing him there. As it was the middle of the afternoon I
found the Club almost deserted. The door-porter having told me
that he was probably in the library, I went up the stairs to the
gallery which overlooks the noble columnar entrance hall. There
I discovered him, with his coat off, at the top of a step-ladder,
cleaning one of the embrowned and more than life-sized portraits
of Victorian Liberal statesmen which are let into the walls. He was
wearing his black silk skull-cap, and looked small and somehow
touching as his tired face brightened to greet me. He was anxious
to hear the result of my expedition to Cambridge. This had been
since the completion of my portrait, with which he was delighted.

I was able to inform him that the Colonel of the Cadet Battalion had agreed to my application for a post as instructor; but I failed to look him in the face when I did so. He said that it was the most sensible thing I could have done. My friends would now breathe a universal sigh of relief at my being prevented from returning to the trenches! The idea of my becoming a teacher of young officers didn't seem to strike him as inappropriate. Personally, I had almost forgotten what a sigh of relief felt like. And I knew that my qualifications for the instructorship were inadequate. My sole purpose, in pretending to accept it, had been to improve my position as a refuser of military service. No one could now say that I had done it to avoid being sent back to the Front. But my duplicity toward Robbie made me feel rather wretched, and he must have noticed that something was wrong, for when I was saying good-bye on the steps of the Club he suddenly asked whether I had anything on my mind, as I didn't look at all well. I muttered something about sleeping badly and London not agreeing with me, and changed the subject to *The Old Huntsman*, which was being reprinted. Robbie told me that he had met Lady Diana Manners in St. James's Street that morning and had presented her with a copy. 'Telling one's friends to buy a book is waste of time,' he remarked airily. 'One has to produce it from one's pocket and press it into their hands. The least one can hope for is that they'll leave it lying about in their drawing-rooms and talk as though they'd read it!'

*   *   *

My experiences during the next three weeks, which ended in my being sent to a shell-shock hospital, have already been related in *Memoirs of an Infantry Officer*. I am thankful not to be obliged to drag my mind through the details again. Being fourteen years older than when I wrote Sherston's subjective account, I am now more inclined to analyse and investigate the inner history of a course of action that I have never regretted and for which there was no apparent alternative. While at the Front I was able to identify myself with my battalion. But, once I was back in England, I had to do something to relieve my state of mental tension. In my note-book there is an entry dated May 21st. 'I still think that I'd better go back as soon as possible unless I can make some protest against the War.' Had there been a chance of my getting passed for general service at the end of my June leave, I might conceivably have tried for it in a spirit of self-destructive bravado. But there seemed no likelihood of my being sent out again for several months, so I plunged headlong into my 'protest'. When I sent my statement to Arnold Bennett he replied at some length, with typical tolerance and good sense. He pointed out that I was not in a position to judge the situation, and was arrogating to myself a right to which I was not entitled—the right to be free from my obligations as an officer whenever I happened to conclude that the War ought to be over. 'What is the matter with you is spiritual pride,' he affirmed. That may have been true. But he was unaware that my action was the climax of a progression of ideas and emotions which had begun almost a year before, and that my behaviour was in accordance with the temperament which had led me to perform reckless exploits in the front line. His judgement was duplicated by a writer in the *Army and Navy Gazette*. 'It is obvious that soldiers, even if they have reached the exalted rank of Second-Lieutenant, cannot be permitted to decide when the time has come for them to discontinue fighting, and the military authorities would appear to have taken a commendably mild view of the case of the young officer in question in adopting the medical suggestion that his extraordinary action is due to the fact that at the time he entered upon it he was suffering from shell-shock rather than from a sudden impulse of insubordination of a particularly grave kind.' There were others who considered my behaviour admirable and inspiring. The incomparable author of *Mr. Britling* wrote that he agreed with me that the War was going on through the sheer stupid inability of the responsible people to crystallize out in a plain statement the peace wishes that were practically the same in the minds of reasonable persons everywhere. He said he would like to find some means of backing me. Anyhow his letter was more than enough to counteract the urbane disapproval of the *Army and Navy Gazette*. Meanwhile the Under-Secretary for War had told the House of Commons that I was suffering from a nervous breakdown, unavoidably ignoring the fact that people in such a condition don't usually do things requiring moral courage. I must add that in the light of subsequent events it is difficult to believe that a Peace negotiated in 1917 would have been permanent. I share the general opinion that nothing on earth would have prevented a recurrence of Teutonic aggressiveness.

VI

One morning at the beginning of August, when I had been at Craiglockhart War Hospital about a fortnight, there was a gentle knock on the door of my room and a young officer entered. Short, dark-haired, and shyly hesitant, he stood for a moment before coming across to the window, where I was sitting on my bed cleaning my golf clubs. A favourable first impression was made by the fact that he had under his arm several copies of *The Old Huntsman*. He had come, he said, hoping that I would be so gracious as to inscribe them for himself and some of his friends. He spoke with a slight stammer, which was no unusual thing in that neurosis-pervaded hospital. My leisurely, commentative method of inscribing the books enabled him to feel more at home with me. He had a charming honest smile, and his manners—he stood at my elbow rather as though conferring with a superior officer—were modest and ingratiating. He gave me the names of his friends first. When it came to his own I found myself writing one that has since gained a notable place on the roll of English poets—Wilfred Owen. I had taken an instinctive liking to him, and felt that I could talk freely. During the next half-hour or more I must have spoken mainly about my book and its interpretations of the War. He listened eagerly, questioning me with reticent intelligence. It was only when he was departing that he confessed to being a writer of poetry himself, though none of it had yet appeared in print.

It amuses me to remember that, when I had resumed my ruminative club-polishing, I wondered whether his poems were any good! He had seemed an interesting little chap but had not struck me as remarkable. In fact my first view of him was as a rather ordinary young man, perceptibly provincial, though unobtrusively ardent in his responses to my lordly dictums about poetry. Owing to my habit of avoiding people's faces while talking, I had not observed him closely. Anyhow, it was pleasant to have discovered that there was another poet in the hospital and that he happened to be an admirer of my work. For him on the

58

other hand, the visit to my room—as he subsequently assured me —had been momentous. It had taken him two whole weeks, he said, to muster up enough courage to approach me with his request. I must add that, in a letter to his mother—shown me many years afterwards—he reported me as talking badly. 'He accords a slurred suggestion of words only. . . . The last thing he said to me was "Sweat your guts out writing poetry." He also warned me against early publishing. He is himself thirty. Looks under twenty-five.' This must have been written a few days later, after he had diffidently shown me a selection of his verse, for he describes me—I am thankful to say—as 'applauding some of it long and fervently' and pronouncing one of his recent lyrics ('Song of Songs') 'perfect work, absolutely charming', and asking him to copy it for me. I record my thankfulness, because I have an uncomfortable suspicion that I was a bit slow in recognizing the exceptional quality of his poetic gift. Manuscript poems can be deceptive when handed to one like school exercises to be blue-pencilled, especially when one has played thirty-six holes of golf and consumed a stodgy hospital dinner. I was sometimes a little severe on what he showed me, censuring the over-luscious writing in his immature pieces, and putting my finger on 'She dreams of golden gardens and sweet glooms' as an example. But it was the emotional element, even more than its verbal expression, which seemed to need refinement. There was an almost embarrassing sweetness in the sentiment of some of his work, though it showed skill in rich and melodious combinations of words. This weakness, as hardly requires pointing out, he was progressively discarding during the last year of his life. In his masterpiece *Strange Meeting* he left us the finest elegy written by a soldier of that period, and the conclusive testimony of his power and originality. It was, however, not until some time in October, when he brought me his splendidly constructed sonnet *Anthem for Doomed Youth*, that it dawned on me that my little friend was much more than the promising minor poet I had hitherto adjudged him to be. I now realized that his verse, with its sumptuous epithets and large-scale imagery, its noble naturalness and depth of meaning, had impressive affinities with Keats, whom he took as his supreme exemplar. This new sonnet was a revelation. I suggested one or two slight alterations; but it confronted me with classic and imaginative serenity. After assuring him of its excellence I told him that I would do my best to get it published in *The Nation*. This gratified him greatly. Neither of us could have been expected to foresee that it would some day be added to *Palgrave's Golden Treasury*.

It has been loosely assumed and stated that Wilfred modelled his war poetry on mine. My only claimable influence was that I stimulated him towards writing with compassionate and challenging realism. His printed letters are evidence that the impulse was already strong in him before he had met me. The manuscript of one of his most dynamically descriptive war poems, *Exposure*, is dated February 1917, and proves that he had already found an authentic utterance of his own. (For some reason, he withheld this poem from me while we were together.) Up to a point my admonitions were helpful. My encouragement was opportune, and I can claim to have given him a lively incentive during his rapid advance to self-revelation. Meanwhile I seem to hear him laughingly implore me to chuck these expository generalizations and recover some of the luminous animation of our intimacy. How about my indirect influence on him? he inquires in his calm velvety voice. Have I forgotten our eager discussions of contemporary poets and the technical dodges which we were ourselves devising? Have I forgotten the simplifying suggestions which emanated from my unsophisticated poetic method? (For my technique was almost elementary compared with his innovating experiments.) Wasn't it after he got to know me that he first began to risk using the colloquialisms which were at that time so frequent in my verses? And didn't I lend him Barbusse's *Le Feu*, which set him alight as no other war book had done? It was indeed one of those situations where imperceptible effects are obtained by people mingling their minds at a favourable moment. Turning the pages of Wilfred's *Poems*, I am glad to think that there may have been occasions when some freely improvised remark of mine sent him away with a fruitful idea. And my humanized reportings of front-line episodes may have contributed something to his controlled vision of what he had seen for himself. Of his own period of active service he seldom spoke. I was careful to avoid questioning

him about the experiences which had caused his nervous breakdown, and was only vaguely aware of what he had been through
in the St. Quentin sector and elsewhere. Fourteen years later,
when reading the letters quoted by Edmund Blunden in his finally
authoritative Memoir, I discovered that Wilfred had endured
worse things than I had realized from the little he told me. On
arriving at the Western Front he had immediately encountered
abominable conditions of winter weather and attrition warfare.
But of this he merely remarked to me that he wished he'd had my
luck in being inured to the beastly business by gradual stages.
His thick dark hair was already touched with white above the
ears.

As I remember him during those three months we spent together at Craiglockhart he was consistently cheerful. Dr. Brock,
who was in charge of his case, had been completely successful in
restoring the balance of his nerves. He seemed contented and had
found plenty to occupy him. He edited *The Hydra*, the fort-
nightly hospital magazine, and was an active member of the
Field Club. In a number of *The Hydra*, the proceedings of the
Field Club include the following unexpected item: 'An interesting paper on the classification of soils, soil air, soil water, root
absorption and fertility was given by Mr. Owen on October 1st.'
My sonnet *Dreamers* made its first appearance in the magazine,
thus inconspicuously inaugurating a career of frequent quotation
and reprinting. It is also worth noting that it was only through my
urgent instigation that he printed a short poem of his own. This
was in accordance with his essential unassumingness. Though not
clearly conscious of it at the time, I now realize that in a young
man of twenty-four his selflessness was extraordinary. The clue to
his poetic genius was sympathy, not only in his detached outlook
upon humanity but in all his actions and responses towards individuals. I can remember nothing in my observations of his
character which showed any sign of egotism or desire for self-
advancement. When contrasting the two of us, I find that—
highly strung and emotional though he was—his whole personality was far more compact and coherent than mine. He readily
recognized and appreciated this contrast, and I remember with
affection his amused acceptance of my exclamatory enthusiasms

and intolerances. Most unfairly to himself, he even likened us to Don Quixote and Sancho Panza! I have already mentioned the velvety quality of his voice, which suggested the Keatsian richness of his artistry with words. It wasn't a vibrating voice. It had the fluid texture of soft consonants and murmurous music. Hearing him read poetry aloud in his modest unemphatic way, one realized at once that he had an exceptionally sensitive ear. One of his poems begins 'All sounds have been as music to my listening', and his sense of colour was correspondingly absorbent. Sounds and colours, in his verse, were mulled and modulated to a subdued magnificence of sensuous harmonies, and this was noticeable even in his everyday speaking. His temperament, as I apprehend it, was unhurrying, though never languid. Only now and then was he urgently quickened by the mysterious prompting and potency of his imagination. His manuscripts show that he seldom brought his poems to their final form without considerable recasting and revision. There was a slowness and sobriety in his method, which was, I think, monodramatic and elegiac rather than leapingly lyrical. I do not doubt that, had he lived longer, he would have produced poems of sustained grandeur and ample design. It can be observed that his work is prevalently deliberate in movement. Stately and processional, it has the rhythm of emotional depth and directness and the verbal resonance of one who felt in glowing primary colours and wrote with solemn melodies in his mind. It can be taken for granted that there were aspects of him which I never saw. To others he may have revealed much that I missed, since he had the adaptability of a beautifully sympathetic nature. But I like to believe that when with me he was at his best, and I can remember no shadow of unhappiness or misunderstanding between us.

As a letter writer he was—like most of us in our youth—a shade self-conscious and liable to indulge in fine phrases. But if any proof were needed of his physical toughness and intellectual determination it can be found in the wonderful pages sent to his mother from the Front. And he always communicated vividly what was uppermost in his thoughts at the moment.

Wilfred's face will be known to posterity by a photograph taken in uniform, and to some extent disguised by the animal health of

army life. It shows him very much as he was when I was with
him. He wasn't a fine-drawn type. There was a full-blooded
robustness about him which implied reserves of mental energy
and solid ability. Under ordinary conditions it wasn't a spiritual
face. It was of the mould which either coarsens or refines itself in
later life. I cannot say that I ever saw what is called 'a look of
genius' in it. His mouth was resolute and humorous, his eyes long
and heavy-lidded, quiescent rather than penetrating. They were
somewhat sleepy eyes, kind, shrewd, and seldom lit up from
within. They seemed, like much else in his personality, to be
instinctively guarding the secret sources of his inward power and
integrity. His face—what would it have become? While calling
him back in memory I have been haunted by the idea of the unalterable features of those who have died in youth. Borne away
from them by the years, we—with our time-troubled looks and
diminished alertness—have submitted to many a gradual detri-
ment of change. But the young poet of twenty-five years ago
remains his world-discovering self. His futureless eyes encounter
ours from the faintly smiling portrait, unconscious of the privilege
and deprivation of never growing old, unconscious of the dramatic
illusion of completeness that he is destined to create.

*   *   *

'Since mid-September, when you still regarded me as a tiresome little knocker on your door . . . you have *fixed* my life—however short.' These words were in the first letter I received from
Wilfred after he had left Craiglockhart at the beginning of
November. They confirm what I have already indicated—my
slowness in discovering that he was able to be of high significance
for me both as poet and friend. It is indeed sadly certain that only
in those last few weeks I received his fullest confidences and
realized that he could give me as much as I gave to him. Circumstances made this easier, for by October I had a small room to
myself, and our talks were no longer liable to be obstructed by the
presence of a fellow patient. Almost every evening he would visit
me and there was much comfort in his companionship. For I was
enduring the difficult and distressing experience of making up my

mind to withdraw from my 'stop the war' attitude and get myself passed for service abroad. All this has already been described in *Sherston's Progress*, so I need say nothing about it here, or dwell on the inestimable guidance and discernment of my friend and doctor, W. H. R. Rivers. But it seems permissible, at this point, to quote the diagnosis of my case which Rivers made. (The document was given to me after his death.) 'The patient is a healthy-looking man of good physique. There are no physical signs of any disorder of the nervous system. He discusses his recent actions and their motives in a perfectly intelligent and rational way, and there is no evidence of any excitement or depression. He recognizes that his view of warfare is tinged by his feelings about the death of friends and of the men who were under his command in France. At the present time he lays special stress on the hopelessness of any decision in the war as it is now being conducted. His view differs from that of the ordinary pacifist in that he would no longer object to the continuance of the war if he saw any reasonable prospect of a rapid decision.' While this agonizing affair was in process of development Wilfred's wisdom and graciousness of spirit became fully evident. His hero being in sore need, he could bring him gentle and intuitive support, tiding over inevitable moods of bitterness and depression. There was, moreover, a compensating element in the situation. The privacy of my room was making it possible for me to work fruitfully at the series of poems afterwards published under the name of *Counter-attack*, and Wilfred's praises heartened and helped me. It was then that we vowed our confederacy to unmask the ugly face of Mars and—in the words of Thomas Hardy—'war's apology wholly stultify'.

Our final evening together was spent at a quiet Club in Edinburgh, of which Rivers had got me elected an honorary member. Wilfred was leaving for London by the midnight train. After a good dinner and a bottle of noble Burgundy had put us in cheerful spirits, I produced a volume of portentously over-elaborated verse, recently sent me by the author. From this I began to read extracts —a cursory inspection having assured me that he would find them amusing. It now seems incongruous that my most vivid memory of him, on that last occasion when we were alone together, should be of his surrendering to convulsions of mirth in a large leather-covered arm-chair. These convulsions I shared until incapable of continuing my recital.

> *What cassock'd misanthrope,*
> *Hawking peace-canticles for glory-gain,*
> *Hymns from his rostrum'd height th'epopt of Hate?*

It was, I think, the word 'epopt' (the grandiloquent poet's version of epopee—otherwise 'epic song') which caused the climax of our inextinguishable laughter, though the following couplet, evidently 'written in dejection', had already scored heavily.

> *O is it true I have become*
> *This gourd, this gothic vacuum?*

Except for the presence of a dignified gentleman—possibly a Writer to the Signet—who was at the far end of the room, we were unobserved. The more we laughed, the more solemnly he eyed us, and this somehow made our hilarity uncontrollable. 'Laughter at its best,' says Max Beerbohm in one of his amaranthine essays, 'goes so far as to lose all touch with its motive, and to exist only, grossly, in itself.' To that pitch we were reduced. And it is conceivable that behind his outward gravity—and the rustling pages of *The Scotsman*—the elderly gentleman may have envied us, or even have been secretly refreshed by our behaviour.

I have suggested that the remembrance of our laughter now seems incongruous. Perhaps this is because the date of our dinner was November 3rd. Exactly a year afterwards—on the morning of November 4th—Wilfred was killed while leading his company in an attack. Meanwhile it was time for me to be returning to the hospital. When saying good-bye I gave him a letter of introduction to Robbie Ross. Wilfred had no literary connections in London, and during the next few months Robbie made him known to various people who were glad to welcome this new and gifted young war poet. The beginning of these too brief recognitions of his personal qualities by the eminent can best be told in his own words. He wrote from Scarborough, where he had been posted to a reserve battalion. '*November 27th.* I sit alone at last, and therefore with you, my dear Siegfried. For which name, as much as for anything in any envelope of your sealing, I give thanks and rejoice. The 5th Battalion have taken over a big hotel, of which I am Major Domo, which in the vulgar, means Lift Boy. I manage accommodation, food, and service. I boss cooks, housemaids, charwomen, chambermaids, mess-orderlies, and drummers. There were 80 officers when I came, or 800 grouses daily. I had a Third Heaven of a time in London, and should have got into a fourth or fifth if I had not missed you on Wednesday. Were you there for a 'Reading'? I know nothing of it to this day. In Town, then, R.R. gave me a glorified morning at the Reform, and evening at Half Moon Street. When he had steered me to a lunch table I found beside me a man who looked astonished to find himself there. But dear Ross sang out with blessed distinctness 'Mister Arnnoldd Bennettt'. So I stood up and shook hands. Presently I became aware of a pair of bayonet-coloured eyes, threatening at me from over, as it were, a brown sandbag. 'Mr. H. G. Wells'! So I stood up and shook hands. I think these men noticed me because I stood up to them—in two senses. Anyhow I got A.B. into a corner about you, as I will tell you some day.' (From this I inferred that Wilfred had been defending my anti-war gesture.) 'And H.G. talked to me exclusively for an hour. I was only ill at ease with him once, and that was when he tried to make me laugh with him at Bennett's gaudy handkerchief. What sport for my imagination is the idea of *your* Meeting with R. Nichols. He is so self-concerned and vaniteux in his verse that I thought he must efface himself in a room: even as you who write so acid are so—unsoured; and me, who write so big, am so minuscule.'

He continues with some remarks about a batch of newly written poems which he was sending me, wherein I found the compelling distinction of all that he produced in his final flowering. He ends with what must have been a reference to the first time he saw me. 'We have had some strong sunshine; and when it strikes anything blue I see you sitting by the bedside as on That Morning in August. You look round—over my head, which annoys me, so that I go down and rate the kitchen staff of the hotel and insult the new subalterns.

I am Owen; and I am dying.

I am Wilfred; and I follow the Gleam.'

Siegfried's Journey, 1916–1920

The letter also contained comments on my decision to return to the war. With playful urgency he attempted to dissuade me; but by the time he wrote, a medical board had passed me for service abroad. This had been adroitly contrived by Rivers, who profoundly disliked doing it, while wisely agreeing that it was the only solution of my predicament. The purpose of my London visit, to which Wilfred referred, had been to see one of my pre-war friends, a Conservative M.P. who was able to put in an influential word for me with the War Office authorities, to whom my previous record was, naturally, a source of misgiving. While in London I gave the 'Reading' about which he asked, and of which I had said nothing in my letter, though I had apparently sent some account of meeting Robert Nichols. This 'Reading' demands description, for it was my first experience of being shown off as a literary lion—though cub would perhaps be a more accurate word for the occasion. The evening began with a dinner at the Café Royal, to which I had been looking forward, as Robbie had also invited Nichols, whose *Ardours and Endurances*—published in the same month as my *Old Huntsman*—had made him the most successful soldier poet of the year, in fact his sales had much exceeded mine. At the Café Royal all went well, for I liked Nichols, who talked with exuberant energy about poetry, was laudatory of my own work, and made me feel that the longer we sat there the better. I was expecting that we should go on to Half Moon Street to continue the conversation; but Robbie had arranged things otherwise. He had, he confessed, promised to take us to a select party given by Mrs. Colefax. When I protested that I didn't want to go, he begged me not to be difficult, as he had staked his reputation—as a chaperon of soldier poets—on our putting in an appearance. On the way to Onslow Square a horrid suspicion crossed my mind that I was being conveyed thither to read my poems. But I dismissed the idea as improbable. Robbie surely wouldn't let me in for a thing like that without giving me an opportunity to refuse. The party consisted mainly of ladies. I was, however, introduced to Sir John Lavery (who looked rather like a coachman in evening clothes), and to Mr. Pearsall Smith, from whose *Trivia*—I was delighted to be able to tell him—I had derived immense pleasure, as I have since done from all his beautiful prose works. But this propitious conversation was soon cut short, for it became apparent that my fears were to be realized and that a poetry reading was confidently expected. An arm-chair and a small table were placed in the middle of the room, and Nichols— an old hand at the game—proceeded to give an emotional and histrionic rendering of the war poems which had won him reputa- tion. Sometimes his voice was bold and resonant; sometimes it sank to a plaintive pianissimo. He also indulged in gesticulation, and when reading a stanza, the last line of which was 'I look up and smile', he looked up and smiled. In spite of my friendly inter- est in him and his writings, all this caused me acute discomfort, made worse by the knowledge that it would be my turn next. When that moment arrived I did a bit of bashful demurring, but Robbie and Mrs. Colefax conducted me to the chair and *The Old Huntsman* was handed to me. I responded by choosing some of my least ingratiating performances, though so nervous and self-con- scious that my muttered undertones must have been inferred rather than audible. I had never read to an audience before, and felt that I was merely the unwilling object of intelligent curiosity. Robbie was furthering his purpose of getting my poems talked about, but his zealousness had outrun discretion. I didn't want to be paraded before these cultivated and agreeable strangers, and for once I was quite huffy with Robbie. Of course I was impressed by being among socially prominent people. Nevertheless my after- thoughts about them were morose and possibly hypersensitive. To them I was a talented youth who had acquired notoriety by pub- licly protesting that the war ought to stop. To myself I was only in London with the object of making sure that the War Office would send me out again—perhaps to my death. No doubt they attri- buted my behaviour to shyness. Inwardly they made me glad that I had written those savage, hard-hitting poems about civilians. And I was thankful that Wilfred Owen wasn't there as a third reader. I felt that, while the War continued, neither he nor I were designed for fashionable exploitation in a Kensington drawing- room.

VII

That inveterate memoirizer George Sherston has already narrated a sequence of infantry experiences—from the end of 1917—which were terminated, on July 13th, by a bullet wound in the head. His experiences were mine, so I am spared the effort of describing them. We—or, to be strictly accurate, I—left him, on the last of his numerous pages, in a luxurious hospital overlooking Hyde Park. This was the American Women's Hospital in Lancaster Gate, and from that point I will now continue. When we parted from Sherston he had been lying in bed feeling disillusioned about the war—and indeed about his whole previous career—until an unexpected visit from Rivers caused him to take a more hopeful view of the future and the better use he might make of it. But Sherston was a simplified version of my 'outdoor self'. He was denied the complex advantage of being a soldier poet. So my own mental condition, though similar, was alleviated by the reception which was then being accorded my new book of poems. Some of the reviewers were pained and indignant at my insistence on the ugly aspects of war. Robbie, however, when bringing press-cuttings, assured me that a hostile notice often did more good than an adulatory one. Anyhow, there was no doubt that *Counter-attack*, in its blood-red and yellow paper cover, was being bought and discussed. Better still, I was out of the war, and could now write my poems without wondering whether I should be dead and done with before anybody read them! I was liberated to the extent of feeling under no obligation to go back, even if—as then appeared probable—the war went on for another year. Rivers had told me that no-one would expect me to go out for the fourth time, adding that he himself would do all in his power to prevent it.

Yet, in spite of my hatred of war and 'Empery's insatiate lust of power', there was an awful attraction in its hold over my mind, which since childhood had shown a tendency towards tragic emotions about human existence. While at Lancaster Gate I was disquieted by a craving to be back on the Western Front as an independent contemplator. No longer feeling any impulse to write bitterly, I imagined myself describing it in a comprehensive way, seeing it like a painter and imbuing my poetry with Whitman-esque humanity and amplitude. From the routine-restricted outlook of battalion sectors I had seen so little, and the physical conditions were a perpetual hindrance to detached and creative vision. But I had experienced enough to feel confident that I could now do something on a bigger scale, and I wanted to acquire further material which would broaden and vitalize what was already in my mind. There were nights when such war poems were cloudily projected in those mysterious visualizations that reward the extremity of sleepless hours, evolving themselves with an inventive spontaneity over which one has no seeming control. An army on the march moved across the darkness, its doom-destined columns backed by the pulsating glare of distant gunfire. Battle pictures emerged and melted from one to another. I saw the shapes of sentries, looming against the livid and sombre cloud-shoals of forlorn front-line daybreak. Or it seemed that I was looking down on a confusion of swarming figures in some battle-ravaged region—an idea derived, perhaps, from the scenic directions in Hardy's *Dynasts*. These spectral images, seen from the borderland of sleep, brought me a delusive sense of power to put them into words. There was a haunting appeal, too, in the sad anonymous faces which emerged on that dream cinemato-graph, faces pale and passionless, as though from a sculptured frieze. Thus might the dead have returned in apparition, silently censuring the cause for which they had given their lives.

Meanwhile, when morning light reduced these visual phan-tasies to an appropriate relationship with the rational world, there seemed quite a chance that the Ministry of Information might be induced to send me to France with a more or less free hand, as they did with the 'official war artists'. The impetus of my inten-tion allowed me to forget that I couldn't expect to be looked upon as a desirable 'official war-writer'. But when Eddie Marsh came to see me and I divulged my plan he gently reminded me that the tone of *Counter-attack* made it improbable that any such oppor-tunity would be conceded me. It was indeed an impracticable idea, which, even if the war had lasted long enough for me to carry it out, would probably have led to frustration and failure. Short poems are my natural means of expression, and for sustained description I have come to prefer prose. While at Lancaster Gate I wrote eight vigil-haunted lines, *The Dugout*, which are probably more memorable than anything I could have achieved in confederacy with a Propaganda Ministry. I was evidently aware of this when, early in October, I received a letter from someone in the Ministry of Information, provisionally offering me a post on Lord Beaverbrook's secretarial staff and asking me to state my credentials. To this I replied, with reprehensible impudence, that as far as I knew my only qualification was that I had been wounded in the head. (The offer now seems to have been a remarkably tolerant one; but I suspect that the Deputy Minister, Arnold Bennett, was responsible for it.) Although capable of repulsing the blandishments of officialdom with such petulance, I was developing a more controlled and objective attitude towards the War. To remind people of its realities was still my main purpose, but I now preferred to depict it impersonally, and to be as much 'above the battle' as I could. Unconsciously, I was getting nearer to Wilfred Owen's method of approach. (For it was not until two years later, when I edited his poems, that I clearly apprehended the essentially compassionate significance of what he had been communicating.)

While in Palestine and France I had heard from him occasionally. In August, when I was half-way through my four weeks at Lancaster Gate, he was in London for a short spell of leave and we spent the whole of a hot cloudless afternoon together. We met at the house of Osbert Sitwell, to whom we had both of us been introduced by Robbie. Osbert, whose talent for hospitality has since become proverbial, was doing duty as a Guards officer at Chelsea Barracks. But at his house in Swan Walk he made us temporarily oblivious of Armageddon in its fifth year. He had arranged to take us to see Mrs. Gordon Woodhouse, who gave us a concert of harpsichord music, entrancing us by her incomparable art, and looking like some exquisite eighteenth-century marquise. These immaterial delights he supplemented with a sumptuous tea which culminated in—was it raspberries and cream?—and ices of incredibly creamy quality. After this delectable negation of war-time conditions we sauntered happily in the charming old herb-garden which is overlooked by the houses in Swan Walk. It was indeed a sybaritic afternoon. My only opportunity for intimate talk with Wilfred was while he saw me back to the hospital. I parted from him in deluded ignorance that he was on final leave before returning to the Front. About three weeks later, when on his way to France, he wrote to say good-bye. The news caused me consternation, but I did my best to be impersonal by telling him that it would be 'good for his poetry'. The letters I received from him during September and October are quoted in Edmund Blunden's Memoir. To transcribe them here would cost me many heavy sighs. The only consolation in them is that they begin 'Very dear Siegfried' and 'Dearest of all Friends'. With the last of them he enclosed a Special Order of the Day issued by his Army Commander. 'There are indications that the enemies' peace offensive is creating the danger which is its object, namely, to divert the attention of officers and men from their single task of defeating the enemy. All ranks are warned against the disturbing influence of dangerous peace talk. Peace talk in any form is to cease in the Fourth Army and Commanders of all formations and units will take immediate steps to ensure that this order is obeyed both in the spirit and in the letter.' His only comment on this admittedly needful document was, 'Full of confidence after having taken a few machine-guns (with the help of one seraphic lance-corporal), I held a most glorious brief peace talk in a pill-box.'

After the Armistice I waited to hear from him, not daring to ask myself, during those weeks of lively distraction, why no letter arrived. Several months elapsed before I was told about his death. I have never been able to accept that disappearance philosophically. A blank miserable sense of deprivation has dulled my mind whenever I have thought of him, and even now it has needed an effort of will to describe our friendship. Recognition of his poetry has steadily increased; but the chasm in my private existence remains. I am unable to believe that 'whom the gods love die young'. Perhaps the Grecian writer who coined the saying had it in mind to hint that the less men see of life the pleasanter their opinion of it must be. My own conviction is that 'whom the gods love' are allowed to fulfil the early promise of their powers.

*   *   *

In his last letter, Wilfred, whose battalion was out of the line after some heavy fighting, observed that 'while you are apparently given over to wrens, I have found brave companionship in a poppy, behind whose stalk I took cover from five machine-guns and several howitzers'. Writing from a convalescent hospital near Coldstream, I had described how, early one morning, a golden-crested wren had appeared in my bedroom and perched on my pillow, thereby affording me the innocent pleasure of releasing it at the open window. Reading his rejoinder to this almost maiden-auntlike piece of news, I probably told myself that war experience was mainly composed of acute contrasts, of which this—in conjunction with his—seemed a classic example. Anyhow there was nothing to be gained from rebuking oneself for being visited by such a charming little creature—evidently an exhausted straggler from a migrating flock—while half asleep in Lady Clementine Waring's delightful house in Berwickshire on a fine September morning. And I could claim that—less than two months before— a five-nine shell had scored a direct hit on my company headquarters; its nose-cap, protruding within a foot of me, leaving me in no doubt as to how my career would have ended if it hadn't happened to be a dud. At Lancaster Gate I had been in a state of overstrained nerves. I had felt as though part of me were still commanding a company in France, and thoughts of that company had often been with me. It was only decent to feel like that, after a long period of self-identification with a set of men, most of whom one liked, and all of whom one did one's best to look after. Arriving at Lennel towards the end of August, I had at once dropped into a comparatively cheerful and unspeculative frame of mind. Before long I was a liberated and irresponsible person, bicycling many miles during the day, doing a little peaceful versifying in the evenings, and getting on quite comfortably with my fellow convalescents, of whom there were about a dozen. Exonerated from any possibility of my name 'living for ever' on the village War Memorial, I could be comfortably conscious of success

73

as a poet, even though that success had been substantially achieved by shocking and aggravating a good few of the older generation. For a while I could find refuge in the little world of one's own whereby human beings contrive their fundamental felicity—the self-contrived contentment of a child making a dam in a brook, or Robinson Crusoe putting the final touches to the palisade of his fort. Bicycling about Berwickshire, I sought to identify the districts described by Surtees in *Mr. Sponge's Sporting Tour*. For these ingenuous explorations there was adequate material. The country had been hunted by that Lord Elcho to whom 'Sponge' was dedicated, and Surtees had enjoyed many a season with his hounds. Lennel had been Lord Elcho's hunting-box, and part of the house could be recognized in one of Leech's illustrations, where Lord Scamperdale is seeing Jack Spraggon into the dog-cart at his front-door. One afternoon when I was meditating in a lonely churchyard not far from Flodden Field, I actually discovered the name John Spraggon on a weather-worn tombstone. In this way I sedulously allowed my mind to relax in day-dreams, gazing across grand stretches of hunting country to the green Cheviots and the dark remoteness of the Lammermoor Hills. For, like my beloved Edward FitzGerald, I had been 'all my life apprentice to the business of idleness', and I could now safely admit that army life had persistently interfered with my ruminative and quiet-loving mentality. I may even have been aware that most of my satiric verses were to some extent prompted by internal exasperation.

Looking through my War diary I have found some lines, written at the beginning of that year after a conversation with a bemedalled and congenial brother officer who took a gloomy view of his prospects of coming through alive.

> *Saved by unnumbered miracles of chance,*
> *You'll stand, with war's unholiness behind;*
> *Those years, like gutted villages in France,*
> *Done with; their shell-bursts drifting out of mind.*
> *Then will you look upon your time to be,*
> *Like someone staring over a foreign town*
> *Who hears church bells and knows himself set free,*
> *And to the twinkling lights goes gladly down.*

Siegfried's Journey, 1916–1920

I hadn't much fancied my own chances of survival when I sat there, in a cold little room in Limerick Barracks on a frosty January night, failing to evolve the last six lines of a rather feeble sonnet. Yet here I was at the end of my journey, apparently none the worse for it, and refusing to bother about the immediate future. My 'time to be' didn't look like a foreign town, and what I went gladly down to was a series of excellent meals presided over by Lady Clementine, who managed her supposedly nerve-disordered guests with undeviating adroitness and good humour. I had to remind myself, however, that my sense of deliverance was still incomplete. Emergence from hospital life would probably be followed by some form of war service, though I had ceased to contemplate that obligation seriously. In the Lennel library there was a handsome octavo edition of Hardy. The pages had been uncut until some omnivorously reading but culpably careless officer had done so, evidently with his fore-finger. I spent most of a pouring wet day trimming the ragged edges with my nail-scissors. Renewed respect was owing to the Wessex novels, I felt. And it was just the sort of tranquillizing occupation I wanted. But the greatest luck I had was in finding among my fellow convalescents one who wrote poetry. His name was Frank Prewett. Everyone called him 'Toronto', that being his home town. He was a remarkable character, delightful when in a cheerful frame of mind, though liable to be moody and aloof. This could be explained by his having served in the Ypres Salient, from the horrors of which he had been delivered by a huge shell bursting near him. His alternations of dark depression and spiritual animation suggested a streak of genius. He was quite young, and the verses he was writing were blurred and embryonic, but there was a quality in them that interested me and raised expectation. This was justified by the small volume which he published about five years later. Thoughtful and sensitive in their nature observation, these poems have a distinctive strangeness of tone and expression. It was a disappointment when he abandoned poetry and became a farmer. Hitherto almost neglected, I can well believe that *The Rural Scene* will some day be rediscovered by a discerning anthologist. In the meantime our friendship was mutually advantageous. I encouraged and advised him in his writing, and he provided pleasant company for bicycling expeditions. The usual object of these was to go as far as we could just to see what it was like when we got there, and since my stamina exceeded his, Toronto often returned tired and taciturn. Late in September, however, we made a memorable journey to Lindisfarne, which was in itself worth the long ride. Mr. Heinemann had been staying there with Edward Hudson, the proprietor of *Country Life*, to whom the castle then belonged. He motored over to Lennel to see me, bringing an invitation to spend a day at the castle. But it so happened that by the time I took Toronto thither both Mr. Hudson and Mr. Heinemann had been called back to London on business. After driving across the wet sands to the island at low tide, we spent the afternoon with the only occupant of the castle. This was none other than Madame Suggia, who enchanted us by her immense vitality and charm. It needs no saying that Suggia on the concert platform has been the loveliest and most romantic of modern executants, in addition to being one of the most magnificent. How then can one find words to describe her playing a Suite by Bach in the reverberant chamber of a lonely and historic castle—her 'cello's eloquence accompanied only by the beat and wash and murmur of waves breaking against the rocks below the windows? This was an experience which I shall always remember with gratitude. It seemed as though I had arrived at the end of a pilgrimage, to find peace and absolution in an hour of incomparable music. For it was the first time I had felt completely remote and absolved from the deadly constraints of the War.

VIII

Towards the end of September I received a letter from Eddie
Marsh in which he asked me to come to London as soon as possible. He had been talking about me with Winston Churchill, who
was interested in my poems and would probably offer me a job in
the Ministry of Munitions. This proposition, though incompatible
with my ideas of such war work as would suit me, was well-timed
for asking Lady Clementine to allow me a few days absence from
her hospitality. I made the most of it by staying four nights with
Eddie in Gray's Inn, diverting myself with a series of lunches and
dinners at which I met several distinguished people for the first
time, among them being Lytton Strachey, Maurice Baring, Edith
Sitwell, and Desmond MacCarthy. The interview for which I had
come to London was not until the morning of the third day. It can
be assumed that while Eddie and I were on our way to the Hotel
Metropole I was nervous and excited. Not that I had any immediate reason for nervousness, since I wasn't foreseeing that the
interview would affect my military future. I had, of course, been
elated by hearing from Eddie that 'Winston knows several of the
Counter-attack poems by heart'. But I realized that to be working
in the Ministry of Munitions would be inconsistent with my previous outburst against the prolongation of the War and the views
I had expressed in my poems. Nor had I any illusions about my
non-existent qualifications for such work as might be found for
me. I supposed that I should merely find myself in an office,
filling up forms; and what sense was there in that? What I
wanted was to be doing something which would provide human
experience equivalent to what I had acquired at the Front. Anyhow, when Eddie shepherded me into the lofty sanctum which
contained his Chief I wasn't expecting to occupy much of the
Ministerial morning, nor was it presumable that the Minister
would receive me with anything beyond official graciousness. But
before many minutes it was manifest that he was in no hurry to
be quit of me. His manner was leisurely, informal, and friendly.
Almost at once I began to feel a liking for him and to forget that I

was with one whom I had hitherto thought of as an unapproach-
able public figure. He had heard from Eddie that I was keen on
hunting, and was pleased that we had that in common. The only
other fox-hunting poet he knew was his old friend Wilfrid Blunt,
with whose political opinions, he added with an expressive smile,
he profoundly disagreed. He then made some gratifying allusions
to the memorable quality of my war poems, which I acknow-
ledged with bashful decorum. Having got through these preliminaries, he broached—in a good-humoured and natural way—
the subject of my attitude to the War, about which—to my surprise—he seemed interested to hear my point of view. Still more
surprising was the fact that he evidently wanted me to 'have it
out with him'. Overawed though I was, I spotted that the great
man aimed at getting a rise out of me, and there was something
almost boyish in the way he set about it. My shy responses were,
however, quite out of character with the provocative tone of the
war poems, which may have led him to expect an exhibition of
youthful disputatiousness. It would, of course, have been absurd
for me to match myself against such a pre-eminent controver-
sialist and war historian. I am not by temperament an arguer, and
have always found difficulty in producing logical ideas rapidly.
Such quickness does not belong to a reflective mind.

Nevertheless he was making me feel that I should like to have
him as my company commander in the front line, and under the
influence of his candid geniality I was discarding shyness and well
on the way towards behaving as my ordinary self. There came a
point, however, when our proceedings developed into a mono-
logue. Pacing the room, with a big cigar in the corner of his
mouth, he gave me an emphatic vindication of militarism as an
instrument of policy and stimulator of glorious individual achievements, not only in the mechanism of warfare but in spheres of
social progress. The present war, he asserted, had brought about
inventive discoveries which would ameliorate the condition of
mankind. For example, there had been immense improvements in
sanitation. Transfixed and submissive in my chair, I realized that
what had begun as a persuasive confutation of my anti-war convictions was now addressed, in pauseful and perorating prose, to
no one in particular. From time to time he advanced on me, head

thrust well forward and hands clasped behind his back, to deliver the culminating phrases of some resounding period. It was the spontaneous generation of a speech which would probably be fully reported in the press before I was many weeks older. Before this he had definitely offered to find me a post in his Ministry if I wanted one, and had told me to think it over. He now spoke with weighty eloquence of what the Ministry was performing in its vast organization and output, and of what it might yet further achieve in expediting the destruction of the enemy. In love with his theme, he was elaborating a full-bodied paragraph when the secretarial countenance of Eddie appeared in the doorway to the ante-room, announcing that Lord Fisher had arrived. But the information went unheeded. The Winstonian exposition continued until Eddie reappeared with an apologetic intimation that Lord Fisher was growing restive. As I went out I was introduced to the famous Admiral—a small man with a queer Mongolian face, who had obviously come there with lots to say. In my afterthoughts I naturally felt a bit bewildered by having spent a full hour with Winston Churchill. He had made me feel that he was extremely likeable as a human being (as he has since done to the majority of the English-speaking race). There was the added and highly influential fact that he had shown interest in—and even friendliness towards—myself. Yet there was no doubt that I disagreed with almost every opinion he had uttered about militarism. Had he been entirely serious, I wondered, when he said that 'war is the normal occupation of man'? He had indeed qualified the statement by added 'war—and gardening'. But it had been unmistakable that for him war was the finest activity on earth. Had I been capable of disputing with him, I might have well quoted four lines from *The Dynasts*.

> *I have beheld the agonies of war*
> *Through many a weary season; seen enough*
> *To make me hold that scarcely any goal*
> *Is worth the reaching by so red a road.*

This passage, which I had copied on to the first page of a manuscript book containing poems written since *Counter-attack* went to the printers, occurs in the poet's version of an oration in the House of Commons by an 1815 advocate of peace, subsequently dismissed by Lord Castlereagh as 'hackneyed forms of speech upon war's horrors'. Uttered in the context of our conversation, the lines would have sounded rather priggish and inconsonant. Churchill would rightly have replied that, in 1918, we had to choose between reaching the goal and losing the war. But I might well have suggested that it was the business of politicians to discover some less destructive method of improving sanitation. War having since then become more than ever 'the normal occupation of man', I need not waste any words on the subject. And any comment on Churchill as a national figure in 1940 and after would be a failure to express unqualified admiration. Hardy himself was far from being optimistic about the preservation of peace. I remember asking him—one evening when staying at Max Gate —whether he believed in the League of Nations or any such design for the prevention of war. Rather diffidently, he expressed his view that wars came about almost like atmospheric disturbances, adding that he had sometimes felt that they were caused by supernatural agencies and were beyond human control. This, of course, was an idea on which he had exercised his epic genius in *The Dynasts*. And in one of his last poems he speaks of nations making war

> *not warely or from taste*
> *But tickled mad by some demonic force.*

It must be hoped that some imaginative mind, comparable with his, will one day give the world a dramatic masterpiece wherein our present shocks and disasters are set in proportion to human history as a whole, warning a less insane epoch against the errors which debase the kindlier arts of life-development and consign the wisdom of the ages to the refuse dump. Meanwhile, as I strolled bemusedly along the Strand, no such coherent and elevated ideas were in my mind. I merely told myself that to have been hobnobbing with Winston Churchill was a jolly good step upward in the world. I was on my way to call on Mr. Heinemann at his office in Bedford Street. He increased my complacency by telling me that more than three thousand copies of *Counter-attack* had already been sold, also intimating that it had narrowly escaped being suppressed by the Censorship. When I described how I had been spending the morning he expressed satisfaction and reassurance, not unmixed with amusement.

After this I went on to the Waldorf Hotel where I was to have lunch with a young officer of my regiment. We had been together in the Spring Offensive of 1917, and I had good reason to know how imperturbable he could be under the most unpleasant conditions. He had lost an arm, but was the same smooth-haired whimsical philosopher as ever. Bad though those days had been, he remarked—when we were half-way through a bottle of 'bubbly'—it had been an improvement on a lot of the aimless things one did in peace-time. Some of the best men had gone west, but he was thankful to have known them. Fixing his monocle, he observed that he'd rather be out in France than with most of the civilian birds at the tables around us. Falling in with his humour, I agreed that there was a lot to be said for the ups and downs of active service. When I gave him the gist of what Winston Churchill had said to me, he gazed reflectively at his tilted wine-glass and remarked—with the habitual stammer which made his utterances meaningful—'I've never had much use for the hot-air of politicians; but in spite of war being so absolutely bloody he's right about it bringing out the best in some of us.' I had to confess that I had frequently felt the same, when my pacifism hadn't got the upper hand of me. To this he very sensibly replied that it didn't do to think too much while there was a war on. That was the advantage of being out there. As soon as one got home one began to worry, and that had been my main trouble. We then adjourned to the Coliseum and saw the ballet 'Carnaval'. At that time the Russian Ballet was giving single performances in the variety programme. On this occasion we remained till the end, and by then I was conscious of having done about enough for one day. By my present standard of controlled and discreetly assimilative experiencing, I certainly had! But I'd come to London for liveliness, and had been assiduously over-entertaining myself all the week. To be dining with Maynard Keynes at his club was, of course, an agreeable occasion, and need not have tired me if I'd talked less and given myself an hour's rest beforehand. I had got to know him through the Morrells. As he was a highly important figure in the Treasury I felt that I was yet again in contact with national affairs, though he made no parade of his eminence and was charmingly friendly. It was after dinner that the exertions of the day began to tell on me. We went to the Russian Ballet. This time it was 'Cleopatra', which had such a stimulating effect on my emotions that I afterwards wrote a poem about it. By itself, the Ballet would have been a respite from fatigue. But further social efforts were demanded of me, for Lady Ottoline was there with Lytton Strachey, Roger Fry, Mark Gertler, and several others. We all went behind to see the leading dancers, and by the time that was over I had a splitting headache and seemed to have been living in a disordered dream where Lady Ottoline, in one of her hugest headgears, towered above Massine and Idzikovsky, who were much smaller in real life than on the stage. Such was my rather overwrought condition when I went on to Half Moon Street for the very special purpose of saying good-bye to Robbie, who was about to leave England for several months in order to give the Melbourne Art Gallery the benefit of his expert advice. It was only about half-past ten, and my headache would clear off when I arrived, I hoped; for he always had a calming effect on me. We would have a nice quiet talk about my visit to the Ministry of Munitions and all the other things I had been doing. He had told me that he would be spending the evening alone, as his preparations for departure had worried and over-tired him. I found him sitting at his table reading a little red-bound Bible. He explained that he wasn't getting ready to meet his Maker; he had a fondness for the Old Testament because there were such a lot of good stories in it. I lit my pipe and began to feel more like relaxing. It was therefore most unfortunate that Charles Scott Moncrieff should have chosen this moment to come in, bringing with him a tall thin youth whose name meant nothing to us. I had met Moncrieff a few times before, and had tried to get on with him as he was an intimate friend of Robbie's. But he had never liked me, and had shown it by reviewing *The Old Huntsman* with unconcealed acrimony. Knowing that he was in hospital badly wounded (he was lame for the rest of his life) I artfully responded by writing to congratulate him on the Military Cross which he had been awarded. He had sent me a graciously apologetic reply; but in spite of this he now seemed as surly as ever. I knew that before long we should be at loggerheads about something, with poor Robbie trying in vain to mend matters. Moncrieff had a scholarly and rather pedantic mind, and my impetuous and often ill-considered opinions about poetry never failed to aggravate him. I must add that in after years I became fully grateful to him for his masterly translations of Proust; but friendship cannot be sustained by Proust alone. Meanwhile disagreement was avoided. He sat by the fire conversing glumly with Robbie. The 'boy actor'—for such he had announced himself to be, was being almost excessively appreciative to me about my war poems, telling me that he had quite lately read them aloud to a lady novelist while lying on the rocks in Cornwall. This only annoyed me. I was feeling too much 'on the rocks' myself, and his behaviour struck me as too gushing. It became evident, also, that his effusiveness made an unfavourable impression on Robbie, who, for once, lacked his usual liveliness as host. I had now reached a condition of nervous irritability when I was capable of contradicting everything I believed in, and some of my remarks to Moncrieff were, no doubt, unpardonably petulant. But the youthful stranger rattled brightly on, making smart remarks, which I considered cheap. There were several copies of *Counter-attack* on Robbie's table, one of which I sourly inscribed for him at his request. His name—I can no longer conceal it—was Noel Coward. I must hasten to qualify this account of him by saying that our episodic and too infrequent meetings during his brilliantly successful career have been entirely delightful and stimulating. When I subsequently reminded him of that first encounter he went so far as to exclaim that he 'must have been pretty shattering'. But even then he was the only sprightly element in an otherwise shattering hour which ended in my confessing that my head was splitting. I said good-bye to Robbie with tormented abruptness, and when I was downstairs and about to let myself out of the front door he came quickly down and stood beside me. He said nothing, but took my hand and looked up at me for a long moment. His worn face, grey with exhaustion and ill-health, was beatified by sympathy and affection. The memory of it will always remain with me. How should I forget that look, with what afterwards seemed to have been its presentiment of final farewell? At the time, however, I only wondered whether I should be able to see him again before he started for Australia. Walking along Piccadilly in quest of an elusive taxi to take me back to Gray's Inn, I was reminded, when passing the top of Berkeley Street, of an incident he had described to me. Returning home one night during a noisy air raid, he had observed a perturbed and solitary old lady standing on the pavement opposite the Ritz. Unable to think of any other method of reassuring her, he put up his embrella, offered her his arm, and gravely escorted her across to the shelter of the Ritz arches. There had seemed nothing ridiculous, he said, in his holding the umbrella over her, and it evidently gave her a sense of security.

Many such actions he had performed, both considered and impulsive, through his instinct for gay and chivalrous behaviour. But I was never to hear his voice again. The next evening, while resting before dinner, he died of heart failure. It seems reasonable to claim that this was the only occasion on which his heart failed him, either in personal courage or in generosity towards his friends. For them his death made a difference which could only be estimated in sorrowful conjectures. It deprived us of an ever-ready helpfulness that might have changed many human discords to harmony.

My portrait of him can be most fitly concluded by quoting some words by Edmund Gosse, who knew him, with deep affection, during the last twenty-five years of his life. 'He dwells in the thoughts of a multitude of men and women who feel life emptier for his absence. His character, which was a very strange one, invites analysis, but may easily evade it. He loved to support lost causes and to advance paradoxical opinions. He had a passionate horror of injustice, and a wild determination to correct it, without any counting of the cost. He was not, in the first instance, a writer, but a talker. Conversation was the natural medium of communication with him, and in the rapidity of his mental movement, his fantastic flights of paradox, and the astonishing breadth of his knowledge, he was truly remarkable. What, however, will be remembered longest is not his laughter, nor his easy erudition, nor even his extravagant ideals, but his quixotry of self-denying generosity. He wore himself out in deeds of active kindness. He was disinterested almost to excess, and indefatigable in practical beneficence.'

IX

On November 5th I went to London to stay a night with Eddie Marsh, who had asked me to dine at the Savoy to meet a somewhat distinguished Colonel. I had left Lennel three weeks before, and had remained quietly at Weirleigh during the acceleration of events which was bringing the war to its conclusion. I had been granted the usual four weeks' leave; but my career as an officer was at an end, for—although not officially 'placed on the retired list' until the following March—I received no further order to report myself for duty. In his letter, Eddie had merely told me that this Colonel had done wonderful things in the Hejaz campaign (about which I was quite hazy, though I had often focused my field-glasses on the distant mountains of Moab while in Palestine during the previous March and April). I gathered that he wanted to know me, and vaguely wondered why. When arriving at the Savoy, I expected to find a conventional military character with whom I should have little in common; so the small fairhaired, youthful-looking person to whom I was presented came as a surprise. His demeanour was reticent and precise. Evidently unwilling to be drawn out about his military exploits, he inscrutably dissolved my shyness and led me on to tell him about my own interests. Eddie, however, directed the conversation towards Arabia, and before long we were talking about C. M. Doughty. It was his poetry rather than his prose that we discussed, and the first time the Colonel laughed was when I described how I had once written to inform the author of *The Dawn in Britain* that I had read his epic 'all through'. He expressed a strong preference for Doughty's dramatic poem *Adam Cast Forth*, a strange contorted work of genius which had impressed me deeply when it appeared, almost unheeded, ten years before. Eddie thereupon interposed a justifiable protest against the poet's style. His remarkable gift for memorization enabled him to quote a line in support of his opinion. 'Spouse-father, It am Adama I that speak.' He 'simply couldn't believe it necessary for Eve to talk such stilted archaic jargon, even to produce a primitive effect'. It transpired that the Colonel had also corresponded with Doughty, and had actually been to see him. It was apparent that he wanted to talk only about men of letters. Henry James was another who cropped up, allowing Eddie to delight us with anecdotal reminiscences, including his evergreen imitation of the great man enunciating— with immense effort—one of his convoluted sentences.

Much perplexed by the personality of the Hejaz celebrity, I reached a point when, emboldened by good wine, I looked across the table and exclaimed, 'What I can't understand is how you come to be a Colonel!' In after years I realized that I could hardly have said anything more likely to please and divert T. E. Lawrence—for he, of course, it was! Subsequently there was some talk about politics and peace settlements, to which I could only listen with respectful curiosity. I was astonished when Eddie spoke with a strong bias against President Wilson; for, like most uninformed people, I still regarded him as the heaven-sent leader of the Allied Nations. Lawrence reserved his opinion, demurely remarking that Wilson wanted to give Mesopotamia to Portugal. This I duly noted down in my diary; but I am now inclined to doubt whether the statement was intended to be taken seriously. The impression left on me by Lawrence was of a pleasant unassuming person who preferred to let other people do most of the talking. As he often did, he was subduing that power of stimulation which could lift others above and beyond their habitual plane of thought and action by communicating his mysterious and superlative vital energy. Had I been told that I was meeting one of the most extra-ordinary beings I should ever know and idolize, I should have refused to believe it. He was, I briefly informed my diary, 'the Hejaz general, a little Oxford archaeologist, who admires Doughty and called him "a Viking".' A few weeks later, however, Society was agog about him and his romantic military adventures. An intrepidly enterprising hostess buttonholed me at a party with a wildly hopeful eye, exclaiming, 'Oh, Mr. Sassoon, I hear you know Colonel Lawrence. Can't you bring him to lunch? I'm longing to talk to him about *Arabia Deserta* and all that!' But she might as well have asked me to produce the King of the Cannibal Islands, even if I'd felt like contributing to her menagerie!

Siegfried's Journey, 1916–1920

It now seems odd and almost incredible that while in Lawrence's company I should have said nothing about Thomas Hardy. How, I wonder, did I get through the evening without its somehow transpiring that I was on the eve of an inaugural visit to Max Gate? How, on the other hand, could I have guessed that Lawrence honoured him—as I did—beyond any other living writer (although it was not until 1923 that he became, probably, the most admired and valued friend of Hardy's last years)? My own association with Max Gate had begun early in 1917, when I wrote to ask him to accept the dedication of *The Old Huntsman*. In doing this I had been encouraged by my uncle Hamo Thornycroft's having known him for many years, and by the fact that Mr. Gosse had assured me that the request would give pleasure to 'True Thomas', as he called him. Since then I had received half a dozen letters from him, in which he had shown considerable interest in me and liking for my work. When I was about to return to the Front, at the beginning of 1918, I had sent him a photograph of the Glyn Philpot portrait, feeling that to be there in effigy was better than nothing, especially as I might be dead before I had an opportunity of visiting him in person. The photograph had reached him in advance of my explanation. In acknowledging it he had written, 'We divined it to be you, but I was not quite certain, till a friend told us positively only a day before your letter came. It has been standing in my writing-room calmly overlooking a hopeless chaos of scribbler's litter. I shall be so glad to see you walk in some day.' Ever since then I had been looking forward to the time when I should be free to 'walk in' on the author of *The Dynasts*, who so unassumingly referred to himself as a scribbler.

I began the awaited day by going to the Ministry of Munitions with Eddie. There I spent a few minutes with a Winston who was now in boisterous spirits and full of victory talk. I noted that he was 'still conversing rather like a leading article and just off to a Cabinet Meeting'. He was, however, as friendly as ever, and my own spirits were in fine fettle while I travelled towards Dorchester in bright frosty weather. Naturally, my mind was full of speculations as to how far the Mr. Hardy of Max Gate would harmonize with the writer whose works I had absorbed so fruitfully. But—as in one of his most beautiful lyrics—

88

Siegfried's Journey, 1916–1920

What would bechance at Lyonesse
While I should sojourn there
No prophet durst declare.

For in spite of his letters to me I still looked on him as such an eminent and almost legendary figure that it was puzzling to imagine oneself with him in any ordinary human relationship. He was seventy-eight, too, and I could only approach him agape with veneration. I had a notion that he was a modest sort of man; and Mr. Gosse had told me that, of all the famous writers he had known, Hardy was the least likely to say anything which one remembered afterwards. The nearest I had got to picturing him 'in real life' was through an anecdote of Robbie's. He had described how—more than twenty years before—he had spent a rather dull evening with the Hardys at a flat they had taken in Kensington. He had been discussing with Mr. Hardy the methods by which authors coped with the laborious process of writing their books. Mr. Hardy having remarked that he had written one of his early novels on his knees, Robbie wittily replied, 'We *read* it on our knees.' Whereupon the late Mrs. Hardy had exclaimed in reproving tones, 'Don't flatter Mr. Hardy in that foolish way!' This wasn't much to go on, and I felt that the first Mrs. Hardy would have taken a similar view of my own mental attitude to her husband. I had left London soon after midday, but my bemused condition caused me to remain in the wrong part of the train, which was left behind at Bournemouth. So I had to go on by a slow one, preceded by an apologetic telegram. Next day I wrote as follows in my note-book.

November 7th. Arrived 6.45 in darkness. Horse cab rumbled up to porch of small house among trees. Found little old gentleman in front of fire in candle-lit room; small wife with back turned doing something to a bookcase. Both seemed shy, and I felt large and hearty. First impression of T.H. was that his voice is worn and slightly discordant, but that was only while he was nervous. Afterwards it was unstrained, gently vivacious, and—when he spoke with feeling—finely resonant. Frail and rather wizard-like in the candleshine and dim room, with his large round head, immense brow, and beaky nose, he was not unlike the 'Max' caricature, but

89

more bird-like. He knelt by the log fire for a bit, still rather shy. They both gained confidence, and then there was a charming little scene of 'which room is he in, dear?' 'The west room, my dear,' though of course he must have known. He lit me up the narrow staircase with a silver candlestick, quite nimble and not at all like a man of almost eighty. Already I felt at ease with him. (I think he had feared that I should be a huge swell and come down to dinner in a white waistcoat. That Philpot portrait is so misleadingly Byronic!)

I had arrived on a Wednesday, and stayed until midday on Friday. 'Both days were bright and frosty. T.H. became more lovable all the time. A great and simple man.' That was all I found time to say in my diary, though I might well have added a few words in praise of Florence Hardy, who was always the best of friends to me. In one of his letters he had told me that he didn't know how he should have endured the suspense of this evil time if it were not for the sustaining power of poetry. And it was mainly of poets and poetry that we talked. It was the beginning of a genuine friendship, and of my experience of his evergreen persistency in vitality and mental resilience. The door of his mind always remained open to the ideas and speculations of the young. Those of my generation were his new hope for that war-weary world in whose sane reconstruction he did his best to believe. Thus I soon found myself forgetting the disparity of years and achievement that divided us. He was enlivened by my exuberant youngness, and enjoyed being with me because we could always drop into a comfortable chat about quite ordinary matters. It may be said that I gained his confidence by not trying to seem clever, and through my interest in everyday humanity. He liked good talk, of course, but preferred people not to be vividly intellectual at the tea-table. What I was offered at Max Gate was homeliness. On that basis we discussed Shakespeare and Shelley, Keats and Browning, with uncritical gratitude for their glories. When I asked him why 'Ah, did you once see Shelley plain?' is such a memorable poem, he replied, 'Because Browning wrote from his heart.'

Meanwhile I was learning a lesson which has leavened my imperfections ever since. He was giving me a demonstration of the simplicity of true greatness. By this I do not mean that he was simple, when viewed apart from his writings, though his modesty sometimes misled superficial observers into thinking so. This modesty was instinctive and quite unaffected. For example, he once remarked to me—with one of his wistful little sighs—that he didn't suppose he'd have bothered to write *The Dynasts* if he could have foreseen the Great War. The comment may have been only half serious; yet no one but he could have made it. It was impossible to imagine him talking for effect, and he was adroit at declining to be drawn out by visitors angling for oracular utterances. J. M. Barrie had a story of him at the Savile Club, where the secret of style was being discussed by a group of writers. When all the others had set forth their views, Hardy was unable to produce any explanation except some quite trivial remark. He was interested in cleverness but not attracted by it. The homely strength and ripe integrity of his nature were somehow apparent in his avoidance of the brilliant and unusual. When he did say something profound he contrived to make it seem quite ordinary. He was, in fact, a wise and unworldly man who had discarded intellectual and personal vanity. He has described himself as 'a private man', which merely meant that he liked to live quietly, shunning active competition with his contemporaries. He regarded authorship as an unobtrusive occupation rather than a struggle to attract attention. He had written his novels to earn a livelihood. He wrote poetry to please himself, and even in 1918 was not fully aware of the admiration for his verse prevalent among other poets, both old and young. Anyhow, what I carried away from Max Gate, both then and thereafter, was an impressive awareness that Hardy—who was, as I remarked to myself, 'the nearest thing to Shakespeare I should ever go for a walk with'—had no vestige of vanity, and wore his illustrious laurels with no more concern about them than if they had been his hat. The pessimism which has often been imputed to him was—in his own words—merely 'the sad science of renunciation'. In spite of what Meredith called his 'twilight view of life', he was not a melancholy man. He had a normal sense of humour and could be charmingly gay. The bitterness in his writings was meditative and impersonal. He was disappointed rather than disillusioned in his attitude to life. Instinctively compassionate, he had suffered deeply through the apparently fortuitous victimization and injustice in many human happenings. I was often astonished by an octogenarian agility and quickness which matched his alertness of mind, and can remember how—at eighty-four—when discussing some variant reading in Shakespeare, he went up to his study to fetch his facsimile edition of the First Folio. As he re-entered the room with it under his arm I realized that he must have run both ways—had at any rate performed his errand at a lively trot! His movements were brisk, purposeful, and compact. He always chose a straight-backed chair to sit in, and carried himself with an almost military erectness. Seen in a strong light he looked all his age—a bird-like ancient whose monumental head might well have belonged to some ex-Mayor of Dorchester, some local worthy—though obviously derived from the fine stock of a naturally noble ancestry. Hob-nobbing with him of an evening I could almost forget that he was anything more than a dear and delightful old country gentleman. But I have watched him when he was in shadow and repose, and have held my breath in contemplation of what seemed the wisdom of the ages in human form. For that time-trenched face in the flicker of firelight was genius made visible, superhuman in its mystery and magnificence. This was the face of the life-seer who had transmuted the Wessex country into a cosmogony of his imagination, who had humanized it and revealed its unrecorded meanings and showings with patient power and mastery of half-tones and subdued colours, who had learned the secret of under-emphasized radiance and the rich significance of shadows, over-hearing the semitones of sounds in Nature, and observing the qualities and characteristics of his native country until he had made them all one with the English heritage of recreated life. Here was the real Hardy, unmeasurable by intellectual standards, who will haunt the civilized consciousness of our race when the age he lived in has become remote as the Roman occupation of Britain. He was sitting with one arm around his old friend 'Wessex'—that unruly and vociferous sheep-dog whom he has enshrined in a poem. But when he gazed down at 'Wessie' he ceased to be Merlin. The face of the wizard became suffused with gentle compassion for all living creatures whom he longed to defend against the chanceful injustice and calamity of earthly existence.

*   *   *

From Max Gate I journeyed to Garsington, where I had been invited to stay as long as I liked. Reading the papers in the train I must have found plentiful historic reportings to distract me from observing 'the Hardy country' through which I was travelling. But for some reason I am unable to bring to mind how it felt to be living through that final week of the War, which was made memorable for me in other ways. This process continued next day, for Lady Ottoline had arranged that I should go to lunch with the Masefields. There had been no previous communication between Masefield and myself. I was, of course, eager to know him; and there was the added excitement of hearing that he would be taking me to call on the Poet Laureate. Everything seemed to be happening at once, I thought, while making my way towards Abingdon in cold sunny weather on a borrowed bicycle. The distance, however, proved greater than I'd calculated, and it took me so long to get up Boar's Hill that I arrived, perturbed and perspiring, some time after they had finished lunch. Masefield brought me a steaming plate of roast mutton and potatoes, and my equanimity was soon restored by his serene and unassuming manners. While swallowing my meal I told him how I had been to stay with Hardy. His courteous and deliberative replies must have been an amusing contrast to my impetuous utterances, which in those days had a habit of falling over one another almost before I had decided what I intended to say. Anyhow, while he listened and concurred, with downward glances and gentle deference, I felt conscious of giving him pleasure by my presence and was much exhilarated by the cordiality of the occasion. In other words, we got on famously, and I felt quite sorry when our talk was interrupted by his reminding me that it was time to make a move in the direction of the Laureate. During the short walk to Chilswell he told me that since the house was burnt down Bridges had been living in the gardener's cottage. Having heard that he was liable to be abrupt and even arrogant towards new-comers, I was rather nervous. But I had loved his poetry ever since I was twenty, and nothing could have been more decorously deferential than my state of mind when we entered the cottage.

He was seated at a table in the small room, which wasn't getting any of the afternoon sunshine. My first view of his magnificent bard-like head and fine patrician features was a pleasantly impressive recognition of the portrait frontispece to his Collected Poems. Masefield having pronounced my name with dulcet distinctness, I meekly awaited the response. There was, however, no welcome in the way he looked at me, nor did he stir from his chair. After an awkward pause he told us to sit down. Then, having inquired of Masefield whether there was any credibility in the report that the German Emperor had abdicated, he glowered in my direction and gruffly made one of the most surprising remarks I have experienced. 'What did you say his name was— *Siegfried Digweed*?' Masefield met this embarrassing situation by repeating my name with submissive politeness. Personally I was so taken aback that I wasn't even capable of realizing that we had been so unlucky as to find the Laureate in one of his grumpiest moods. There was, however, an element of absurdity in the episode which saved me from feeling completely crushed, especially when I caught Masefield's eye. The name Digweed, by the way, is to be found in the letters of Jane Austen. The Digweeds were neighbours of her family at Steventon and Chawton. There was a certain Mrs. Digweed of whom she often makes gentle fun. A brother of Jane Austen's married a daughter of Sir Brook Bridges (1767–1829).

I had innocently expected to hear the Poet Laureate discourse about literature. But he had other matters in mind, and was resolved to ventilate them. Talking at—rather than to—us, his main theme was 'those Socialists', in whom he found nothing to applaud and much to admonish. He was particularly severe on German Socialists. 'Look at them!' he exclaimed, showing us a row of photographs in some newspaper which had predicted possible ingredients for a Democratic Government in Germany. 'Did you ever see such a parcel of pudding-faced dullards?' he added, with the slight retardation of his consonants which wasn't exactly a stammer. We were obliged to agree that, as human types, they showed little promise of refinement or intelligence. Meanwhile I wondered why I should be hectored like this; for it seemed that his remarks were aimed at me as a reprehensible supporter of Socialist opinions and that he had awaited my arrival with the intention of taking me down a few pegs! And although he mellowed towards me afterwards, I departed with a disappointingly unfavourable first impression, for which I could hardly be blamed.

Seen in the light of subsequent experience of him, it was all quite characteristic. He was proud, self-conscious, and often aggressively intolerant. There was something of the self-contradictory schoolboy about him. (When presenting himself at the Palace to receive the Laureateship he remarked to the lord-in-waiting that he 'didn't want any of their Stars and Garters', an assertion which was afterwards rewarded—most deservedly—with the Order of Merit.) It was, I think, his unrestrained naturalness which caused these somewhat petulant exhibitions of rudeness. He hated pomposity, and consistently refused to stand on his dignity. And this same naturalness was the mainspring of his geniality, which could be glorious. One who knew him well has described him as 'delightfully grumpy'. 'He mentions thing after thing which is commonly believed and says that of course it's not so. He's always right. His intellect has been so completely self-indulged that it now can't understand rubbish.' He wasn't 'always right'. I have heard him dismiss the works of Landor—with whom he had affinities—as 'rather bosh'. But, once one understood him, there was no need to declare that his nobility of mind atoned for his inurbanities of behaviour. In his writings he showed splendid control of self and spirit, undeviating devotion to his art, and the gracious purity of one who 'uttered nothing base'. In the man there was an unreserved and abundant humanity, and no-one but a fool could fail to love him for it. The 'Digweed' episode was the only time I saw Robert Bridges in a bad humour. During the next ten years I was not with him often, but I can claim that he liked me, and my admiration for him ripened to affection. He will always be among the living dead whom I have known and honoured. Remembering him as he appeared on that November afternoon, I mildly rebuke my young self for not understanding that this was a man of high courage and sensibility, remarkably vigorous at seventy-four, who had endured several years of brooding inactive melancholy, and had also had his comfortable house burnt down. It should have occurred to me that he had suffered in spirit. As it was, I resented his war-talk and thought him a bigoted reactionary. Not long afterwards he made a magnanimous public gesture of reconciliation towards German men of learning and letters. And while staying with him some years later I discovered in his library an anti-German book, and was touched by finding that he had erased the word *Hun* throughout, substituting *German.*

Meanwhile I left Masefield playing a twilight game of hide-and-seek in his garden with his two children and one of the Bridges girls. Bicycling easily back to Garsington I drew comparisons between Max Gate and Chilswell, which ended in a decision that no two illustrious septuagenarians could be more different. But I'd had such a long day that in contrasting them I got no deeper than the fact of T.H. being a non-smoker, while Bridges puffed a full-flavoured pipe.

X

Walking in the water meadows by the river below Garsington on the quiet grey morning of November 11th, I listened to a sudden peal of bells from the village church and saw little flags being fluttered out from the windows of the thatched houses on the hill. Everyone had expected to hear that the Armistice was signed; but even now it wasn't easy to absorb the idea of the War being over. The sense of relief couldn't be expressed by any mental or physical gesture. I just stood still with a blank mind, listening to the bells which announced our deliverance.

Had I been my present philosophic self I should thankfully have remained in that peaceful place, keeping as far as possible from metropolitan rejoicings. But, being what I then was, it seemed imperative for me to rush up to London, though more for the purpose of observing the celebrations than of sharing in them. My former front-line associates were the only people with whom I felt any inclination to be festive. None were available. So I wired to an Air Force friend of Robbie's. He had a flat off Bond Street, and had offered me a room whenever it suited me. I didn't know him well; but he had shown an ardent enthusiasm for my war writings, and could be relied on to agree with my attitude towards the jubilations.

I was prepared for an orgy of patriotic demonstrations, but the reality went far beyond what I had foreseen. There is no need to describe the extraordinary spectacle of the London streets on Armistice night. It was a humid and rainy evening, and I had to carry my suitcase from Paddington to Cork Street, which didn't make me any more amiable towards the flag-waving of the surging and congested crowds which had taken possession of the main thoroughfares. I felt no wish to shake hands with anyone, and a quiet evening at my club seemed the best solution, though St. James's Street would be impartially invaded by the uproarious populace. My Air Force friend, however, had already arranged to take me to Chelsea, and although he assured me that the social status of the people we were dining with was considerable, I

D   97

wasn't in the mood to meet conventional strangers, agreeable though they might be. Nor, when it came to the point, was he. The party consisted of four other men and several women. They were, most of them, rather silly and excited, and 'much moved' by the demonstrations, which they—not unnaturally—considered worthy of the occasion. The chorus was led by an effusive American woman journalist, who confided to me that she had never before known such a sense of high-plane emotion-release. This was probably an accurate description of her feelings, but I accepted the statement rather glumly. Now it so happened that my friend and I were the only members of the party who had seen any active service, while two of the others were of an age which suggested that they might likewise have done so, had their now exuberant patriotism prompted them to the adventure. Towards the end of an excellent dinner this unfortunate cleavage became conspicuous. We were involved in an inimical argument with a youngish gentleman whose war services (as I afterwards ascertained) had been devoted to assisting on the Central Liquor Control Board. Our moral advantage over him made the situation awkward. It was, no doubt, the wrong moment for me to exclaim that the War had been a loathsome tragedy and that all this flag-waving couldn't alter it; but he wasn't in a position to support the opposite view with fine phrases. We left the house extremely unpopular, and as we walked away I told my friend that his Armistice night entertainment had been a ruddy wash-out—an assertion which won his cordial assent.

The next day I dined quietly with Rivers, who was an ideal moderator of victorious agitations. He had watched the wild scenes in the streets with ethnological eyes. It was more or less what he'd expected, he remarked, while admitting that mass-emotion was definitely overdoing it. This was fully obvious to me while once again I lugged my bag through the inebriated throngs which were parading Regent Street. No taxis or buses were visible, and by the time I trod wearily up the stone stairs to Eddie Marsh's flat I was in no mood for making new acquaintances. But it happened that John Drinkwater was also staying the night there, and he arrived a few minutes after me. The sensations and events of the last two days had told even on indefatigable Eddie. Drinkwater, however, had plenty of energy in reserve. Friendly and unfatigued, he had very soon opened an important-looking leather portfolio which contained manuscripts of his latest poems. It was taken for granted that the editor of *Georgian Poetry* was both willing and anxious to hear them read aloud before retiring to bed, so we solemnly sat ourselves down, resolved to be wide awake and appreciative. The purposeful and practical-minded poet was at a table, reading by the light of a shaded lamp. His diction, like his verse, was urbane and accomplished, but the poems were numerous, and his unhurrying and self-satisfied voice produced restful rather than rousing results. Eddie remained bolt upright in his chair with monocle firmly fixed, while I did my utmost not to lapse into a lolling attitude. Murmurings of polite approval followed each item. At about 1 a.m. there came a longish consignment of somewhat soporific blank verse which I was unable to follow attentively. This was followed by a graceful lyric ending

> *While Rameses and Romeo*
> *And little Ariadne sleep.*

At this point Eddie, no doubt intending to utter some phrase of approbation, failed to suppress the well-earned yawn. The fact was that both of us were so tired that we could hardly keep our eyes open, and it seemed that if the recital lasted much longer we should be imitating the persons mentioned in the poem. However, the hint was taken by the imperturbable author. Himself realizing that it was growing late, he liberated us by replacing the manuscripts in his portfolio.

In the morning he conducted me to the Poetry Bookshop, introduced me to its poet-proprietor Harold Monro, and gave me an inscribed copy of his play *Abraham Lincoln*. He was anxious to be friendly, but somehow the acquaintance never matured. Now I come to think of it, at our subsequent meetings I almost always heard him read his works aloud. This prejudiced me against him, owing to my preference for bards who hide their lights under bushels. Drinkwater never did that, though he was much liked by those who knew him intimately.

From the Poetry Bookshop I walked across Regent's Park to have lunch with the Gosses. It was more than a year since I had seen Mr. Gosse, who had viewed my anti-war activities with disapproval and distress. The success of *Counter-attack* had, however, afforded him a sort of scandalized satisfaction. He had praised its 'power and originality', and there had been no abatement in the affectionate tone of his letters to me. (In a letter to J. C. Squire, who had reviewed me with moderation, he perceptively remarked, 'You are very kind and just to poor S.S. It is profoundly true that he writes these horrors simply because fortune won't let him alone to write about the things he loves.') I was now welcomed as a triumphant prodigal, no reference being made to my pacifist aberrations. He was in bed with bronchitis, but after a nice non-literary lunch with Mrs. Gosse and her daughters I was taken to his room to find him in his most charming conversational form. It was, I think, the first time I had felt completely comfortable when alone with him. He listened with delighted interest to my lively account of the visit to 'True Thomas' at Max Gate, and the anecdote about the Laureate and 'Siegfried Digweed' was almost too successful, since it brought on a paroxysm of coughing.

A shadow of sadness fell across us when he laid his hand on a stout folio volume on the table by his bed. This, he explained, had been bequeathed him by Robbie. It was a seventeenth-century epic poem—Heywood's *Hierarchie of Angels*—a long-neglected work, impenetrable to the modern reader, which Robbie had acquired for the sake of its elaborate engraved plates. Not long afterwards, when writing about it, he began his essay with the character portrait from which I have quoted a passage in a previous chapter. On this occasion he allowed what we both felt to remain unsaid. Robbie's death was too recent—his absence too poignantly in our minds—and Edmund Gosse was a sensible avoider of the funereal, being too eager a lover of life to allow his mind to dwell dolefully on the subject of extinction. It pleases me to remember that during our talk he strongly urged me to undertake a long poem which would serve as a peg on which—for the general public—my reputation could hang. He suggested that I might draw on my sporting experiences for typical country figures—the squire, the doctor, the parson, and so on. He was, of course, partly influenced by anxiety that I should divert my mind from the War. At the time I thought the idea unworthy of serious consideration. I doubted my ability to produce a long work in verse, and also believed that I ought to address the age on more startling and momentous themes. Ten years later Gosse's critical intuition proved to have been correct. The peg on which my popular reputation finally suspended itself was—though written in prose—essentially in accordance with his advice. Meanwhile, having betaken myself to Chelsea to have tea with Osbert Sitwell, I told him—with the blinkered effrontery of youth—that dear old Gosse had been egging me on to write a long dull poem about bucolic characters and hunting people. Quite a good joke against my eminent old friend, I thought it. Surely, with life beginning all over again and a splendid new Social System in the making, I could find something more important to say than that! From Swan Walk I rushed back to Raymond Buildings, for I was to dine with Eddie at Brooks's Club and go on to a party given by Lady Randolph Churchill. One advantage of still being in uniform was that it saved one the trouble of dressing for dinner. Also, I decided, it suited my personality when I was being trotted out as a soldier poet.

It will be remembered that, on the third night, the rejoicings continued, though they had ceased to express anything beyond determination to keep the shindy going as long as possible. The progress of our taxi along the Strand was much impeded by uproarious crowds. Oddly enough, I have few distinct recollections of what I saw while going about London during those days. In fact the only incident which I can authentically visualize is Eddie's embarrassed and slightly apprehensive countenance when several tipsy soldiers climbed on to the roof of the taxi while it crawled through Trafalgar Square. At Brooks's, of course, we found a sanctuary of comfort and decorum, and the dinner was such that I felt myself to be celebrating Victory with delectable exhilaration, reminded that there was more to be said for privileged than for proletarian standards of behaviour.

I had already become known to Lady Randolph at the Lancaster Gate Hospital, where she acted as a sort of Olympian headmatron. She had visited me several times and we had got on very agreeably, except, perhaps, on one occasion when—with what appeared a misdirected pride in her countrymen—she announced that American casualties in France had reached fifty thousand. Meanwhile it is probable that, while approaching her evening party, I was rather encumberingly conscious of making my début in 'Eddie Marsh high-life'—as I should then have called it. When nobody at all, I had sometimes wondered what it would feel like to be in those circles as a literary somebody, though I couldn't see myself as a brilliant success. At this moment of 'arrival', however, there seemed no need to be anything beyond my ordinary self. Modesty was the safest policy. I would imitate Mr. Hardy, leaving the game of smart cleverness to others. It wasn't a large house, so the party was formidable only in what I assumed to be the distinction of the guests. Most of those in the drawing-room would have been recognizable to me, a few years later, as belonging to that section of society which interests itself—when not otherwise occupied—in the arts. It was a fairly representative gathering of persons who had got through the War without having been outwardly inconvenienced. Among them, 'Mr. Marsh' was regarded as a supreme authority on new poets and their poetry. He could tell them about the poets, and they sometimes bought—and even read—the poetry. In other words, it was that unpausing world which Henry James—after prolonged investigation—had diagnosed as 'singularly uncommemorative of whatsoever it had pursued and discussed only a few months before'. I mention this in no spirit of censure, but merely to indicate my total ignorance, at this little climax of my momentary success, that I had a lot to do before I could hope to impress myself durably on the mercurial consciousness of what Henry James further described as 'the society most wedded by all its conditions to the immediate and finite'. Nothing, of course, could have been pleasanter than the contrast between such a civilized assemblage and the rampant rowdiness of the mob in Trafalgar Square. No immediate demands were made on my manners, for there was a concert of chamber music during which I gradually became half forgetful of my surroundings. The César Franck Quintet and the Debussy Quartet were so beautifully performed that it no longer mattered where I was or who happened to be observing me while occupying a gilt chair in an inconspicuous corner. Lying awake at Raymond Buildings that night, I came to the conclusion that being a newly arrived literary light was less difficult than I'd expected. I had been introduced to a number of people, all of whom had beamed on me as though I'd never written a bitter or disagreeable line in my life. I did not pause to ask myself how soon soldier poets would be out of fashion, or whether ladies of culture and high degree would continue to be thrilled by anti-war satires. Uppermost in my mind was the immense geniality shown me by Winston, who had talked to me for a long time, eulogizing my war exploits—such as they were—more than they deserved, and winning my heart by his engaging friendliness. Apart from liking him personally, I felt that his was a resounding recognition bestowed from beyond the social scene of ephemeral adulation (even though he did happen to be sitting on one of his mother's sofas). There was an exciting quality in his commendations which made them different from the approval of admired men of letters. It is always slightly intoxicating to the vanity of a private individual when notice is taken of him by some famous political figure. I was, in fact, rather snobbishly gratified by Winston's unaffected amiability. My afterthoughts now dwelt on two other incidents. General Sir Ian Hamilton, when shaking hands, had said that he was proud to meet me. I had seen him once before, when he came to Canterbury to review the Yeomanry in August 1914. For a fraction of a second, as he rode along the line wherein I figured as an untrained recruit, his gaze had seemed to alight on the clumsily-rolled overcoat on the front of my saddle. Contrasting our two encounters, I felt complacent about the progress I had made during those intervening years. But Sir Ian was well known as a man of literary taste and talent, and while conversing with me had made me think that if all Generals were of his type and temperament there would be fewer indignant anti-war poets.

The second episode was my introduction to Mrs. Charles Hunter, to whom, as I was well aware, a copy of *The Old Huntsman* had been presented by Robbie. Mrs. Hunter was, of course, an exceptionally gifted and generous hostess, and the valued friend of several illustrious writers and artists who were averse to being lionized in the usual way. But on this occasion she rather overdid it with the allusive archness of her greeting. 'Where have you been, South Wind, this May day morning?' she exclaimed, wagging her fan at me playfully. Since she was quoting the first line of one of my most innocuous poems, I was myself answerable for the archness. Had I been an adept at drawing-room technique I should, supposedly, have made a rapid choice between responding with the next line—which would have indicated that I had been 'with larks aloft or skimming with the swallow'—and jocosely replying that I had, on this November morning, been 'with Drinkwater at the Bloomsbury Poetry Bookshop'. As it was, I felt rather nonplussed, and merely made some inaudible acknowledgement of the salutation. And we were soon talking reasonably, about Robbie, to whom she had been admirably loyal when he most needed it. But herein, I now cogitated, was another of time's rewards. For the South Wind poem had been written one May day morning in 1914, in my room in Raymond Buildings. It was a period when I felt rather forlorn about my future. And the poem, submitted to *The New Statesman* (then in the first flush of its eagerly-perused youth) had been rejected as 'too much of an exercise in versifying'. Yet here was the famous Mrs. Hunter spouting it at me in the middle of a brilliant evening party! With this consoling reflection I lapsed into 'dateless oblivion and divine repose'.

*   *   *

Two evenings later I resumed my series of 'excursions to the homes of celebrated authors'. John Galsworthy had asked me to contribute a poem to *Reveillé*, a magazine which—with his usual generosity—he had consented to edit. He was hoping that it would enable the younger generation to obtain a hearing in the post-war world; but it came to an end after three distinguished numbers. Meanwhile it had brought me a cordial invitation to dine at Grove Lodge, his beautiful old house in Hampstead. Thither I went, tuned to concert pitch for yet another memorable occasion. Memorable it was, but mainly through an atmosphere of achieved serenity. The only other guest was a shyly uncommunicative young lady writer, and the whole evening appeared designed for the promotion of comfort and kindliness. Even when I had got to know him, Galsworthy produced an impression of being a reticent revealer of himself, for he was essentially modest and unegotistical. At our first meeting his reserved but shiningly sympathetic manner made me—partly owing to politeness—so talkative that I felt more like an impulsively informative nephew than a contributor to the next number of *Reveillé*. As he sat at the dark polished dinner table his strikingly handsome face and unassuming dignity seemed somehow avuncular, suggesting that, when we had finished our discussion of Turgenev and Thomas Hardy and I was sipping a second glass of the '87 port, he would inquire, with a subdued smile, whether a slight increase in my college allowance would meet with my approval. By the end of the evening I almost felt that I ought to call him 'Uncle Jack'. Mrs. Galsworthy, too, seemed well qualified to become 'Aunt Ada', for she was full of charm and lively intelligence. After dinner I was induced to try their lovely piano, on which I discreetly performed a Bach sarabande. I departed feeling that the creator of the unforgettable Forsyte family was exactly what I would have wished him to be.

During the ensuing week I was in such a vortex of accepted invitations and met such a hotch-potch of old friends and fresh acquaintances that it makes me positively dizzy to contemplate that scene of mentally indigestible experience. What I accomplished in those seven days would now be enough to satisfy my normal social needs for a twelve-month. But by many people that brief bout of long-vanished activities would not be considered exceptional. Nor can my mellowed maturity deny that—since the combination of youth and circumstance was making things lively for me—a rabble of disordered occurrences was inevitable. What bothers me about that kaleidoscopic young man is the remembered inconsistency of his responses to various individuals. Never the same with any two people from one lunch or dinner to the next, he now strikes me as almost too deplorably chameleonic an ancestor for my present self to be descended from! And, although some facetious inward monitor reminds me that even now the infirmity of multiple personality may not have been finally overcome, I am sure that if, for example, my Gosse, Galsworthy, Marsh, and Arnold Bennett selves could have been interchanged, some perplexity would have been present in their acutely observant minds. I resembled the character in a Pirandello play who was told, 'Your reality is a mere transitory and fleeting illusion, taking this form to-day and that to-morrow, according to the conditions, according to your will, your sentiments, which in turn are controlled by an intellect that shows them to you to-day in one manner and to-morrow . . . who knows how?' What was I like with Walter de la Mare? I wonder. For it was to him that I made an expedition at the end of the aforesaid week of festivities. But what he was like with me is an obviously preferable subject for retrospection; and, let me add, a subject to which I could joyfully devote several chapters, were this volume more voluminous.

To be composing but a prelusive page or two about de la Mare brings remembrance of the crowding enchantments of his word magic. I must indeed begin by recording that I took a suburban train to the Crystal Palace on a raw foggy November evening, and then went along to Anerley in a clanking tram. But even that humdrum journey associates itself with a couplet of his.

> *Flee into some forgotten night and be*
> *Of all dark long my moon-bright company . . .*

After that I see myself ringing the front-door bell of a dimly discerned house in a quiet side street. It was necessary that Mr. de la Mare should live somewhere in the Postal Directory. Thornsett Road happened to be the label attached to his terrestrial habitation. Yet my mind was unwilling to be convinced that he permanently existed anywhere away from the timeless province of his imaginations. Anerley was merely the (somewhat inaccessible) device he had adopted for making himself accessible to ordinary mortals. And, at first sight, it seemed that he was even doing what he could to disguise himself from identification as the de la Mare of his books. In my ardency of admiration I had expected to receive an immediate impression of poetic genius, to discover in his face some implication of ghostly communings. There was, however, nothing mysterious about the humorous and hospitable Mr. de la Mare whom I found in the midst of his family. He was as homely and natural as Hardy, and as neighbourly in his attitude to the details of everyday existence. One had to be alone with him before he began to make known things miraculous, setting one's dull wits moving to the music of his mind. On that evening two other poets were there—John Freeman, who also lived at Anerley, and Wilfrid Gibson, whom I had already met and liked and who wore the uniform of an Army Service Corps private, since he was still performing his uninspiring duties—at the Crystal Palace, of all places! Freeman, for whose muse I felt more respect than enthusiasm, appeared to be a sensitive unobtrusive type of literary man, though, as a matter of fact, he led two separate lives, being the head of an important insurance office during his daylight hours. On this occasion he began the after-dinner talk rather disappointingly for me by pinning the conversation to Coventry Patmore's prosodial experiments. I have always found prosody a perplexing and unassimilable subject, and my appreciation of the immaculate author of *The Unknown Eros* was as yet insufficient. And even when I had managed to produce my only trump card by divulging my visit to Hardy, I wasn't able to say anything illuminating about it. Freeman soon superseded me with modestly discriminative opinions of the novels, though de la Mare remarked, in a meditative undertone, 'Lucky you—to be inside Max Gate!' Thereafter they went into the problems of 'the later Henry James', of whom I had then read so little that I could only remain mute and mystified. Of *What Maisie Knew* I knew nothing, and *The Awkward Age* I had never even heard of. It was while they were appraising his shorter stories, however, that I caught a momentary glimpse of the de la Mare whose word-wizardry had long since put its spell on me. Speaking of *The Turn of the Screw*, he recalled a particular episode in that macabre masterpiece, referring to the terrific effect created when the governess narrator, watching from a window, sees the boy out in the bright moonlight staring up at the apparition of the infamous Peter Quint on the tower above. De la Mare's face was half in shadow, and it was then that I saw the haunting and haunted presence of genius in his eyes, and overheard in his voice the allurement of supernatural solicitings.

His all-human everyday self could reveal and combine intellectual curiosity, fanciful ingenuity, sweet reasonableness, and strong commonsense. He could capture the enchantments of childhood and interpret the oddities of the old. But within him was the poetic daemon whose promptings are incalculable and whose elements 'lost in the uttermost of eternity'. He has stated somewhere that 'any writing about poetry, however well-intended it may be, cannot but resemble beating the air. It can do little but attempt to give reasons for a delight that needs none.' The delight of knowing the poet de la Mare needs no translating into logic. But I must testify to one gift wherein he outshines anyone I have been lucky enough to meet. He has wisely warned us to 'look thy last on all things lovely every hour'. To this I can add that I have never been in his company without a sense of heightened and deepened perception. After talking to him, one goes away seeing the world, for a while, with rechristened eyes.

XI

After three weeks of pilgrimages to poets, post-Armistice parties, and other diversions, it was natural that the pendulum should swing back to the outdoor element of my two-fold experiment with time. It was a relief to be reminded that there were people for whom I was still merely 'Old Sig', even though that wayward individual had—as his hunting associates probably put it—'gone off the deep end writing wild and woolly poems'. It was therefore with a sense of escape that I betook myself to Rye for a few days' golf; and the trusted friend who joined me there happened to be the right one for this particular juncture of events. Apart from being a scratch golfer, he was a progressive-minded observer of political affairs, and also one of those sensible readers whose judgement is able to be unaware that their favourite authors are out of fashion with the advanced intellectuals. He belonged to a firm of stockbrokers, and had been doing the work of two absent partners. When I had first known him he was a tutor at the cramming establishment where I spent a year before going up to Cambridge. Readers of *The Old Century* will remember him there, admiringly delineated as 'George', and will understand that he was well qualified to counteract any swollen-headedness caused by climbing literary and social ladders to success. When with him I became the impulsive and unaffected person he had known in the past, glad to be guided by his integrity and good sense. His thoughtful detachment from the commotion of contemporary cleverness had a salutary effect, when contrasted with the monkey-house sophistication of some of the talk I'd listened to in London. His deductions, like his drives and iron-shots, were sound and unspectacular, well in the middle of the fairway. He just made them, picked up his bag, hunched his shoulders, and went on towards the green with his pipe in the corner of his resolute mouth.

My own game, like my ways of thinking, was erratic, as I hadn't touched a club for twelve months. (It felt a good deal more than a year since I had left Craiglockhart; but so much had happened since then, and the sudden ending of the war had made time seem inconsecutive and unadjusted.) In most of our matches George played the best ball of David Ayton and myself—myself not making much difference to the result. Ayton was looking more like a Scottish music-hall comedian than ever, especially when cleaning his ball with his tongue. One of the last survivors from that period when a potential open champion was willing to earn half a crown by carrying someone's clubs, his own set of clubs would now attract attention in a museum; but he used them in a canny, classic style that was a delight to watch.

Thus, for two or three days, I submitted to an illusion that Rye had ceased to concern itself with the agitations of the outer world and that I also had contrived aloofness. It was my favourite golf course, and George and I had played many a round there together before the War. So we had much for remembrance, and nothing to worry about except such mishaps as my topped drives and socketed approaches, and even these weren't taken seriously. This refreshing condition of mind was interrupted by a letter which caused me some astonishment and perplexity. The handwriting being unfamiliar, I left the envelope unopened until after our morning round. Over a plate of cold beef in the club-house I read it through twice, and then handed it to George. It was from Max Plowman, a soldier poet of whom I had first heard in the autumn of 1917, when he followed my example by refusing to perform any further military duties, after serving with the infantry in France. Since then he had remained an uncompromising pacifist. He was a man of fine intellect and high moral courage. He wrote to ask whether I would be willing to speak for Philip Snowden at the General Election. If such a thing appealed to me, he had reason to believe that my action would be singularly appreciated. 'The Government,' he explained, 'have put up a V.C. to oppose Snowden, hoping to unseat a sincere and honest opponent by what I regard as the political exploitation of a man's bravery. I believe you could stop the rot.' It was only a few days since the General Election had been sprung on the country by the Prime Minister. Assuming it to be an inevitable sequel to the conclusion of the War, I had paid little attention to it until George surprised me by deprecating it as premature. He supposed it to be a political manœuvre designed to play on popular feeling and break up the

Liberal Party led by Mr. Asquith. Nothing could have been more remote from my mind than the idea of taking any active part in it. My first thought, after reading Plowman's letter, dismissed the suggestion as preposterous. I had felt grateful to Snowden for his anti-war attitude in Parliament, and had been angered by the abuse thrown at him. All my political sympathies and convictions were with him; but the notion of my going in to 'stop the rot' at the Blackburn election seemed absurd. I half expected that George would hand the letter back with a jolly laugh. Had he done so, I should have regarded the matter as settled and put the request away without even indulging in a sigh of relief, for there would have been nothing to be relieved about. But after a deliberate perusal of the document, he remarked with a cheerful smile that it would be quite a stout effort on my part if I went there. In his opinion Snowden was too much of an extremist, though deserving of respect. He advised me to think it over before making up my mind. 'But damn it all,' I exclaimed, 'I've never made a speech in my life, except to my platoon, and the N.C.O.s of my company last summer. I should be no more use to Snowden than old Ayton!' George thereupon pointed out that my being an unpractised speaker wouldn't matter. The main support would consist in my appearing on the platform as an officer who had been at the Front. He added that, as far as he could see, this was going to be rather a demented election, and he'd like people with Snowden's views to be given a fair show. As a result of this impartial advice I allowed the project to percolate my mind, and by the evening had cogitated myself into feeling that it would be quite a fine gesture. Moreover it would annoy people who rabidly disagreed with me about the War. This was an inducement, even though it was also unlikely that many of my friends would approve the performance. But it was with no self-confidence that I telegraphed to Plowman offering to help at the election. The ingredients of my political utterances were a muddle which I didn't dare to contemplate. While still at Rye I received from Snowden a grateful acceptance of my offer. I then wrote to warn him of my inexperience as a speaker. His reply was reassuring. 'You ask me to say what I should want you to do. I should leave it to you to say what you felt moved to say. You would not be expected to make a long

111

speech. I am emphasizing the need for a clean, non-vindictive peace which will establish permanent good international relations.' He enclosed an election leaflet which enumerated the work he had done in Parliament during the War. What impressed me about his record was the continuous effort he had made on behalf of private soldiers and their dependants. This was a subject on which I had earned the right to feel strongly, and I foresaw my platform personality making use of that line of argument. Leaving Rye about a week before I was due at Blackburn, I went to the other side of Sussex for some hunting. While staying with my sporting friends I was aware of the incongruity of the situation. But I defied their Tory-minded disfavour, and they treated my venture with outward tolerance and good nature. Though already puzzled by my pacifism, this, they felt, was merely what might have been expected. If I chose to be 'a budding Bolshevist' and go and get rotten eggs chucked at me, someone remarked, it was my own look-out! At this bit of fun my temper flared up. If the Lloyd Georgeites started throwing things, I proclaimed with bravado, they'd get plenty in return. This caused general hilarity and cries of 'Good old Sig! That's the stuff to give the ruddy voters!' During my journey to the industrial North, however, I was feeling by no means 'on my toes'. There was a sinking sensation in my midriff. Before I knew where I was I should be facing my first meeting, and most thankfully would I have exchanged it for a meeting even with one of my least favourite famous authors! But there could be no turning back. I had set my hand to the plough—or Plowman had set it there for me—so I sought stability by absorbing political hyperboles from the weekly journals. Night had fallen when I reached Blackburn. A room having been engaged for me at an hotel near the station, I was intending to find my way thither, but as I came carrying my bag along to the exit I was met by a friendly man in seedy clothes who said he'd been told to take me to the Prince's Theatre, where Mr. Snowden was addressing a big meeting. This was too sudden for my equanimity. In dazed silence I accompanied him a short distance through dark and narrow streets. We entered the theatre by the back way. Somewhat breathless—for my guide had been in a great hurry—I found myself behind the stage. Snowden's voice sounded very

loud and rather grating. He was saying that what Mr. Lloyd
George had promised the people of this country whom he had
gulled was a palpable and ridiculous absurdity. There was nothing
in President Wilson's Fourteen Points about exacting an indem-
nity of two and a half billion pounds from the Central Powers, and
if this was put before the Peace Conference it meant that we had
broken our pledged word and committed a crime as great as . . .
At this point I was nudged on to the platform, to be greeted by a
smile from the speaker and a hearty round of applause from an
audience of about fifteen hundred women. Shy and nervous, I sat
there while Snowden resumed his exposure of Mr. Lloyd George's
ministerial misrepresentations. The thought crossed my mind
that I was breaking the King's Regulations by appearing at a
political meeting in uniform. A few minutes later I was beckoned
off the stage by an excited lady who bundled me into a cab, after
informing me that I was to address 'a hostile meeting at St.
Giles's School'. This proved to be a large dreary gas-lit room containing about a hundred people. Address them I did, in halting
style, mainly on the irrefutable virtues of Wilson's Fourteen
Points, the implications of which I understood as little as they did.
Their hostility wasn't actively apparent, and there was nothing in
my speech to provoke opposition. They listened with a sort of
gloomy attentiveness while I went lamely on, feebly paraphrasing
an article from *The Nation* which I'd read in the train. Those in
the front row stared up at me from behind school desks, looking as
if they'd partaken of a heavy 'high tea' and were now failing to
digest it.

After this depressing début I was driven back to the theatre,
which I found an inspiriting contrast. In a brief speech, punctu-
ated by laughter, I presented myself—not always audibly—with
an admission that I was 'no good as a speaker'. I adopted a demure
jocosity of manner, 'touching quite lightly on the issues of the
election', and acquiring confidence through the good-natured way
in which my remarks were received. 'Had some cocoa with the
Snowdens at their hotel and got to my own—The Old Bull—
about 11.15. I like them and am thankful I came here,' says a
pencilled scribble in my diary. When lying awake with a mind
which revolved in perorative electioneering phrases—containing,

113

I fear, a minimum of constructive ideas—it was difficult to believe
that I was the person who had been out hunting with the Southdown the day before. Early next morning I heard the clatter of
clogs in the cobbled street outside. The electors were on their way
to work, unaware that a new adherent to the Labour Movement
had arrived among them. During five days spent in Blackburn I
addressed a dozen meetings. I must have been an extremely bad
speaker, but the audiences were always well worked up when I
arose to contribute my little amateur turn. I enjoyed the excitement of the contest, and became quite a popular figure with
Snowden's supporters. In the only printed record of my utterances which I have preserved I was but briefly reported. 'Captain
Sassoon remarked that the soldiers on active service in France and
elsewhere had not a dog's chance of registering their vote at the
election.' Miss Margaret Bondfield followed me, asserting, with a
more professional expansiveness, that 'Government control had
not affected the crucial evil regarding the distribution of the
wealth of the world'. I have, however, kept some of the notes I
made for the big meetings. These suggest ambitious flights of
oratory when stimulated by the auditorium of the Prince's
Theatre. I even went so far as to quote Whitman, while affirming
my belief in the better and happier world in store for us after the
triumph of the Labour Movement. I urged the electors towards a
policy of Reconciliation with Germany. . . . But what I urged—or
intended to urge while making my notes—now makes rather
mournful and nonsensical reading, though I wasn't alone—either
then or thereafter—in declaring myself 'utterly opposed to the
continuance of compulsory military service in any form whatever'. (Cheers.) When taking the constituency into my confidence,
there was one subject which I prudently omitted to dwell on.
Having nothing to do in the mornings, I had explored the district
in tram-cars, without ever emerging from a horizonless unity of
grimy houses and dismal gas-smelling streets. In so far as Blackburn, Burnley, and Accrington were concerned, there seemed no
prospect of a better world until they had been demolished and
rebuilt. I had been spouting about freedom of thought, emancipation from social and industrial injustice, and the need for a
clean Peace. But what use was a clean Peace to people whose

bodies were condemned to such dirty conditions? How could the plans and promises of politicians have any meaning for their minds until Social Reconstruction had improved these places? The issues of the Khaki Election did not include this inescapable social problem which was brought to my notice on those drizzling dingy November mornings, and I surmised that some of the inhabitants would be offended if I told them that they were living in what had once been a nice bit of Lancashire and was now unfit for any community of human beings, industrial or otherwise. My final day at Blackburn being 'the eve of the poll', I spent the afternoon driving round to the local committee rooms with the Snowdens. The town was quiet, and there were no unfriendly demonstrations except when a few children hooted our car as it passed. Most of the voters had become forgetful of their surroundings while watching league football. Snowden was tired and untalkative. Once, however, he turned to me and said, 'I began in this town by speaking at street corners. Ever since then I have fought to improve working-class conditions here. And that's what I've come to now!' He pointed with his stick to an opposition poster which was to be seen all over Blackburn. 'Vote for the Two Britishers.' It was the first time I had heard him refer to the campaign of misrepresentation and abuse which his opponents had been conducting. Both in his speeches and in private he had shown consistent dignity and forbearance. My heart went out towards this man of bleakly uncompromising convictions, crippled with lameness, and fighting a losing battle against a frenzied intolerance whose catchwords were 'Hang the Kaiser' and 'Make the Germans Pay'. 'Snowden, the Arch-Pacifist' was reviled as though he were a public enemy. But the admirable energies of his wife were in all ways devoted to sustaining him, and at the moment she was cheerfully admonishing him with 'Now, Philip, you shouldn't talk like that. You know quite well that you'd go through all those years again ten times over for what you believe in. And some day people will be ashamed of this mad election.' To which, with a grim little smile, the Arch-Pacifist signified his assent. At the committee rooms, optimism was being outwardly maintained. By an extra effort it was just possible to believe that Snowden would be 'returned for the fourth time'. He himself

could probably have predicted the result within a few hundreds
of the exact figures. He knew that it was merely a matter of how
many votes he would lose by. In the evening there was a crowded
and enthusiastic finale at the Prince's Theatre. Snowden made an
impressive speech, in which he showed more of his essential
humanity than he usually allowed himself. The meeting culminated in a high-pitched oration by Mrs. Snowden, who was a most
effective speaker. It wasn't an occasion for under-emphasis, and
her peroration was a masterpiece of electoral appeal which lifted
the future of the Independent Labour Party to dizzy heights of
rhetorical prefigurement. My diary claims that my own performance, which filled the gap between the principals, was much the
best I had given. 'I felt absolute confidence and never hesitated
for a word.' Were those words extant, however, I should hesitate
before reproducing any of them. Unaccompanied by the thunders
of applause which they evoked, I am afraid they would sound
somewhat spurious. My self-identification with the cause of
Labour was too recent to justify such lofty pronouncements. What
I said about Snowden, on the other hand, was genuinely felt, and
may even have been adequately expressed, since he thanked me
afterwards with touching gratitude.

My experiment in electioneering concluded with tea and
kippers at the Snowdens' hotel. After the first day, this supper with
them and their friend Miss Isabella Ford had been a sort of family
party, and I felt quite sorry that it was all over. In spite of my
shortcomings as a speaker, I hadn't been a failure, and there was
no doubt that I had helped to keep their spirits up. Mrs. Snowden,
in the warmth of her heart, even went so far as to say that I had
been 'like a great big brother' to them. And Miss Ford had told
me that I had a gift for getting in touch with audiences, so I had
visions of myself as a Labour Leader, swaying multitudes by my
inspiring personality. But much as I liked Miss Ford, who was an
experienced suffragist and a wise, humorous woman, I do not
regard my subsequent avoidance of political oratory as a mistake.
Ink has always been the appropriate medium for my impulse to
address those who care to listen. Anyhow, when saying good-bye
to Snowden I felt sure that we should meet again. But somehow or
other we never did. I have often regretted that our ways of life

116

diverged, but so it was. The result of the election didn't surprise me. Out of 75,000 votes he only received a fifth of the number. Meanwhile, in all my experience of time's revenges, none has given me more satisfaction than the ultimate triumph over his detractors which transformed him into a nationally-acclaimed Chancellor of the Exchequer and thereafter created him the first Socialist Viscount. This made me doubly glad that I had supported him at the climax of his unpopularity.

XII

Towards midnight on the last day of 1918 I was sitting with my feet on the fireguard in the little ground-floor room at Weirleigh. Topper, who had been overfed and under-exercised during my long absences from home, was curled up on the sofa snoring. On a small table beside me was a three-branched candlestick. The electric light hadn't yet modernized us. I liked soft candleshine better than an oil lamp, and my eyesight was arrogantly good. Although I had been conscientiously studying Beer's *History of Socialism*, its unbeguiling pages had only sent my mind rambling in other directions. The book lay open on my knees, but I was well away on a New Year's Eve rumination which ranged over the past two months in a somewhat moody audit of overcrowded experience.

Rivers, who had been staying with us for a few days since Christmas, had departed that afternoon. Most of the doings I had described to him had been received with a reticent amusement which reduced them to their right proportions. He had made me feel that I must begin 1919 with at least one good resolution—not to be bamboozled by having scored a bit of a success. While approving my intention to join the Labour Movement, he warned me that my support of Snowden was merely a fortuitous gesture, though consistent with my war attitude. He laughed when I told him that, within twenty-four hours of returning from Blackburn as an ardent Socialist, I had been hob-nobbing with Lady Randolph at an evening party, and a couple of days later had lunched with the Asquiths. 'You'll have to decide which party you really belong to!' he remarked, whereupon I regretfully realized that there wasn't much likelihood of my hob-nobbing with Winston again. For, after all, the Blackburn episode had shown me which side I was on. Rivers suggested that the less I was in London the better. I was now considering my future arrangements. It wouldn't have suited me to remain at home for the remainder of the winter. Weirleigh had become a sort of repository for my defunct pre-war self. Its unlively atmosphere

118

oppressed me, and was too much of a contrast to the gaieties of London. But the chief uneasiness at that time was caused by a conflict of prejudices between me and my mother. Mine were fluid and experimental. Hers were obdurate and unchangeable. She did her best to be tolerant of my new interests and experiences, but I was often aware of disagreements looming up between us. My association with Snowden had pained and displeased her deeply, and it wasn't possible to speak about him. I was, of course, a prime example of the unforbearingness of youth towards supposedly bellicose civilians. My poor mother had to suffer for her habit of denying the Germans any attribute except devilry and her inability to believe anything blameworthy about the British. She looked upon many of my recently-acquired acquaintances with disfavour, suspecting that if they weren't Socialists they were at any rate Radicals! Since then I have been taught a sympathetic comprehension of middle age and its war-time endurances. I am prepared to be submissive in the presence of the returned warrior. It was, in fact, the situation which must have been creating disharmony in many a home. The demobilized young felt that it was no use attempting to explain to their elders the realities of an experience from which they had been excluded, or that those elders had any right to express opinions about it.

Anyhow, Rivers had provided a safe and comfortable subject for conversation. My mother had what I can affectionately describe as a weakness for the medical profession. For her, any doctor was difficult to disbelieve in, and ever since I could remember I associated the arrival of the family physician with her efficient, though rather fussy, enjoyment of the treatment of minor ailments. Rivers had earned her gratitude by curing me of being a militant war-resister, and she could discuss my general health with him to her heart's content. The fact that he had given up hospital work many years ago to become an anthropologist and F.R.S. didn't seem to have clearly impressed itself on her mind. She preferred to think of him producing a stethoscope from his pocket and listening to one's chest. Meanwhile, enlivened by his visit, she made me realize what a good talker she was. Not long afterwards, when I stayed with him at Cambridge, he said that he had seldom met anyone with a more direct and humorously simplifying intelligence or better intuitive judgement of essential human questions. Even from him, however, such testimony failed to persuade me that she could be right about those matters whereon we disagreed. I couldn't then see that her intolerances were on the surface, irrelevant to the sterling sagacity which—in a single idiomatic and original phrase—could sum up the strength or weakness of human beings and works of art. She had watched modernities and 'advanced' movements come and go, and could see through slick and second-rate cleverness at a glance. I, on the other hand, was rejecting almost everything I had been brought up to admire. All that my mother believed in must be superseded by what I was discovering for myself. It must be added that it was only in politics that we were seriously at variance. And her political opinions, as Rivers remarked, were a habit of mind which she wasn't young enough to alter.

But I have digressed from the point where my ruminations about 1919 were interrupted by Topper stretching himself and giving me a fox-terrier look which meant that he was ready to be let out of the front door for a sniff round. Beer's *History of Socialism* fell on the floor, and I was too lazy to pick it up. The rosewood timepiece which I had bought for my Gray's Inn rooms in the spring of 1914 stared silently at me from the shelf above the fireplace, indicating that 1918 was ended. I could hear the leisurely tick of the grandfather clock in the front hall. It seemed to be presiding over the quietude of the house without concerning itself about my future. There it had stood all my life, keeping an eye on my comings and goings. It had struck all the hours of the War, including those of my intensified revisitations, when I had more than once given it what might have been a final glance while the village taxi was waiting to take me to my train. I was fond of its eighteenth-century brass face, and respected it as an old friend; but it would have ticked on just the same if I had never come back from the War. Like Hardy's notion of Nature, it was unconscious and impercipient. A subject, I mused, suitable for one of his poems, wishing that I could make something of it myself, as I vaguely remembered those summer days of childhood, and how 'the hall clock' had been the arbiter of my unruly existence when I rushed in late for meals, after a drink from the tap in the pump-yard outside, where the smell of the wide-spreading fig-tree on the wall seemed to bring to mind all I had ever known of sunlight and garden freedom. The clock on the mantelpiece was, ostensibly, quite alert and inquisitive about my unformulated future. Wind me up once a week, it seemed to be saying, and I'll tick you on to achievements which may make an unusually significant clock of me. For it was a cheerful young chronologer, dating from a time when I was unhopeful of making a reputation, and I associated it with my period of progress. A day or two ago it had overheard Rivers advising me to go and stay in Oxford to study political economy. I had suggested Oxford because it was near Garsington, and had now written to Lady Ottoline asking her to find me some 'rooms. Rivers considered that political economy would be a useful preparation for my participation in the Labour Movement, though, for once, he was mistaken in assuming that I could absorb economics. I was already aware that my mind recoiled from such practical knowledge, just as it had done when I was studying Law at Cambridge. I was also discovering that I felt least confident when meeting writers of my own generation. They expected an intellectual sophistication which I did not possess, and made me feel clumsy and uninformed. But most of them had learnt to find their way about the literary world before they were thirty. When talking to Hardy I had felt no such inferiority. Being what he was, he had freed me from self-consciousness, and had conversed with me as if I could tell him things he didn't know. On the mantelpiece was the framed portrait he had given me, propitiously inscribed with my name as well as his own signature. When sitting to the photographer about five years before, he had contrived to intimate that he wasn't such a great man as his admirers imagined. There was a just discernible expression of amusement in his eyes and about the region of the moustache. Except for the majesty of his brow, Hardy the poet had evaded the camera. That photograph, I now told myself, was something to be lived up to. It was the hall-mark on such recognition as my poetry had so far achieved. For there was no one, among living writers, whose approval could have the significance of his. Ten years ago the farthest flight of my day-dreams would have been a few words of encouragement from Swinburne or

121

Meredith. Even to have seen either of them would have been a wondrous experience. And here I was, complacently ensconced in a feeling of actual friendship with the inheritor of their fulfilled renown!

At Max Gate I had induced him to talk about Meredith, and he had described their earliest meeting, in the back room of the publisher for whom Meredith was reading manuscripts. When receiving generous admonitions about his first novel he had no idea who the frock-coated critic was. The anecdote (subsequently well known through the biographies of both) had given me a pleasant sense of being ahead of the literary historians, combined with the strangeness of its having happened more than fifty years ago, when Meredith's hair was not yet grey and Hardy was a shy young man in an architect's office. This brought to mind a scene in my own recent history. For, about a week before, I had been introduced to Meredith's daughter. Meanwhile my rememberings will be more effectively continued if I substitute my present self for the fireside ruminator, who hadn't advanced far enough along the years to be able to divulge much beyond the fact that he had met the lady at a dinner party given by Frank Schuster. When meeting Mr. Schuster for the first time, at a luncheon given by Osbert Sitwell in the previous November, I had found him very pleasant and congenial, but should have been astonished had I foreseen that he would afterwards become one of my closest friends. Unconscious of the vista of concerts and operas that I was destined to hear in his company, I didn't even know that for many years he had been a notable figure in the musical world. He was at that time well past sixty, but had evidently decided to be no older than he felt. For the present, however, I need say no more than that he was wealthy, a superfine gastronomist, and a giver of superlative parties. To entertain, and be entertained by his discriminative enjoyments—this had been his *métier*, and he had no intention of allowing it to lapse, since he belonged to that fortunate period when social pleasures were unrestricted. The Great War had caused an inevitable reduction of his entertainings, interrupting his continental career in pursuit of sunshine and memorable musical events; but nothing could diminish his desire for the delectable or his ingenuity in attaining it. The fancy-dress ball which he had given two days before Christmas had been his rejoicing demonstration of emergence from the War and of his renewed resolve to regale himself and his friends with exquisitely organized hospitality. I had received my invitation on the day I went to Blackburn, but as I wasn't in the mood for such revels and had no means of devising a fancy dress I left the card unanswered. Shortly after, however, Glyn Philpot asked me to stay with him for it, which resulted in my being elaborately rigged-out as a Tartar prince in a gold turban. By the time he had finished I scarcely knew myself, for he insisted on painting two black curls and round pink spots on my cheeks and chin. Needless to say, this made me feel delightfully dissociated from my normal self. He himself was an Elizabethan Spaniard in black velvet. His face powdered dead white, white spur straps on long black boots, and large green gem rings on his fingers, he had transformed himself immeasurably away from the accomplished painter of Academy portraits. He had escaped into that imaginative environment for which he had a self-defensive predilection, and looked more suitable for a canvas in the Prado than for Schuster's elegant house in Old Queen Street, Westminster. There we found about thirty guests assembled, and soon afterwards I was sitting at the dinner-table between Madame Vandervelde, the vivacious red-haired wife of the eminent Belgian politician-patriot, and a lady of no particular period who was plentifully adorned with tricolour ribbons and rosettes, from which I inferred that she impersonated La Belle France. This was Mrs. Sturgis, Meredith's daughter, to whom Schuster had presented me in characteristically opulent style. (His introductions were always apt to be rather florid and effusive.) Next to her was 'Dodo' Benson, an Apache with a stubbly grey moustache. Opposite us, Lady Randolph as a Holbein Duchess in black velvet, was in appropriate partnership with Glyn Philpot. Our host was in ordinary evening clothes, over which he afterwards donned a hooded cloak. There were a good many young people, wearing the motley disguises of jesters, harlequins, pierrots, Dresden shepherdesses, and suchlike. In this atmosphere of masquerade it felt rather inept to be so eager to talk about the author of *Love in the Valley* and *The*

Ordeal of Richard Feverel. Mrs. Sturgis was probably a bit tired of people who wanted to discuss her father, although anything she might have told me of him would have been welcomed with avidity. But it was not to be. I soon realized, with disappointment, that I was conversing with a typical society woman, witty in a smart and worldly way, and superficially opinionated. Moreover, her manner towards me was noticeably antagonistic. Almost at once she tackled me about my views on the War. Unwilling to argue, I allowed her to clinch the matter by asserting that she hoped there would be conscription for the next hundred years. The reason for this infelicitous episode, as I afterwards discovered, was that she believed me to have been a conscientious objector throughout the War. It was a pity that she knew so little of me, for she had the reputation of being good-hearted and genuine. It must be added that I was unjustified in resenting the ultra-militaristic views to which she had treated me. I ought to have known that Meredith himself was a strong advocate of National Service. In 1878, when England's relations with Russia were so ominous, he wrote to a friend that 'ultimately it will come to conscription, and the sooner the better'. In 1918, however, I had no tolerance for those who fought their country's battles from arm-chairs. And since that evening was designed to gladden the hearts of the demobilized, it seemed surprising that Mrs. Sturgis, with her highly-developed social sense, should have obtruded the subject of conscription. I am glad to say that I succeeded in reminding her of the large laurel wreath which I had sent to her father's funeral, so she may have admitted that there was something to be said in my favour after all.

But the band was striking up in the gallery of the oak-panelled music-room, and all was in readiness to receive 'Frankie Schu's' guests. Soon the ardent revelry was in full swing, 'with plume, tiara, and all rich array'. In other words, the company had begun 'jazzing' and 'one-stepping' for all it was worth. Ambulating rather than revolving, they exhibited pedestrian persistence more than poetry of motion. Waltzing was a thing of the past, and as I lacked experience of these innovations I remained an outsider. When Schuster offered to find me some partners I pleaded my disability, asking him why he didn't insist on a few minutes of

'The Blue Danube' to relieve the monotony. 'My dear boy, I simply dare not!' he exclaimed. 'They would howl me down.' As a young man he had studied the piano in Vienna, and he disliked these dreary American importations as much as I did. A diversion was then created by the entry of Roger Fry, impersonating a witch-doctor of forbidding aspect. Later on Diaghilev, white-faced and imperturbable, arrived with some of the leading members of the Russian Ballet. This led to my being a subject of mistaken identity. I was standing by a doorway in my usual attitude of an uncommunicative Mongolian when a rather effeminate Roman Emperor asked me, with ingratiating archness, 'Are you going to dance for us? We are all thrilled with expectation!' For a moment I was somewhat bewildered, nothing being farther from my thoughts than taking the floor for a solo performance. I then realized that he had assumed me to be one of Diaghilev's troupe. I shook my head with a dignified evasiveness which implied that I might be willing to oblige if sufficient pressure were brought to bear on me, and he passed on, leaving me with an indefinable sensation of having scored an unsolicited personal success. Soon afterwards the expected thrill was provided by a new Spanish dancer, with much bravura stamping and finger-snapping.

One other memory returns to me from that evening, intensified by the intervening years. The ball was coming to an end, and the John Peel Galop—as a concession to the outmoded past—was being danced with exuberant gaiety. Looking up, I observed the grey-cloaked figure of Frankie Schuster, who was watching from the musician's gallery. His face, relaxed and oldened by the fatigue of entertaining, peered unsmilingly from under his quaint crumpled hood. It may have been that he himself was conscious only of his patent leather shoes pinching his tired feet and a desire to have his head on the pillow. But for a moment I saw him with the mask of social sprightliness discarded, and as though he were comparing this latest evocation of festivity with those many others which had gone their way of impermanence with the caravan that starts for the Dawn of Nothing when the door is closed behind the last departing guest. It was a face world-weary and saddened by the pursuit of pleasure, yet still in love with life, still demanding stimulation from the spectacle of youth in action. In after years I often saw him thus, when he believed himself unobserved, and I used to wonder whether the words 'vanitas vanitatum' were in his mind. On that first occasion, however, the cloak and hood made me perceive him as a sort of party-giving Prospero. Were he to clap his hands, I thought, the whole rout of merry-makers might suddenly vanish, and he be left alone with his beautiful empty house and the solitude of his Epicurean philosophy.

XIII

While reconstructing the contrasts and inconsistencies of what might conceivably be called a simpleton's progress, I am often doubtful in deciding what is significant to the story. Anxious to impose coherence on the patchy integument of chuckle-headed immaturity, one observes how the actions of undeveloped character, especially when governed by emotion, vary between reversions to juvenility and anticipations of the self-knowledge towards which one was being conducted by the educative process of making mistakes and refusing to admit them. From this top-heavy paragraph of perspicuity it will be seen that—in assembling my material for the first months of 1919—I have been indulging in elderly deprecations of remembered silliness. Nevertheless there are moments when sedately-compromising maturity seems no more praiseworthy than the imprudent predecessor who scorned to count the cost of his actions and vaguely aspired towards altruism and unworldliness. In fact I can imagine him 'giving me up' as a hopeless case of full-blown fogeydom. 'Easy enough for you', he might say, 'to be sitting there making memoirs out of my inexperience and palavering about my chuckle-headed inconsistency. And look at you now—popping-in a safeguarding clause against yourself just to prove your sublime impartiality!' To which I can only reply that no one regrets my loss of initiative more than I do. Seeing all round a subject doesn't always produce illuminating results. One can but sigh and continue the chronicle. . . .

Leaving Weirleigh in the middle of January I went to Oxford. After inspecting the pleasant rooms in Merton Street which Lady Ottoline had engaged for me, I spent a night at Garsington, where I listened to a philosophical discussion between Bertrand Russell and George Santayana. As far as I can recollect, they were investigating the reality of Reality, or something equivalently beyond my powers of comprehension. On my return journey to Oxford the only conveyance available was Philip Morrell's milk-float, which I shared with Santayana. The jogglesome reality of this

127

vehicle wasn't conducive to conversation, and the shy, fragile-looking philosopher could only acknowledge my remarks with nervous nods. I was on my way to Raymond Buildings, where Eddie Marsh was giving a dinner party for a dozen people, most of whom were what I designated 'titled blokes and blokesses'. Since I now regarded myself as a revolutionary, my attitude to the aristocracy was theoretically inimical, and this feeling was aroused by an unlucky incident. It so happened that the evening papers had announced the murder of Karl Liebknecht and Rosa Luxemburg. During dinner, Eddie mentioned this, adding that no one would miss them—an opinion which, naturally enough, passed undenied by those who overheard it. This was too much for my fiery political feelings, and I exclaimed that I wished I were half as brave as Liebknecht. The awkward moment was tactfully tided over. But judging by Eddie's scared expression, my demeanour must have been a bit volcanic.

Later in the evening, when about twenty people had joined the party, I sat on the floor watching the famous General Freyberg, with his V.C. ribbon, and a dozen wound-stripes on his sleeve, while Ivor Novello, in an elegant uniform, sang some of his own compositions.

> *I'd like to die, but die a little death only.*
> *I'd like to die, but look down from the window.*
> *I'd like to die, but walk with the procession. . . .*

he informed us, with graceful and engaging youthfulness. But I was still feeling too pro-Liebknecht, and couldn't share the spirit of my surroundings as I should have done, which was unfair to Eddie and his gifted and agreeable guests. Viola Tree's impersonations made me laugh, but I couldn't forget those two anti-militarists riddled with bullets in a Berlin hotel. For Liebknecht had been the same sort of pacifist in the German Parliament as Snowden in ours. It wasn't 'a little death' that he had died, and in my estimation he was as much a hero as Freyberg.

Next day I went to Cambridge to stay with Rivers at St. John's. Dining in Hall I sat between him and a venerable don, with whom I made experiments in small talk to which he listened with rather absent-minded civility. This was Dr. Liveing, the President—or vice-master—of the College. Since his silver beard was still tinged with brown, I assumed him to be a well-preserved septuagenarian, and put forth bright efforts to interest him in contemporary events. Gazing at me from time to time, he appeared to be wondering, with kindly acquiescence, what surprise I should offer him next. What I did ultimately ask him was 'Have you been to the Russian Ballet?' With a faint smile he replied that it was several years since he had been away from Cambridge. Evidently the existence of the Russian Ballet was as yet unknown to him. I became aware that my question was causing a ripple of amusement among those who had overheard me. For Dr. Liveing was in his ninety-second year. He was a very distinguished scientist who had made important discoveries in spectroscopy, but his career had been mainly devoted to chemical research. He had been appointed the first Professor of Chemistry to the University in 1861! Rivers told me all this while we were on our way to the Combination Room. In that beautiful dark-panelled gallery I sipped my coffee among the buzzing assemblage of begowned fellows, who looked rather queer and crepuscular, since candles were their only illumination. Arnold Bennett, when staying with Rivers after I had brought them together, commented disparagingly on the absence of electric light; but I found the candlelight pleasantly appropriate to the traditional collegiate atmosphere. At the end of the room, Dr. Liveing was sitting alone by the fireside, elbows on knees and both hands outstretched as he gazed at the flickering flames. His tall, sparely-built figure, half-hidden by the folds of his gown, made a memorable picture of patriarchal repose. The long dim room was murmurous with present-day discussions; but his mind had withdrawn into far-vista'd musings, and while watching his face—so nobly refined and so becalmed by reverie— I remembered the lines of Landor, who himself lived to be nearly ninety.

> *I warmed both hands before the fire of life;*
> *It sinks, and I am ready to depart.*

But Dr. Liveing continued active for several more years. It is recorded that when ninety-six he read a paper to the Cambridge Philosophical Society on *The Recuperation of Energy in the Uni-*

verse. Within three years of his century he died as a result of being knocked down by a lady bicyclist.

Talking to Rivers late on the following evening, I remarked that during the past twenty-four hours I had met more Fellows of the Royal Society than in the whole of my previous career. Counting the F.R.S.s on my fingers I found that there were six, including Dr. Liveing. I asked him to enumerate their achievements in science. (I must mention that I was in the habit of making jokes about the vast erudition of his friends and colleagues, and these levities were a stock source of amusement to him.) He began with Dr. Bonney, a lively geologist who had been to the summit of the Matterhorn and was still a rock-climber at eighty-five. What was his special subject, I inquired. Rivers thought it was probably volcanoes. Next came Seward, the Master of Downing, with whom we had been to tea. He was a botanist, and a great authority on fossil plant-life. I had also been taken to call on Haddon, the eminent anthropologist, a big man whose powerful head had struck me as having something of the noble savage about it. We had lunched with Sir Horace Darwin, who apparently specialized in being human and delightful. At dinner in college I had sat next to Sir Joseph Larmor. He was a professor of Mathematics and Natural Philosophy, and M.P. for the University. Evidently unaware that I had written anything, he talked about nothing in particular; to which I listened respectfully, careful not to ask whether he had been to the Russian Ballet. Afterwards Rivers took me to the rooms of Cyril Rootham, the composer, where I was persuaded to read a few of my poems to a silent but seemingly appreciative circle of undergraduates. It had indeed been a socially strenuous Sunday.

*　　　*　　　*

On the first day of February I was digesting an early dinner in the smoking-room of the Reform Club, to which I had recently been elected. It was a Saturday evening, and I was on my way to Oxford to begin the vaguely visualized spell of student life which would, I hoped, improve my unpreparedness for lending a hand in the Labour Movement. On this particular day the Movement had

been providing conspicuous evidence of liveliness in the shape of
an ugly outbreak of rioting in Glasgow. The evening papers were
making the most of it, and although the situation seemed well in
hand the news had caused an electrical disturbance in the public
mind. Even the legal-featured Reformers around me were looking
less oracular than usual after their perusals of the tape-machine in
the front hall. While sitting there I was joined by H. W. Massingham, from whom, as editor of *The Nation*, the affair would
demand a penetrative article in next week's issue. I had a great
regard for Massingham. He had been a good friend to my poetry,
and was an energetic supporter of the young. With eager interest
I listened to his denunciations of the Government and his gloomy
predictions of the blunders which would be perpetrated at the
Peace Conference. These riots, he asserted, were the first fruits of
the Khaki Election. His private sympathies were with the demon-
strators, but it was, of course, his business to discover the extent of
the trouble and whether it was likely to be followed by further
eruptions. 'I wish I could get hold of someone to go up there and
find out what's happening. If I were a younger man and not tied
to the office I'd go myself,' he remarked, glancing unbenignly at a
dozing club nonentity as though suspecting him of being an
enemy to social reconstruction—which he probably was. Impulsively I offered to go there next day if he thought I should be any
use to him. He gladly accepted, and at once wrote me a couple of
letters of introduction. He gave me no definite instructions,
merely saying that I could pick up all he needed in a couple of
days by going about and keeping my eyes and ears open. On my
way to Oxford I felt much elated that such a pre-eminent editor
had permitted me to act as his special correspondent in a crisis.
My only regret was that I couldn't get there before Monday
morning; and I went so far as to hope that things wouldn't have
quieted down by the time I arrived.

I must now confess that I have quite forgotten the origin of the
commotion which I was then so earnestly resolved to investigate.
There must have been a lot more in it than broken windows and
free fights between the police and the proletariat, but my mind is
a blank as to what it was all about, and I was too busy to jot down
the details in my note-book. I see myself getting a smoke-drifted

glimpse of Glasgow from the train, in the dismal beginnings of daylight, and then betaking myself to More's Temperance Hotel —why, I cannot say—unless it was recommended to me by my cabman! After a morning spent in futile search for first-hand facts, I began to feel rather desperate about providing Massingham with anything that wasn't already in the newspapers. There seemed nothing to discover, except that it was all over and the centre of the city looked a bit deserted. Where did the professional reporters find their copy, I wondered, when everything appeared so ordinary? While lunching at the hotel, however, I observed, at the other end of the long table, a group which seemed likely to be newspaper men, since one of them was scribbling on a note-pad. I was thinking that my only hope was to hitch on to them and try to cadge some material, when a young man came in and took the place next to me. He had a sensitively intelligent face, and before long we had struck up an acquaintance. It transpired that he knew all about me and was there for the same purpose, though not representing any particular paper. His name was John Langdon-Davies, and I gathered that he was an ardent anti-militarist and wrote poetry. His uncle was a well-known member of the Independent Labour Party, so he was fully informed and could take me behind the scenes of what had been happening. I really don't know what I should have done without him. For the next three days we were inseparable, and I was exempted from all exploratory initiative. We attended at the police court when David Kirkwood, the Clydeside Workers' leader, was remanded in custody. His head was bandaged and he said nothing. He looked strong, kindly, and sensible. I should have liked to shake him by the hand. A contrast was provided by the magistrate, a meagre, parchment-faced person with a droning, lifeless voice. We also witnessed a session of the City Corporation, made eventful by shouted interruptions from the extremist members. One of the Bailies was frog-marched out of the stately Chamber. On the following day, using a letter of introduction given me by Massingham, I visited Weir's engineering works. The manager showed me round civilly, but I came away little the wiser, except for having picked up the phrase 'shop-stewards'; for I was totally ignorant of Trade Union technicalities.

Siegfried's Journey, 1916–1920

That the 'Reds' of the City Corporation had reason to be indignant was grimly impressed on me when I was conducted through
the worst of the slum areas. I had thought of slums as wretched
and ramshackle, but had imagined them mitigated by some sort
of Dickensian homeliness. These courts and alleys were cliff-like
and cavernous, chilling me to the bone. The few unfortunates
who scowled at us from doorways looked outlawed and brutalized.
Here the thought of comfort never came, and there was a dank
smell of destitution. Cold as the stones we trod was the bleak inhumanity of those terrible tenements. Appalled, and more than
willing to ask why such things should be, I felt thankful to get
back into the thriving city streets. I had no wish to enter the
Cowcaddens again. Does that rent-producing monument of misery
and social injustice still exist, I wonder? Or has the work of people
like Kirkwood for Labour Housing conditions been effective in
condemning the Cowcaddens as unfit for human habitation?
Meanwhile my special-correspondent report had to be composed
and dispatched. Ably drafted by Langdon-Davies while I puffed
my pipe and blessed his professional phraseology, it probably contained a fair number of suggestions made by me. But I cannot
quote from it, as no copy is preserved in the archives of my
literary career.

A couple of unforgotten incidents seem worth appending.
Most of the people we talked to in the hotel were enthusiastic
Socialists. One of them—a warm-hearted middle-aged woman
with whom we became friendly—remarked, while discussing me
with Langdon-Davies, 'It's easy to see that *he* didn't acquire the
teachings of Karl Marx with his mother's milk!' She might have
added that neither then nor thereafter was I likely to assimilate
one particle of the Marxian doctrine from the impenetrable pages
of *Das Kapital*. Another of our acquaintances was a loquacious little
man from whom I gained an impression that he lived for nothing
except wholesale social reform. The workers of the world must
unite; and he and I were already doing so while consuming
sausages and bacon and strongly-brewed tea. On my last evening
he drew me aside to divulge, in a mysterious manner, that he had
something he particularly wanted to show me. I vaguely assumed
that it must be some document connected with subterranean

political activities. Subterranean it appeared to be; for he led me nimbly down some steps to the basement of the hotel, and unlocked a door. Nothing could have been more unexpected than what met my gaze in the vault-like room which we entered. It was filled with a fleet of perambulators. He had, of course, no intention of trying to sell me one. He was proud of them, and they were all he had to show me. The perambulators were very nice ones, and he was a very nice little man; but they were an anti-climax, though I felt touched by the simplicity with which he demonstrated their merits, and expressed adequate appreciation.

My report to *The Nation* earned me unmerited commendations from Massingham. It was exactly what he had wanted, he said. Conscience rebuked me for failing to mention Langdon-Davies; but as my name hadn't been attached, I allowed myself to believe that some of the credit had gone to him.

*   *   .*

Arriving in London by the night train from Glasgow, I went to the '1917' Club, to which Mrs. Snowden and Miss Margaret Bondfield had been responsible for my election. Membership, of course, implied association with Labour Party politics, and this was my first appearance there. The '1917' lacked the spacious amenities of the Reform; but I was tired and untidy and felt that my tousled unshaven condition was appropriate evidence of my exertions as a Socialist. The smoking-room was empty, except for a couple of rather invertebrate-looking young men whose conversation I couldn't avoid overhearing while I glumly consumed some coffee. Before long, one of them mentioned my name and asked his companion whether he knew anything about me. 'Not much,' he replied, 'but I've heard he spends a hundred a year on scent.' Without waiting for further fabulous revelations of my mode of life, I departed to catch the next train to Oxford. Brightened by the polychromatic curtains which Lady Ottoline had chosen for me, the Merton Street rooms held out hopes that the rest of the winter would pass in peaceful acquisition of mental equilibrium. I foresaw undistracted mornings, spent at my writing-table by the window, which looked across the gardens of Merton toward Christ Church meadows. There I should absorb constructive information about Capital and Labour and how to create social equality for all. In the afternoons I should go for walks in the country. At night I should read poetry or emerge to be invigorated by the progressive ideas of brilliant young dons and undergraduates. And I could always go out to Garsington when I needed home life combined with high thinking. What I didn't foresee was that I should at once become involved in a series of tea parties with Oxford poets, some of whom induced me to give talks to literary societies. Instead of slowing down my existence, as Rivers had advised, I was seldom alone, and did much more than was good for my unsettled state of mind. Wearing corduroy trousers and a bright red tie, I went about exploiting my Labour Movement personality and my reputation as an anti-war poet. Now and again I reverted to riding-breeches and a loud check cap, a form of dress which caused me to be more my authentic self than I realized. For the fox-hunting man was irrepressible, and the superficially adopted Socialism—though generous in impulse and intention—required more than corduroy to conceal its inadequate repertoire. I must have talked a lot of nonsense, but I remember one sensible speech I made, which can be quoted in full, owing to its brevity. I had persuaded Masefield to bicycle down from Boar's Hill to address the literary undergraduates of Balliol. When asked to contribute my views on poetry-writing, I felt unwilling to compete with the unassuming excellence of what he had told them; so I merely remarked that I had but one thing to say: 'When in doubt, cut it out.'

Osbert Sitwell was often in Oxford to visit his brother, and this led to my oddest experience there. One afternoon in February they took me to see Ronald Firbank, who was living in a house opposite All Souls. None of us had met him before, but his impressionist novels had led us to expect a somewhat peculiar person, so we weren't surprised when he received us in a closely-curtained room lighted by numerous candles and filled with a profusion of exotic flowers. A large table was elaborately set out with a banquet of rich confectionery and hothouse fruits. Firbank, whose appearance was as orchidaceous as his fictional fantasies, behaved so strangely that all attempts at ordinary conversation became farcical. His murmured remarks were almost inaudible, and he was too nervous to sit still for more than half a minute at a time. The only coherent information he gave me was when I heavily inquired where his wonderful fruit came from. 'Blenheim,' he exclaimed with an hysterical giggle, and then darted away to put a picture-frame straight, leaving me wondering how peaches were grown at Blenheim in mid-winter. The Sitwells were more successful in mitigating his helpless discomposure, but even Osbert's suavely reassuring manner failed to elicit anything except the disconnected utterances which were his method of evading direct explanations. For instance, when Sacheverell spoke appreciatively of his latest novel, *Caprice*, he turned his head away and remarked, in a choking voice, 'I can't bear calceolarias! Can you?' Could this have any bearing on the book, I speculated, from the other side of the table, where I was now a mere cake and fruit consumer. There was an enormous fire, and the warmth of the flower-scented room made me drowsy while Firbank, who was shedding some of his agonized shyness and its attendant affectations, confided in the Sitwells that he had no servants in the house and lived almost entirely on cold chicken. Watching him through the jungle of orchids, I found it hard to believe that this strange being could have any relationship with the outer world. He was as unreal and anomalous as his writings, and the room—with its exquisite refinements and virtuosities of taste—seemed a pathetically contrived refuge. I afterwards discovered that he had travelled widely, and was much more business-like than he made himself out to be. But when I once ventured to ask what was his favourite country, he could only answer 'Lotus land, of course!' He had a horror of particularities, and my more literal-minded approach to life was too great a strain on him.

A few days later I invited him to tea, for I was curious to observe how he shaped by daylight and away from his 'highly stylized' surroundings. Rather to my surprise he accepted. Anxious to entertain him appropriately, I bought a monumental bunch of grapes, and a glutinous chocolate cake. Powdered, ninetyish, and insuperably shy, he sat with eyes averted from me and my well-meaning repast. His most rational response to my attempts at drawing him out about literature and art was 'I adore italics, don't you?' His cup of tea remained untasted, and he quailed when I drew his attention to my large and cosy pile of crumpets. As a gesture of politeness he slowly absorbed a single grape. In subsequent years I met him at intervals—mostly intervals at the Russian Ballet—and he sent me copies of his books, wittily inscribed in violet ink in his bold, feminine handwriting. The last time I talked to him he happened to be in a communicative mood. 'I am Pavlova, chasing butterflies,' he exclaimed; and then added with mock seriousness, 'You are Tolstoy, digging for worms.' His earlier books had amused me, but I regarded them as the elegant triflings of a talented amateur. Misled by their apparent lack of construction, I failed to see that he had a deliberate technique of his own. I was often charmed by his sensitive and diverting word-play, and in his later works I found a sort of opulent beauty and decadent gaiety. Firbank's writings, though leaving a superficial impression of exquisite accomplishment, never achieved the tenuous mastery which he aimed at. His chicness is too pervasive, and his improper innuendoes seem to me tittering and tiresome. Nevertheless he ranks high among nonsensical novelists, and might be described as having a genius for subtle silliness.

*   *   *

Early in March a letter arrived which took me completely by surprise. It was from Gerald Gould, the associate-editor of the *Herald*, which had been a politically dissentient weekly during the war, and was now about to become the daily organ of Labour. Gould, whom I only knew through his graceful Stevensonian lyrics, offered me the literary editorship of the paper. It seemed a providential opportunity to put an end to my purposeless existence at Oxford; but when replying I pointed out that I had no journalistic experience whatever, and had never reviewed a book in my life. He assured me that this would be no disadvantage. What they needed was 'someone who would bring a fresh mind to the literary page', and it appeared that ignorance was, so to speak, a qualification. I therefore accepted the job, at a salary of five pounds a week, and had soon persuaded myself that the literary page was going to be unlike anything that had happened in Fleet Street before. Provided that I was allowed a free hand, this seemed not improbable.

XIV

Sanguinely announcing itself as 'The Paper with its Face towards the Future', and foretelling a minimum circulation of 250,000, the *Daily Herald* was born on March 31st. My own promotion to literary editorship was heralded by a pleasantly-printed eight-page pamphlet devised by Francis Meynell. Its object was to ensure that the publishing trade sent us review copies, and to stimulate competition for the privilege of advertising on my page. It is possible that the pamphlet made an agreeable impression on the publishers, but there was one notable exception. Meynell had reprinted four of my poems without obtaining permission from Heinemann, who at once wrote indignantly demanding the destruction of all undistributed copies. 'A Literary Editor for the New London Daily Newspaper' thus achieved immediate scarcity, and it is now one of the least accessible items in my bibliography. Though always friendly to myself, Heinemann looked on the *Herald* as a menace to the fabric of the social system. He was pained by my appointment to its staff.

It had been arranged that book reviews should appear on Wednesdays and Saturdays. When discussing this with Gould and Meynell I urged that one whole page a week would give me more elbow-room. I did not want my territory to be invaded by extraneous ephemeralities, and even went so far as to deprecate the intrusion of advertisements. Why shouldn't my page be a journalistic work of art? I inquired—the impermanence of reviewing being an idea I had so far failed to comprehend. To me, a review was something one pasted into a press-cutting album for pious preservation. Although in youth I wasn't actively observant, I suppose I am by nature a recorder, being one of those people who like to know exactly what they were 'doing this time last year', or this time ten years ago! So I wondered why Gould and Meynell laughed when I asserted my intention of making the book page memorable every time, and why they were even more amused by my suggestion that a review of any work of literary distinction ought to stand alone, surrounded by empty columns symbolizing the unimportance of anything else that week. Gould then gently reminded me that some rather dull books would have to be noticed for their subject matter. As evidence of this he handed me the proof-sheet of a thousand weighty words by Havelock Ellis about Professor Nicolai's *Biology of War*. He felt sure that there was no likelihood of my failing to make the page bright and enter-taining, adding that I couldn't be too lively in my literary notes. From this conference I returned to Weirleigh confronted by the problem of composing my inaugural column of these notes. It was a task which I approached with diffidence and perplexity. Since brightness was demanded of me, I decided that the best tone to adopt was a sort of cheeky jocularity, and the outcome of my efforts appeared in the following paragraphs.

'It is easy to write literary notes. The writer need only possess the following accomplishments: a sound and comprehensive understanding of all branches of literature; a fluent and graceful style; an acute perception of what the publishing trade likes; a brilliant, creative, and facetious intellect; and an eye for the advertisement columns. The life of a literary editor is like a fairy tale. He gets up at a not unreasonable hour: on his way to work he pops in to see a few eminent and sympathetic publishers. Finally, he drifts down Fleet Street like a ray of sunshine and arrives at the office, where he finds that people have sent him presents of lovely books. After glancing at a few of these, he writes some literary notes and goes away to spend his salary.

'In spite of the predicted slump in war books, they are still booming. Lord Jellicoe's *Grand Fleet* (Cassell, 31s. 6d. net) is having a thundering success, and *Open Warfare*, by P. Gibbs (Heinemann, 10s. 6d. net) is also doing well. And we are pro-mised a book by Lord French. Novelists still go in for Armageddon titles. The undermentioned have already caught my eye: *When the World Shook*, H. Rider Haggard (Hodder & Stoughton); *The Law of the Gun*, Ridgewell Cullum (Chapman & Hall); *The Thunderbolt*, George Colmore (Fisher Unwin); *While Guy was in France*, Thomas Cobb (Stanley Paul).

'There is usually something topical about the name of a best seller. H. G. Wells's new novel, *The Undying Fire* (Cassell) will not appear until May 22nd; but proprietors of coal mines should not fail to secure a copy (provided that they can afford the six shillings). Another intriguing announcement is *The Price of Things*, by Elinor Glyn (Duckworth), which will be ready by Easter, and will probably coincide with the advent of warmer weather.'

To this somewhat puerile performance I appended a list of our team of reviewers—twenty names, all well known, and some of them pre-eminent in the literary world. I announced that, although the spring lists of publishers were brilliant beyond belief, our scribes would tackle the masterpieces with unflinching self-confidence. Turning over the pages which I have preserved and perusing the sporting intelligence on the other side of them, I am reminded that our racing expert 'Templegate' gave so many winners during that April that many unliterary people took to buying 'The Paper with its Face towards the Future' for that reason only. Our editor, George Lansbury, who disapproved of betting and had reluctantly conceded racing tips as a feature, was reputed to be quite upset about 'Templegate's' sequence of successes.

*   *   *

One evening in the middle of April I had an experience which seems worth describing for those who are interested in methods of poetic production. It was a sultry spring night. I was feeling dull-minded and depressed, for no assignable reason. After sitting lethargically in the ground-floor room for about three hours after dinner, I came to the conclusion that there was nothing for it but to take my useless brain to bed. On my way from the arm-chair to the door I stood by the writing-table. A few words had floated into my head as though from nowhere. In those days I was always on the look-out for a lyric—I wish I could say the same for my present self—so I picked up a pencil and wrote the words on a sheet of note-paper. Without sitting down, I added a second line. It was as if I were remembering rather than thinking. In this mindless recollecting manner I wrote down my poem in a few minutes. When it was finished I read it through, with no sense of elation, merely wondering how I had come to be writing a poem when feeling so stupid. I then went heavily upstairs and fell asleep without thinking about it again. But next morning I felt so pleased with the lines that I sent them to Masefield, asking him to let me know whether they were any good. He replied with the generous comment that it was the only adequate peace celebration he had seen. The poem was *Everyone Sang*, which has since, become a stock anthology piece. No one has ever said a word against it, and it is now almost as well known as Yeats's *Innisfree*. What I have been unable to understand is that there was no apparent mental process during its composition. Many of my shorter poems have been written with a sense of emotional release and then improved by revision—often after being put away for a long time. Others have been produced by mental concentration and word-seeking which lasted two or three hours. But there was usually a feeling of having said what I wanted to with directness and finality. *Everyone Sang* was composed without emotion, and needed no alteration afterwards. Its rather free form was spontaneous, and unlike any other poem I have written. I wasn't aware of any technical contriving. Yet it was essentially an expression of release, and signified a thankfulness for liberation from the war years which came to the surface with the advent of spring. Many people, by the way, have interpreted the poem as referring to soldiers singing while on the march, so I take this opportunity of stating that no such idea was in my mind.

> *My heart was shaken with tears; and horror*
> *Drifted away . . . O, but Everyone*
> *Was a bird; and the song was wordless; the*
> *Singing will never be done.*

Thus I saluted the post-war future and my own part in it. Not many weeks before, I had written an effective recitation-poem which ended 'Look down, and swear by the slain of the War that you'll never forget'. This, I hoped, was to be my last word on the subject, for I assumed that War 'as an instrument of national policy' was completely discredited. The singing that would 'never be done' was the Social Revolution which I believed to be at hand. In what form that Revolution would arrive I cannot now remember foreseeing—possibly because its form was invisible to me. No doubt I anticipated that there would be some comparatively harm-

141

less rioting, but on the whole I merely thought of it as the sunlight of Liberty spreading across the landscape and Everyone being obliged to admit that the opinions of the *Daily Herald* were, at any rate, worthy of their serious consideration. Most of my arguments in favour of it were denunciations of the Rich, supported by extremely imperfect acquaintance with the Poor.

It astonishes me now that I could have felt so strongly about it, or have been so oblivious to the obdurate unprogressiveness of semi-civilized mankind. The old might shake their heads and talk about Freedom broadening slowly down from precedent to precedent; but the new world was going to be made by the Young, and I was one of them. Going up to the *Herald* office on Tuesdays and Fridays, I felt comfortably optimistic about my own career and the outlook for human affairs in general. It was indeed the right time of year for feeling hopeful. The Weald of Kent was doing what it could to revive my confidence in its dawns and sunsets. I had never seen the cherry orchards look lovelier in blossom, and every time the train took me to London I was that number of miles farther away from the War. I had just enough employment to interest me and provide a sense of stability; and the world as I saw it seemed to be settling down to recuperation and recovery of its forcibly interrupted habits. A few of my new friends were invited to Weirleigh for week-ends, and their enjoyment of the place made me freshly aware of its charm. Having, as I imagined, said good-bye to my pre-war self, I took it for granted that there would be no horses in the stable and that I shouldn't be playing any cricket this season. I spent a lot of my time reclaiming the lawns, which had been much neglected, for the two war-time gardeners had been inefficient—one of them had absent-mindedly destroyed the fine magnolia tree by the front gate. I also experimented in sleeping out of doors, but soon gave this up. A cuckoo insisted on calling me in the silvery haze of summer dawn as I lay in my military 'flea-bag' under the cedar tree.

Meanwhile my mother maintained a noble reticence towards my association with the *Daily Herald*, which she had been known to refer to as 'that rabid and pestilent rag'. I had bought a new bicycle, and it was with a refreshful feeling of something worth-while ahead of me that I used to free-wheel down the hill to the

station on those sweet-smelling mornings. Pleasant was it also to
be sauntering along Fleet Street as an enterprising literary editor,
and, having arrived at the office, to skim through my correspondence and sort out the review copies which filled most of the available space in the small but sacrosanct compartment wherefrom
the mind of Labour was being leavened with a love of Literature.
By the end of April, however, the accumulation of unreviewable
volumes was becoming oppressive. Now and again the experts in
the office would carry away some of the heavy specialist stuff on
economic problems, but there remained a lot of dull and diffuse
reminiscences, inferior fiction, and the miscellaneous propaganda
issued by arid ideologists. There was also a good deal of common-
place poetry, sent me by writers desirous of encouragement. Contemplating overcrowded shelves and their overflow on the floor,
I felt inclined to pen a pungent literary note urging authors and
publishers to cultivate continence; but my part-time secretary,
Miss Clephane, who was young and sympathetic, voted this inad-
visable. She suggested that the usual procedure was to sell them
for what they were worth, which was something less than half-
price. So I took to dumping weekly consignments into a taxi and
depositing them with a stoical bookseller who dealt in discarded
review copies. The profits went towards a summer outing for the
office staff. Miss Clephane also lent a helpful hand with the make-
up of the page—much needed, owing to my ignorance of the
technicalities of typography. But it was as a dictator of correspondence that I was most liable to indiscretions. 'Are you sure you
want to send that?' Miss Clephane would inquire, with pencil
poised above shorthand notes, when I had addressed some exuberant facetiousness to an eminently solemn contributor, or ironically
rebuked an influential publisher who had failed to send us a copy
of an important new book. For I was readily provoked by any
symptom of hostility to the *Herald*, and at that time my overstrained nerves made me irritable when at all tired. It was safer
for me to do the dictating at the start of my mornings, when the
worst that could happen was a lapse into leg-pulling.

Interruptions by visitors were fairly frequent. Some of them
were authors well worth meeting, but they had an inconvenient
habit of not knowing when to go away. Besides this I suffered from

the attentions of several unemployable literary journalists who counted on taking advantage of my inexperience. Impervious to polite refusals, they returned again and again casting hungry looks at the review copies. One of them—a dreary and devitalizing person whose works had been much remaindered—offered to write my literary notes for me, and sent in some sickeningly chatty sample paragraphs. In fact far too many people wanted to write for the book page, and I wasn't qualified to handle the situation. Five years earlier I had found it impossible to get into the London literary world at all. Now ⅰ began to wonder whether I wasn't getting too much of it at once. I had intended to learn my way about by degrees; but all these clever would-be contributors made me wish that I could do my editing in an ivory tower. On one occasion, however, a successful novelist was misled by my apparent innocence and received a shock. He called on me to explain with oily alertness that his forthcoming novel, *Eddies of the Day*, had been written as a sort of manifesto in support of everything that the *Daily Herald* stood for. Not unnaturally, he expected a long and laudatory review, and even suggested that the book should be given publicity on the leader page. It contained a flattering reference to me, and one of my war poems was quoted in full. Vaguely aware of finding his personality unpleasant, I nevertheless accepted an invitation to lunch with him at his club. I then looked him up in *Who's Who* and discovered that he gave 'self-advertisement' as his recreation. During lunch he mentioned Gilbert Cannan, speaking of him with a suave spitefulness which I thought inopportune. 'I wish you'd let me review his new novel,' he remarked, with what I could only consider a nasty look in his eye. I replied that I would bear his request in mind. At that time Cannan was regarded as one of the leading younger novelists. I did not know him, but he was on our list of reviewers. A rapid perusal of *Eddies of the Day* convinced me that it was meretricious and unworthy of serious consideration. I sent it to Cannan, saying nothing except that five hundred words would be enough. They were; for he slaughtered it with gusto. The author, W. L. George, wrote several pages to Gerald Gould, protesting furiously against the perfidious trick played on him. Cannan's novel, *Pink Roses*, a lifeless performance which foreshadowed the tragic decline of his talents, was tolerantly reviewed by someone who did not wish to wound him.

By the end of my second month I had expanded the page to four full columns. It was making quite a name with intelligent readers, and I had endeared myself to the literary journalists by paying 'three guineas a thousand'. But the pace was too good to last. I received a kindly-worded warning from the Editorial Board that 'the literary side' was too expensive and must be abbreviated unless more advertisements came in. This reminder arrived just when I was commissioning a series of special articles, at ten pounds each, from de la Mare, 'Q', E. M. Forster, and H. M. Tomlinson. De la Mare's 'Robinson Crusoe' was already making its proof-sheet magical, and Lascelles Abercrombie had done a column about Hardy which would appear on his birthday. While getting into my editorial stride I had given no thought to the sordid subject of advertisements. Something had to be done about it, however; so I devoted several afternoons to calling at publishers' offices. My interviews with business managers were quite agreeable, and I enjoyed exploring the premises of the Macmillans, Methuens, and other firms, both eminent and enterprising, on my amateur commercial errand. But the outcome was the same everywhere. I was guardedly informed that Sir Frederick, Sir Algernon, or whoever it might be, disliked the *Daily Herald* and its disruptive ideas, and would allow no patronage of its advertisement space. This, combined with an impression that popular novelists were considered more important than poets, had a distinct psychological effect on my attitude to publishers in after years. Towards the end of my campaign I visited various small firms, mainly for the fun of it. On one occasion I was diverted by a remark which now seems to have been my only reward for these unproductive expeditions. I asked the manager what sort of works he went in for. 'Fiction and the future life,' he replied, handing me a badly printed book on Spiritualism. But even he showed no inclination to advertise the immaterial hereafter in 'The Paper with its Face towards the Future'.

I had undertaken to write literary notes once a week, but a month passed before the second batch appeared, for I didn't like doing it, and the cocksure jauntiness to which I unavoidably resorted made me uncomfortable when I saw it in print. That second instalment, however, has always been dear to my memory for the following reason. The next time I went to the office I found, among the usual heap of letters and packages, a small privately printed book of verse—evidently one of those amateur productions which so often depressed me by their sub-mediocrity. Impatiently opening this one at random I was instantly startled by a felicitous line. Within five minutes I knew that I had discovered a poet. Here was someone writing about a Kentish barn in a way I had always felt but had never been able to put into verse. I forgot that I was in a newspaper office, for the barn was physically evoked, with its cobwebs and dust and sparkling sun, its smell of cattle-cake and apples stored in hay, the sound of the breeze singing in the shattered pane and sparrows squabbling on the roof. Here too was description of mill-wheel and weir, beautifully exact and affectionately felt, where authentic fishes basked in glades of drowsy sun.

> *Clear by the tricklings of the dam*
> *Ruddy-finned roach and bronze carp swam;*
> *With here and there a perch blue-barred,*
> *And two foot down a moody pike*
> *Looking with small eyes, small and hard,*
> *At the shoals that lay a yard away,*
> *But far too glutted to strike.*

My literary notes had hooked something exceptional; for these lines had been written at the age of eighteen. In his accompanying letter, modest and homely, and penned in a delightfully clear and graceful script, the author expressed a hope that I might notice his volume in a paragraph. I wrote to him at once, and must have given full evidence of my interest, for he began his reply by saying that he had seldom received a more heartening and encouraging letter. I need only add that his name was Edmund Blunden, and that he has since brought me one of the best and most fruitful friendships of my life.

XV

Early in the summer of 1919 the first number of a Miscellany called *The Owl* made its appearance. Originated and financed by William Nicholson, it was a thin folio containing prose, verse, and drawings finely reproduced in colour. I had the satisfaction of being among the writers and artists whose names were on the delightful pink and black cover which Nicholson had designed. Among those names were Beerbohm, Davies, Galsworthy, and Masefield. But my reason for mentioning *The Owl* is that Thomas Hardy had honoured it with a poem, and that it was necessary to obtain his signature for a couple of dozen copies which were to be autographed by the contributors. This was facilitated by his being in London for a few days at the beginning of May, staying with Sir James Barrie. So I went, one afternoon, to the top-floor flat in Adelphi Terrace with the twenty-four *Owls* under my arm, conscious that the editors were asking a good deal of one who, in his seventy-ninth year, had attended the Royal Academy Banquet on the previous evening, and who was also known to be chary of bestowing his signature. Hardy, however, submitted to the task most indulgently, merely stipulating that he must restrict himself to his initials. Before long he was seated at a table, while I stood prepared to hand him the consecutive *Owls*. Having chosen, and scrupulously tested, a quill pen, he practised a few monograms on the blotting paper. Meanwhile Barrie, almost dwarfish in a very old blue suit, stumped about the room with a big bubbling pipe in his mouth and his hands plunged deep in his pockets. He was taciturn, and I was struck by the expression of melancholy which haunted his queer facial shabbiness. Our most successful living dramatist looked frustrated and disillusioned. But his play *Mary Rose* was in the final process of rehearsal at the Haymarket, and he was probably tired out. By the window which looked across the Thames, Mrs. Hardy was conversing with J. C. Squire, who was meeting the Hardys for the first time. It was characteristic of T.H. that he inscribed each monogram with conscientious deliberation, varying them slightly for his own amusement. The poem he had sent being *The Master and the Leaves*, I playfully remarked—after I had blotting-papered the last of the initials—that its name was suitable for the work we had been engaged on. I could see that *The Owl* was a publication which pleased and interested him, as well it might, since it contained—among other good things—Max Beerbohm's deliciously diverting essay *A Clergyman*.

While with him that afternoon I must have secretly congratulated myself on my share in a surprise which was being prepared for his seventy-ninth birthday. A couple of months before, I had conceived the happy idea of a Tribute to him from the younger poets. Some such token of homage was certain to be forthcoming in the following year; but my eagerness would not wait for his eightieth birthday, and I could therefore claim prime responsibility for the tribute and the form it assumed. Having disclosed the plan to Mr. Gosse, who welcomed it warmly, I set to work as organizing secretary, with him, Walter de la Mare, and Sir Henry Newbolt as the presiding committee. About forty representative writers of all generations were asked to contribute an autograph poem. To each of them was sent a sheet of superlative hand-made paper, and Robert Bridges undertook to write a short foreword. While putting all this into effect I needed advice, and I found an ideal collaborator in Sydney Cockerell, who knew Hardy well and afterwards became one of his literary executors. As an authority on such things, he ensured that the paper and binding were what they should be, and commissioned his friend Graily Hewitt, the eminent calligraphist and gilder, to transcribe the Poet Laureate's beautifully worded page of greeting and felicitation.

I had known Cockerell since August 1915, when I was at Cambridge for a month's course with the Officers' Training Corps. Introduced by a letter from Mr. Gosse, I had spent several evenings at his house—evenings made memorable by the wonderful books he showed me—and from which I returned to my camp bed in Pembroke College in a trance of stimulation after having handled original manuscripts of D. G. Rossetti, William Morris, and Francis Thompson. From the first he had taken a strong and kindly interest in me. On those Sunday nights in the quiet candle-lit room he seemed a sort of bearded and spectacled magician, conjuring up the medieval illuminated missals and psalters on which he was a famous expert, and bringing my mind into almost living contact with the Pre-Raphaelites whom I had worshipped since my dreaming adolescence. Brusque and uncompromising, his light blue eyes regarded me somewhat austerely as he handed me yet another of his treasures to gloat over. People were sometimes offended by his plain-spoken manner; but to be contradicted by Cockerell was an education, and no doubt I offered him numerous opportunities to do so. More often than not, however, he received my incautious demonstrations of ignorance with a lenient laugh. The Poets' Tribute was a labour of love which appealed to him deeply, for he shared my veneration for Hardy. He was indeed a man who had been born to become, through his practical abilities, the trusted adviser of great writers. In this he might be compared with Henry Crabb Robinson, the diarist and associate of the poets of the Romantic Revival. But he will be better remembered for his directorship of the Fitzwilliam Museum, which he re-created, amplified, and enriched through thirty years of selfless service.

In a letter of that year Hardy wrote, to an intimate friend, that he would care more for his birthdays if at each succeeding one he could see any sign of real improvement in the world—as at one time he fondly hoped he had. 'But I fear,' he added, 'that what appears much more evident is that it is getting worse and worse. All development is of a material and scientific kind—and scarcely any addition to our knowledge is applied to objects philanthropic and ameliorative. I almost think that people were less pitiless towards their fellow creatures—human and animal—under the Roman Empire than they are now.' Subsequent history seems to have justified the view he took then. Most of us have increasingly shared his feeling during the past ten years. Anyhow, when I journeyed to Max Gate bearing the Poets' Tribute which I had been privileged to place in his hands, I found him in excellent spirits.

After he had taken it from me and was sitting at a table quietly turning the leaves, I felt that this was as good a moment as any I had known. In a paragraph dictated for insertion in his biography he said that 'the mark of recognition so appealed to

him that he determined to answer every one of the contributors
by letter. . . . It was almost his first awakening to the consciousness that an opinion had silently grown up as it were in the night,
that he was no mean power in the contemporary world of poetry.'
Remembering that visit in conjunction with the sequence of those
that followed it (memories which are not within the scope of this
volume), I realize that it had one element which did not recur. It
was the last time that I was with him as a septuagenarian, and the
occasion was so lit up by the felicity of its attendant circumstance
that he almost seemed to be a hale and active man in his sixties.
Always, when going there again, I was in dread that he would
show signs of his increasing age. Each time, I contrived to persuade myself that he was 'just the same as ever'. But small and
gradual changes came. I had to be more careful of overtaxing him
with talk, and though he never ceased to be a brisk pedestrian we
didn't go so far as we used to do. In his latest years I stayed at an
hotel in Dorchester, so as to avoid tiring him in the evening. To
the end of his life he maintained an astonishing vitality, and the
invasions of his communicative young friend were a stimulation;
but I never saw him quite like that again—as he was when the
Poets' Tribute brought him such profound contentment. And
always, when saying good-bye, the same thought must have been
in our minds. 'Take care of yourself; and go on getting younger!'
I exclaimed on one occasion, with exuberant, emotion-charged
heartiness. 'You'd better come again soon, or you may find me
over at Stinsford churchyard,' he replied. Whereupon Mrs.
Hardy, standing beside him in the porch, exclaimed, 'Don't be so
gruesome, T.H.!'

*   *   *

On a cloudless Saturday afternoon in the middle of June I was
to be seen following Cockerell out of a small branch-line station in
West Sussex. Awaiting us was a light phaeton drawn by an Arab
mare. After going two or three miles along the hot highway, we
turned up a private road. On our left was an extensive oak wood,
and as we ascended the gentle slope we came in sight of a grey
stone house standing well above the woods and the Weald. It was
a largish house and one of the pleasantest I had ever seen, digni-

fied, remote, and friendly. Cockerell, who had spent months at a
time there, pointed it out with an almost proprietary satisfaction
in having brought me there. For this was Newbuildings Place, and
Cockerell was taking me to stay a week-end with Wilfrid Scawen
Blunt, whom he had known intimately for more than twenty
years. I myself knew Mr. Blunt through his admirable sonnets
and Protean love-lyrics, had heard of his famous stud of Arab
horses, and was aware that he had been an adventurous traveller,
an aristocratic man of the world, and a champion of lost causes
who had courted unpopularity by his activities in Irish, Egyptian,
and Indian politics. In an indefinite way I realized that, as a cultivated, picturesque, and contentious character, he was unlike anyone else. He was now nearly seventy-nine and an invalid, but
Cockerell—after interesting him in my writings—had arranged
this invitation, thereby conferring on me what could not fail to be
a most memorable experience, and giving his isolated old friend
an opportunity of running his eye over one of the younger poets.

So far, so good. I am there in the bland June sunshine;
Cockerell is clearly visible, a somewhat tutorial figure in his sober
suit and dark blue hat, conducting me through the arch of a
square-clipped yew hedge, along the flagged path to the front
door, up a flight of steps, and into a small stone-floored and oak-
panelled hall, where I am presented to Mr. Blunt's adopted niece,
Miss Dorothy Carleton, who—together with his devoted nurse,
Miss Lawrence—was responsible for the perfect management of
his house. There, for the present, my twenty-five-years distant
visualization of the scene becomes indistinct. For I was only at
Newbuildings once; and seeing a house for the first time is like
reading a book—a second inspection makes all the difference to
one's retention of detail. At Max Gate, for instance, repeated visits
enabled me to know the place by heart. I now find that to compare
it with Newbuildings is a plausible device for aiding my rememo-
ration of the latter. The difference between them was as notable
as the contrasted temperaments and careers of Hardy and Blunt.
Max Gate, when offered for sale with its two acres, was advertised
as 'a choice freehold residence, built by the famous author in
1885'. The presence of its architect and owner, of course, gave it
unique distinction and atmosphere. Without him, it was what he

would have called 'a red-brick domicile', comfortable, compact, and unassumingly mid-Victorian. As an example of domestic architecture it invited criticism. Deprived of its concealing ivies and creepers, it would have been rather an ugly house. Yet it suited T.H., and one could no more think of him living anywhere else than one could imagine him as Christopher (which was how his parents had first thought of naming him). It was bourgeois when compared with Newbuildings, which had been built as a yeoman farmer's house in the Jacobean period and had suffered no reconstruction since. Medium-sized, plainly proportioned, and aristocratic, its solid simplicity was essentially traditional of the Sussex Weald. Bare oak floors re-echoed the footfalls of past generations; cool panelled rooms were imbued with centuries of quiet summer afternoons. From the dovecote beyond the yew hedges had come innumerable cooings. I could hear those cooings now, and there seemed no reason why they should not go on for ever. Much must have been done in recent years to please the eye, but it now looked cared-for yet uninterfered-with in its mellowed graciousness. Here and there, through faded Persian rugs and trophies of travel, I was reminded of Mr. Blunt's Eastern interests and adventures. But even the Oriental weapons which hung on the walls only made the house more ancestrally English. Meanwhile there was a reason for the sense of stillness, wherein I trod almost like a trespasser and spoke in temperate and unuplifted tones. Mr. Blunt was in bad health; he was upstairs resting. And one was conscious of a curious vacancy, as though the rooms were awaiting the dominating presence of their owner to bring them to life. The very peacocks, which paraded the narrow garden precincts in sleepy sunshine, comported themselves with an aloofness suggesting that they had as yet to accept my arrival as sanctioned by their lord and master. I asked Cockerell whether William Morris had ever been here. Pointing to a tapestry at the end of the hall, he remarked that Wilfrid Blunt had known Morris well. The tapestry, designed by Burne-Jones, was of his weaving. He also told me that the oak table beside which we were standing had belonged to Morris and had been given to Blunt. He had stayed at Newbuildings once, shortly before his death, and the two poets had often been together at Kelmscott. He added, with his abrupt laugh, that they used to go out gudgeon-fishing—a detail which somehow made me see them very clearly. For I had made my own pilgrimage to Kelmscott about seven years before, on a fine June day such as this one, and had wandered by the river, remembering how beautifully the place was described in *News from Nowhere*. The thought of Morris had come into my mind instinctively, for Newbuildings—had it been of earlier construction—was just the type of home he would have used as a background for one of his prologues in *The Earthly Paradise*, or have lovingly incorporated with some prose evocation of the past. Although my thought must have been prompted by the presence of Cockerell, who had been so closely associated with him, there was a William Morris quality in the place, as if he had influenced its amenities. It had now become a house of settled habits and restricted happenings, dependent on the bodily condition of an old man. Much splendid talk had been heard there, from some of the liveliest intelligences of the time. But its great days were done, and I was only there as an afterthought, discovering this quietude that was controlled by the calmly capable vigilance of Miss Carleton.

Many years afterwards that lady, when sending me a volume of Mr. Blunt's Diaries, mentioned my 'passion for climbing trees', and expressed a hope that I still kept up the exercise. And I remembered how—when strolling out with Cockerell before dinner—in a sudden access of energy I had swung myself to the topmost branches of a large oak. I can see him now, staring up at me with amused astonishment, while I waved salutations to the distant Sussex Downs.

It was after sunset when he led me up to the almost monastically furnished room where Mr. Blunt was lying on a narrow bed, propped by pillows so that he could watch the evening sky. I was aware that he had been considered one of the handsomest men of his period, and having been shown a photograph of him in Arab dress I was prepared to see a white-bearded patriarch. But he was more fragile and less formidable than I had expected. His voice was soft. He spoke with grave and languid courtesy, allowing Cockerell the initiative in most of what was said. He was the most perfect example of a thoroughbred human being I had seen, and I particularly noticed the sensitive formation of his hands. His dark eyes observed me steadily with the mournful scrutiny of a proud spirit resenting age and infirmity when confronted by unimpeded youth. There was no feebleness in his movements. His personality was still challenging and capable of quixotic defiance. He brightened approvingly when Cockerell told him that I had been something of a race-rider, and there was a flicker of a smile when he heard that I had climbed one of his trees. To-morrow, he said, he would show me some of his horses. Then he sighed, closed his eyes, and bade us good night.

Separated a little from the main house was a two-storied building built by Mr. Blunt for the use of his guests. Alone in my room there I leant on the window ledge, looking out at a starry sky above the looming trees. In the perfect June weather, any well-ordered country house, arrived at from the noise and heat of London, would have been delectable. But this one, I felt, was an enchantment. Everything about it seemed designed for an idyllic existence of luxurious simplicity. Even in those few hours I had become aware of a fusion of fine taste and fine breeding which ignored the tiresome conventions of hospitality, offering one reasonable and liberated enjoyment. It struck me also that among all the famous men I had visited since the end of the war Wilfrid Blunt—though not the most notable in achievement—was exceptional in his appeal to my imagination. He has been called an amateur of genius; but he was, above all, a man who had done things, and whose philosophy was that 'life's wealth is to do; its loss—to dream and wait'. Combining this with the pathos of the old man as I had seen him, I found it strange that he should be ending his days in this Elysian hermitage after the conflicts and enthusiasms of his romantic and rebellious career. It had not occurred to me before that an old man might be young and adventurous in spirit. This penetrating impression I had instinctively divined from his face, and it has since been confirmed by what I have read in his printed Diaries. Not, perhaps, in any quotable sentence, but from the essence of what he revealed through occasional self-questionings when he was outwardly 'old, weary, and discouraged'.

I cannot remember for certain whether the conversation I had with him next morning was in his room upstairs. Memory—

possibly with an inclination towards descriptive variety—suggests that he was lying on a couch out in the garden when we discussed contemporary poetry, about which he showed strong prejudices and scant appreciation. I now think that these narrow and rather intolerant opinions were an explanation of the failure of his own verse to be quite first-rate. There was always an amateurish quality in his technique, and he was original only in expressing individual experience. Highly dogmatic about poetry as an art, he refused to accept either Bridges or Hardy. Of the ' Georgian ' poets, he conceded merit to Masefield, but thought his verse imperfect. I suspected that he disapproved of my own war poems, for he remarked that ugliness had no place in any of the arts. But I doubt whether he had read any modern poetry attentively. I refrained from reminding him that when Cockerell had sent him my Masefield imitation, *The Daffodil Murderer*, he had replied ' It is better than Masefield in the same way that Swinburne's parody of Browning was better than Browning '—a smart piece of criticism with which many people would disagree! I listened with interest when he spoke of Francis Thompson, to whom he had shown much kindness at the end of his unfortunate life. There is no need to reproduce what he said, since it can all be found in the admirable account he wrote of Thompson as a poetic genius. But I am glad to have heard fragments of it from his own lips. ' The first time Thompson came here I met him at the station with the phaeton. It was a lovely day, but as we drove through the woods the poet of nature never took his eyes off the *Globe* newspaper he had brought with him in the train. He didn't know an elm from an oak.' He also gave me a useful maxim for a young poet to bear in mind. ' Never write unless you have something worth saying which can be said better in verse than in prose.'

After lunch Cockerell and I set off to call on Hilaire Belloc. He was Mr. Blunt's most valued neighbour, and for many years had done much to sustain him by his brilliant powers as a talker and the gusto of his human companionship. Our object therefore was to get him over to Newbuildings later in the day. The walk to Shipley was a pleasant two miles by a field path. We were both of us in the placid Sunday-afternoon condition of mind consequent upon roast beef and gooseberry tart. But the sun was so hot that I felt more like dozing under a tree than climbing one, and not altogether in the mood for meeting yet another famous writer for the first time. Would he be at home, I wondered, when Cockerell had mopped his brow and knocked at the door of a rambling old farmhouse with a disused windmill standing near to it. The door, opened by Belloc, admitted us to a cool, low-windowed living-room—the sort of room which would be equally comfortable in summer or winter, local in character, with its beamed ceiling, open fireplace, and old oak furniture. Belloc received us with glowing hospitality. He had a friend with him—a large, heavy-moustached man, wearing an M.C.C. tie—a full-flavoured frequenter of the pavilion at Lord's, by the look of him. This was E. W. Hornung, a novelist widely known as the creator of 'Raffles, the Amateur Cracksman', whose adventures had thrilled me in my younger years. Sitting at the table with a tankard of beer, he maintained an air of solemn amiability, but said very little. I felt that I could have conversed with him about cricket, for his hero 'Raffles' was a very fine fast bowler as well as a gifted gentleman burglar. Obviously we had plenty in common; but a higher plane of intellectual exercise was called for, which may have accounted for Hornung's tankard-consulting silences. Cockerell having declined all forms of refreshment, Belloc, full of anxiety to make me welcome, poured me a goblet of Burgundy and handed me a good-sized cigar, neither of which I had the heart to refuse. It would have been ungracious to explain that I seldom drank wine except at dinner; to confess that a bottle of ginger-beer would suit me better might have seemed disrespectful to his veneration of august vintages. As a result I was soon feeling somewhat stupefied, and could only produce feeble responses to his stimulating talk. Worse still, I became embarrassed by the inexcusable behaviour of my cigar. 'I hope you are finding that Cabana all right, Mr. Sassoon,' he remarked. But I had been reduced to concealing it under the table, between surreptitious puffs; for it was irreparably apparent that the tactless thing was burning down one side and had no intention of doing otherwise. Altogether I felt that we had chosen the wrong time of day for acclimatization to an atmosphere of Burgundy and flushed conviviality. The circumstances created a social incompatibility which

Belloc's geniality failed to put right. Try as he might, Cockerell couldn't avoid casting a shadow of teetotalism over the proceedings. Meanwhile I contrived to discard my cigar, and Belloc took me to see the view from the top of his windmill. Proud of being a landed proprietor, he pointed out the boundaries of his estate. Broad and sturdy in his black clothes, he was eloquent about the Weald and its local customs and traditions. Observing his fine, ruddy, and uncompromising countenance, I was aware that nothing could be more delightfully Bellocian than his eulogizing of the Sussex landscape. But the Burgundy had made me slightly tipsy, and I suspected that he must be forming an unfavourable opinion of me as a disapproving and unfriendly example of the younger generation. In a clumsy attempt to ingratiate myself, I asked whether there was any hope of persuading him to write something for the literary page of the *Daily Herald*. This proposal he evaded by saying that Lansbury's political credulities were entirely at variance with his own convictions. While walking a little way with us when we departed, he surprised me by speaking rather regretfully of his performances as an author. 'I cannot claim to be more than a successful littérateur. I have been too active in the world to do anything lasting.' As we went on our way I remarked to Cockerell that he surely couldn't have meant it. 'Belloc wouldn't like to have it said to him!' he remarked dryly. Most of us, let me now add, would have been thankful to have written even a tithe of his resonant prose. And a few years ago he produced a long poem which will outlive most of the verse published by his contemporaries. These magnificently perfected couplets were written *In Praise of Wine*.

> *To exalt, enthrone, establish and defend,*
> *To welcome home mankind's mysterious friend:*
> *Wine, true begetter of all arts that be;*
> *Wine, privilege of the completely free.*

Quoted in the present context, these opening lines might seem ironical, since the grape had proved itself a hindrance to my first interview with the poet. Putting that aside, I turn again to the poem and its noble closing apostrophe, which I can never read without emotion.

*   *   *

Siegfried's Journey, 1916–1920

The heat of the day was over when Mr. Blunt came downstairs again and we went to the paddocks to look at some of his horses. Leaning back easily in a little four-wheeled carriage pulled by a pony, he wore a white Bedouin cloak. His appearance was superb; and if anything more remarkable was to be seen in Sussex I should be glad to know where it was. Just as we were starting Belloc joined us, and we all walked beside the carriage. The paddocks were only a short distance from the house, bordered by a big stretch of undulating woodland. Two of the Arab stallions were brought out and led up and down—noble animals with large plume-like tails and arched necks, whose grace and distinction matched that of their owner. Afterwards he sat quietly enjoying the vesperal coolness while shadows lengthened and sun rays glorified the tree-tops. It was the best hour of my visit, for I had begun to feel at home with him, and everything felt harmonized and serene. There are moments in one's life-experience which never lose their felt and memorable freshness. One of them is before me now, seen as I saw it then. Mr. Blunt, tired but reluctant to return to his room, had asked Belloc to sing something. Not having heard of his country songs, I was taken by surprise when, with complete naturalness, he trolled out a ditty in his high tenor voice. It was 'Ha'nacker Mill' that he sang, to a tune of his own, and he made it sound as if the words had come down through long-vanished generations. In fact I assumed it to be an old Sussex ballad, though in print it has more the quality of a modern poem, except, perhaps, in the first verse.

> *Sally is gone that was so kindly.*
> *Sally is gone from Ha'nacker Hill.*
> *And the briar grows ever since then so blindly*
> *And ever since then the clapper is still,*
> *And the sweeps have fallen from Ha'nacker Mill.*

But what returns to me in sunset light is the broad and bulky yet somehow boyish figure of the singer, sitting on a bench close by the old friend whom he was intent on pleasing, and Wilfrid Blunt, listening with half-closed eyes, his face touched to tenderness and regret by the power and pathos of the words. I see them thus together, and so shall always do, as though the moment

158

could never be taken from them and might be re-enacted beyond
the dream of earthly time.

When we said good-bye to him next morning he looked weary
and ill, and spoke as if in pain. He asked Cockerell to pick out a
volume of his poems from the book-shelves above the bed, and
inscribed my name in pencil. From the canopy of the bed hung a
huge ostrich egg—a Mahometan device for bringing good luck.
My memory of his face is unlike any photograph of him in old age
that I have seen. It is gentler and more poetical, less in accordance
with his reputation for tyrannical disagreements and contentious
crusades. I have since heard that he was easy to quarrel with, but
I find it difficult to think of him as such. For me he is the man
who wrote the eloquent poem which begins

> *Love me a little, love me as thou wilt,*
> *Whether a draught it be of passionate wine*
> *Poured with both hands divine,*
> *Or just a cup of water spilt*
> *On dying lips and mine.*

Cockerell, to whom I once referred the question, assured me that
he could not recall a single instance of discourtesy, abruptness, or
lack of consideration on his part during all the years he knew him.
On the contrary, he remembered many acts of thoughtfulness,
kindness, and generosity. I, too, can only believe that he was a
great gentleman and a many-sided spirit whose charm and intelligence outshone his faults and failings. Nothing can alter that
impression of high-bred majesty of mind which I took away with
me when he had relinquished my hand, lay back on the pillows,
and turned his life-renouncing eyes to watch me go.

XVI

The year 1919, which had been welcomed by credulous souls as an ante-chamber to the millennium, laboured under a pervasive disadvantage. Too much was expected of it. It was a year of rootless re-beginnings and steadily developing disillusionments. Few people realized this at the time, and I was not one of them. Up to the end of June I was actively occupied, confident through success, and insolently healthy with youth and summer weather. But a surprise was in store for me, and although it was only a physical one, it symptomized the undoing of my blind belief in the beneficence of 1919. One cloudless morning early in July, while getting into the train to go up to the *Herald* office, I made some sudden stooping movement which brought on an acute pain in my left leg. Unable to believe that such agony could last many minutes, I waited for it to diminish. What right had 1919 to do such a thing to me? The treacherous demon sciatica responded by accentuating its paroxysmal pain. At the office, Miss Clephane fixed up the literary page for me while I supplied an obbligato of groans and conjectures as to what could be done for my relief. Sympathetic and concerned, she could only suggest going home and staying in bed.

But I was due at a large luncheon party in Chelsea, and thither I went, hoping that cultured conversation would cause auto-suggestive alleviation to my leg. Sitting next to the wife of a distinguished Law Lord, I plaintively confided my ordeal to her. This resulted in my being conveyed to her urbane family physician who advised me to wear warm clothes and abstain from red wine which seemed a somewhat academic treatment of the case Couldn't he possibly do something to stop the pain, I asked Whereupon he provided a prescription with which I obtained some pills about half the size of a ping-pong ball. With these potencies in my pocket I hobbled away to Osbert Sitwell's house in Swan Walk. He was out for the afternoon; but his housekeeper— a woman of limitless good nature—after an interlude during which I sat on the stairs with my eyes shut, soon put me between

160

the sheets, and having swallowed one of my celluloid boxes I subsided into oblivion.

I must ask the reader's indulgence for these medical reminiscences. Sciatica is not an enthralling subject; but it was so much the autocrat of my existence for the next few months that it can almost claim to be the constructive element of this chapter. During those months various interesting experiences came my way, but the predominant circumstance was that I could never stoop to pick anything up without suffering a severe spasm. While in bed for ten days at Swan Walk, however, I was tended with the utmost solicitude. Some years later I saw the Sitwells referred to, in some journal, as 'the stormy petrels of modern literature'. Perhaps they were. But towards my sciatica-smitten self both Osbert and Sacheverell behaved like angelic and agitated turtle-doves. Almost always in a hurry, one or other seemed continually to be dashing up the steep stairs to look in and ask 'How are you?' Everything that could possibly divert my thoughts from sciatica was brought into my little room. Their housekeeper (who shared with Eddie Marsh's Mrs. Elgy the distinction of being not only a first-class cook but also an amiable character) plied me with her finest confections. And a highly intelligent doctor called daily to assure me that I should soon be out and about again if I avoided getting hot and exposing my leg to draughts.

There were times when I felt like remaining recumbent as long as possible, for the stiller I kept the less I suffered. Dozing through the warm afternoons, I enjoyed listening to the sounds of the house and wondering what the Sitwells were up to now. There would be a burst of animated conversation, an affectionate farewell, and then the front-door would bang as one of them went out on some social or artistic enterprise. Sometimes I would pretend to be asleep when Osbert looked in—a blond Hanoverian apparition in a frock-coat and top-hat of immaculate grey—was he on his way to the Peace Celebrations, I wondered. Or was he only off to confer with printer or publisher about the latest number of *Art and Letters*, the lively modernist magazine which he was editing? Not for the first time, I was aware that being in bed in someone else's house gives one a great pull over the problems of life and permits the mind to move with unimpeded smoothness. I have always believed in allowing things to take their course without my interference, and being in bed is the nearest one can get to invisibility. Some day, perhaps, the scientists will invent a device for achieving it. This—for persons of my temperament—would afford a providential antidote to the present mechanized progress towards never being in the same place for five minutes. Quietude is essential to human happiness. This fact needs to be comprehensively rediscovered. 'The solitary and contemplative man sits as safe in his retirement as one of Homer's heroes in a cloud, and has this only trouble from the follies and extravagances of men, that he pities them. I think it advisable for every man that has sense and thoughts enough, to be his own companion (for certainly there is more required to qualify a man for his own company than for other men's), to be as frequent in his retirements as he can, and to communicate as little with the world as is consistent with the duty of doing good, and the discharge of the common offices of humanity.' Written by Norris of Bemerton, a seventeenth-century Platonist, these words—although not easily applied to present-day conditions—are worth bearing in mind.

While staying with the Sitwells I found that, among their stimulating and delightful qualities, restfulness was conspicuously absent. I used to complain to Osbert that he never stuck to one subject for more than half a minute. His sallies of wit (not always benevolent when directed at his literary coevals) were a shorthand display which often made me wish that he would be long-winded and prosy instead of twitching me from one thing to another. It was a case where a fusion of our mental ingredients would have improved us both. His intelligence was quick and capricious, while mine functioned in the manner exhibited by these memoirs. He was, in fact, the antithesis of a cavalry captain who had sagely observed to me that the War had taught the French Army what riding-boots ought to be, and who would probably have remarked of Osbert that 'the trouble about these brainy birds is that they think too much'! In reply to which, Osbert would have quoted one of his own poems wherein he made a sportsman express surprise that the Son of God went into the desert for forty days without shooting anything.

Remembering those early days of my association with the

Sitwells, I see myself being rapidly and bewilderingly introduced to the newest fashions in art and literature. The process was a wholesome antidote to my intolerance of the unusual and my instinctive preference for the traditional. Osbert's house was full of pictures which looked peculiar to my inexperienced eyes. In some instances I am inclined to suggest that they were more startling and experimental than well drawn. Wax flowers and other evidences of the vogue for Early Victorianism mingled with totemistic objects which exemplified a new aesthetic tendency to find beauty in the barbaric. This assortment confused my mind, and made me suspect dilettantism in my surroundings. I may well have wondered what the foxhunters would make of it; and it so happened that the test was applied to one of them. My old friend Norman Loder, to whom I had written explaining my inability to go and stay with him at Peterborough, called on me one morning. He entered my bedroom carrying a leather hat-box, and his demeanour implied that the few minutes he had spent in Osbert's drawing-room had given him the surprise of his life. 'Whatever are you doing here?' he inquired, eyeing a Cubist painting near the door as though expecting it to bite him. When in his world I had always behaved as a submissive disciple, and he evidently felt that the sooner he got me away from this one the better. I retaliated by asking what he was doing with that hat-box. He informed me that it contained a perfectly good hunting hat which he had no use for. 'I've just been all the way to Moss's in Covent Garden, and they had the impudence to offer me eighteen-pence for it!' he remarked, looking rather offended when I laughed. Meanwhile his arrival had de-Sitwellized me, and I was soon talking to him in his own idiom. But when he asked, in subdued and almost conspiratorial tones, 'Who *are* these Sitwells?' I could only assure him that, though not quite his sort, they were awfully nice and had both been officers in the Grenadier Guards, which mystified him still more. Any dilemma that existed, however, was more mine than his. Norman never actively disapproved of anyone. He was too good-natured for that. He either accepted people or decided, without comment, that they were no good to him. He had found it difficult to swallow my *Daily Herald* Socialism, and had lectured me a bit about being so pro-German. Now that the

Swan Walk pictures had been too much for his elementary taste in art, he regarded the Sitwell ménage as further proof of my being led astray by the highbrows. My own dilemma consisted in the divided personality which his presence created. We had been friends for nearly fifteen years, and he had dominated the sporting part of my existence. To the Sitwells, though they would probably have thought him a good joke, he was the pattern of that Philistinism against which they rebelled. And here was I, feebly attempting to be on both sides at once. For at that time I was simple-minded enough to want—and expect—all my friends to like one another. Why shouldn't they, if I liked them individually? In the end I found it safer to keep most of them in separate compartments. Anyhow, Norman, who—for all his kindness—didn't understand what acute sciatica felt like, had decided that I only needed fresh air and exercise to put me right. Having made me promise to come and stay with him as soon as possible, he picked up his hat-box and went treading cautiously down the stairs.

Osbert, on the other hand, was less Spartan in his attitude towards my convalescence. He recommended a course of treatment at Bath. So he and I and Sacheverell went there for a week, and I was sweepingly introduced to the eighteenth century. I had always thought of Bath as a dull place where old ladies lived in retirement, but the Sitwells soon put a stop to that. They were insatiable sightseers, and I learnt a lot about the Palladian style of architecture while limping around with them. For me—though not for them—there was a rival attraction in the Bath Cricket Week. Amiable and forbearing, they conceded me at least one afternoon on the County Ground, where I watched the Worcestershire batsmen in difficulties on a sticky wicket, against the eminent slow bowler, J. C. White. The amateurs of the Somerset team were staying in our hotel. Observing them after dinner, I felt—as in my boyhood—that even in private life no first-class cricketer could be an altogether uninteresting person. To the Sitwells, J. C. White lighting his pipe and settling down to a quiet game of bridge was merely a modest, fair-haired man who looked what he was—a jolly West Country farmer. For me, his presence implied that Olympian quality which rightly appertained to one of the best spin bowlers in England. There was, however, someone else in the hotel who afforded the Sitwells much entertainment. This was neither more nor less than another S. Sassoon. My relationship with him was so distant as to be almost invisible, and when identified he proved to be an elderly gentleman of markedly Oriental appearance and frog-like proportions. Osbert attempted to cultivate his acquaintance, but he seemed to be a man of limited intellectual resources, though shyly gratified by our civilities. He spoke with a throaty foreign accent which the Sitwells frequently imitated for my benefit. I was continually asked, 'Are you going to ze krricket to-day?' this being my namesake's invariable greeting when he met one of us in the hotel. It was, apparently, the only thing he could think of to say. I suspect that he would have enjoyed talking about his health and the beneficial properties of the mineral waters, but I never got anywhere near discussing sciatica with him.

Soon after leaving Bath I went to stay with the Loders. My leg was now improving, though liable to stabbing pains if used indiscreetly. I did my best to be my ordinary self, so it was taken for granted that there was very little the matter, and on the morning after my arrival I meekly accepted Norman's announcement that we were all going for a ride. He had got a nice-looking little horse on trial from a dealer, and wanted to see how the animal went with me. If he was too lively I could change on to the one he was riding. There seemed to be some suspicion that the horse was too low-priced and good-looking not to have something wrong about him. Though placid enough when led up to the mounting-block, I noticed that he had a small, sulky, and unbenevolent eye. With sciatic caution I got on to him, inwardly wishing that he were a Bath chair pulled by a donkey. We jogged along quietly until we entered Mr. Fitzwilliam's enormous deer park, and Norman instructed me to canter him on a bit. This I proceeded to do, with the immediate result that he did everything possible to show what was wrong with him. Had I been a cowboy from the Wild West the tussle between us would have proved well worth witnessing. No doubt the cowboy would have got the best of it. I didn't. With his head between his knees, the fiendish quadruped swerved and twisted like an eel, kicking nearly as high as my head. Unable to grip with my sciatic leg, I was very soon shot over his ears, and he galloped away with the reins flapping and Norman in circumspective pursuit. Thankful that my troubles were over, I remained full length on the ground, waiting for my sciatic twinges to abate. As Norman subsequently remarked—when the episode could be treated as funny—'Old Sig lay there on his back like a crusader.' I may as well add that old Sig spent the rest of that day in bed, and for the remainder of his visit took every precaution against being treated as a person in robust health.

XVII

While at Weirleigh during August I busied myself with the unexacting task of arranging my war poems for a complete edition. It was with a comfortable feeling of finality that I put the sequence into its appropriate order. I had said my say; the stimulus of experience and emotion had ceased, and I was glad to be diverting my energies towards something else. I had it in mind to attempt realistic poems about everyday life, and had already produced some lines which described Elliot Smith, the eminent anthropologist, talking about Early Chronology to a select assembly in Rivers' rooms at Cambridge. For, although my existence since the war had been undirected and adrift, my literary instinct was sufficiently wide-awake to warn me against allowing the vehemence of my war writings to become a mannerism.

> *Slowly the daylight left our listening faces . . .*
> *Professor Brown with level baritone*
> *Discoursed into the dusk.*

Thuswise, in the first number of the *London Mercury*, I demonstrated my transition to the new style of versifying which I proposed to cultivate. It was the pattern for a series of descriptive pieces in which I assumed a laconic, legato tone of voice, and endeavoured to be mellow, sophisticated, and mildly sardonic. Some of them were overwritten and little more than exercises in verbal accuracy and adroitness, but they served me well in my resolve to acquire a controlled method of expression.

It was the beginning of November when the small scarlet-bound volume of my collected war poems appeared in the bookshops. By then I had been living for several weeks in furnished lodgings near Victoria Station. Unable to make up my mind where to go, I had come to the conclusion that Pimlico would do as well as anywhere else, and had inspected the rooms uncritically. With winter closing-in it became apparent that they were sunless, stuffy-smelling, dingy, and dispiriting. This added to my dissatisfaction

167

with the year which I had entered upon with such lively expectations.

Meanwhile I was still troubled by sciatica. Two or three times a week I went to a doctor in Wimpole Street for high-frequency electric treatment, which may or may not have aided nature in the process of reparation. Doctor Creasy was a Pickwickian person whose character matched his countenance in smiling amiability. One afternoon I asked him how it was that, leading such an indoor life, he looked so remarkably healthy. He explained that it was due to the ozone generated by his electrical appliance. 'It makes me so hungry that my mouth waters whenever I think of ham,' he said.

My work at the *Daily Herald* office took less of my time than I should have liked. The literary page had simplified itself into an easy routine job, and I sometimes wondered whether my absence would make any difference to it. By writing an occasional review I was gaining experience, but I could have done that without being an editor. Also the space allotted me was being cut down, and I suspected that no-one would mind much if it were reduced to a mere tabloid of two half-columns. I had begun to feel discouraged, and was inclined to complain that Labour was ungrateful for my efforts to provide distinguished literary nourishment.

My projected apprenticeship to politics had made no advance whatever. I was in the situation of being considered a promising recruit by people connected with bodies advocating social reforms. It was assumed that I was prepared to contribute constructive ideas, or at any rate bring an informed mind to such activities. When approached in this way I adopted evasive tactics. It was like being asked to appear on the stage without having had any previous experience of acting, or even learnt my lines. The only Movement with which I became temporarily associated was *Clarté*. Founded and led by Henri Barbusse, its main purpose was to unite the intellectuals of France and England in a confederation to oppose militarism. Robert Dell, the Paris correspondent of the *Manchester Guardian*, had come to London in October to organize *Clarté*, and for several weeks he persistently pursued me about it. He was a charming man, but I was in a false position with him owing to my ignorance of things such as the Quai d'Orsay, to which he frequently referred. In vain I pleaded that I had never been to Paris, that I couldn't speak French well enough to exchange the simplest ideas with the clear-thinking followers of Barbusse, and that I hadn't the ghost of a notion what it was all about. Ingratiatingly his rather foreign voice assured me that I was the man he wanted. More than once he lunched with me at my club. I found that after a couple of glasses of claret he did all the talking; but he continued to exercise persuasiveness, and I was provisionally appointed secretary of the British Branch of *Clarté*. Anyone less internationally qualified could scarcely have been chosen. The climax came when he held a meeting in a committee room at the House of Commons. About thirty of us, old and young, sat round a table towards the end of a foggy November afternoon. Regarded as a gathering of intellects, we were united only by proximity. Speeches were made by Shaw, Wells, and Zangwill. Shaw gave a brilliant and attractive demonstration of inability to be anything except a movement in himself. Wells did likewise. Zangwill, apparently intent on making trouble, protested strongly against the *Clarté* manifesto written by Barbusse, and went on to explain at some length that Free Trade was the only solution for the problem of abolishing war. When invited to voice the views of the younger generation, I rose reluctantly and made some lame and not very audible remarks which somehow ended in a suggestion that everyone ought to read Hardy's *Dynasts*. This, anyhow, must have convinced Robert Dell of my ineffectiveness in the movement, for after that I heard little more from him. And not much more was heard of *Clarté*.

Towards the end of 1918 my poems had been published in New York. Since then *Counter-attack* had sold more than two thousand copies, and I was becoming quite self-important about my American reputation. Taken on their face value, the reviews which had been sent me created an impression that I was an even more powerful poetic personality than I had hitherto realized. Their high-pitched note was most gratifying to my vanity. For one thing, very few of them called me by the name of Mister. To the majority I was Sassoon—a stark and startling apparition from war-stricken England. My soul, to those native critics who mentioned it, had been a polite figure of speech. But in America it was freely expatiated upon in such phrases as 'packed with terror, bitterness, and beauty'. It had acquired a spectacular significance which made me feel much less of a local character. 'The English-speaking world will watch his star as it rises to that zenith where the mighty are clustered—and seen,' exclaimed the *Boston Evening Transcript*. This was indeed something to live up to! There was one writer who dismissed me as 'entirely devoid of intellectual edge'. But I could have told him that myself. For I can remember saying self-defensively to E. M. Forster, 'You *must* realize that I am *not* an intellectual'. No doubt he was already aware of it, and my anxiety that he shouldn't consider me clever evidently amused him (though not as much as his brilliant reviewing for the *Daily Herald* amused *me*).

I must, however, point out that my success in the United States was only due to a temporary interest in war writers. My name had first become known through some generous remarks made about me by Masefield when he was out there on a lecture tour. After that my reputation, such as it was, had been mainly created by Robert Nichols, who had visited America during the latter part of the war with a British Propaganda Mission. For the New York edition of *Counter-attack* he had written an introduction, and had read my poems to audiences wherever he went. The introduction was an effective journalistic gesture, representing me histrionically, almost in the style of a proclamation. His portrait of 'Sassoon the Man' had struck me as likely to be regarded as unrecognizable by those who knew me as an undramatized individual. (He himself had only met me a couple of times before he went to America). To be described as having 'the air of a sullen falcon' was to invite facetious responses from those who knew me well. 'He speaks slowly, enunciating the words as if they pained him, in a voice that has something of the troubled thickness apparent in the voices of those who emerge from a deep grief. . . . And all the while he will be breathing hard like a man who has swum a distance. One would think that he communed with himself, save that, at the pauses, he shoots a powerful glance at the listener.' I knew that I mumbled when shy and was apt to become incoherent and morosely excitable when talking about the war. But to Robert it had seemed that when I spoke of soldiers it was 'with a rapid, tumbling enunciation and a much-irked desperate air filled with pain'. Though obviously overdoing it, he had invented a formidable figure, of which the reviewers made full use. His exposition of 'Sassoon the Poet' sustained the picture with appropriate magniloquence. Anyhow, he had proved himself an admirable impresario, and I was duly grateful for the performance and its results.

One of these results had been a gratifyingly eulogistic letter from a famous Lecture Agency, inviting me to undertake a lecture tour in the United States. This had happened in July. Mr. Jorrocks, when offered the Mastership of the Handley Cross Foxhounds, laid down the letter and exclaimed, 'Werry good indeed—most beautiful, in fact—what honour I arrive at!' My own feeling, although somewhat similar, did not include the idea of acceptance. Since the letter omitted to specify what I was to lecture about, I assumed that a series of professorial discourses would be required of me. Even if I were able to write such lectures, I doubted whether I could deliver them audibly, and I wondered what the audience would do if I modelled my style of utterance on Robert Nichols' notion of it. I therefore replied that owing to inexperience as a public speaker I must regretfully decline the invitation. A few weeks later, however, the lecture agent, James B. Pond, himself arrived in London and renewed his offer, which I still regarded as impracticable. I showed his letter to Osbert Sitwell, who seemed to think that a lecture tour would be rather good fun. 'Why don't you go instead of me?' I asked. As a result of this suggestion I invited Mr. Pond to meet him. He arranged that we should lunch with his friend Mrs. Ronald Greville at her palatial mansion in Mayfair, hoping thereby to impress Mr. Pond. Impressed he no doubt was; but Osbert wasn't the man he wanted, for the Sitwells had yet to become known on the other side of the Atlantic and had still quite a local reputation in England. Anyhow, Mr. Pond insisted on discussing the matter with me again, and at our second meeting I began to wonder why I shouldn't go after all. For one thing, he explained that all I needed to do was to read my war poems and make a few informal comments. For several days I remained undecided. There were two reasons which prompted me to undertake this apparently hazardous experiment.

Siegfried's Journey, 1916–1920

In the first place I had pledged myself to oppose war in every way I could; and here was my opportunity for an active campaign. I may even have told myself that it was a solemn duty to open the eyes of the Americans to those realities of which they needed to be made aware. My second reason emerged in a sudden impulse and longing to escape from the post-war complexities of my existence. I wanted a rest from the overstrain of getting to know so many new people. In America I foresaw myself merely meeting a succession of strangers whom I should never see again. Rivers, when I consulted him, settled the matter by advising me to go. He thought that I should do good by reading my poems and at the same time benefit psychologically by ridding my mind of the war. He himself was going to Baltimore in February to deliver a series of University lectures, so we were likely to meet. My own contract stipulated that I should be in New York by the end of January. Having signed it at the end of July, I allowed several months to pass without giving any serious thought to the matter. In November I gave an experimental reading at the Poetry Book Shop. The room wasn't a large one, but Harold Monro warned me that I was extremely inaudible and urged me to improve my diction before going to America. With this object in view I betook myself to the Central School of Speech Training and Dramatic Art, where I found an able and sympathetic instructor in the Principal, Miss Elsie Fogerty, who knew my poetry well and understood how it could be most effectively spoken. Many an hour I spent with her, acquiring the elements of voice management and extricating myself from that lifelong addiction to rapid undertones and blurred articulation which had been so vividly portrayed by Robert Nichols. The School of Speech Training was (and still pre-eminently is) in the upper regions of the Albert Hall. This made me feel that I was in professional contact with the world of public speaking. The Albert Hall and I got to know one another quite intimately. It was rather like getting to know a celebrated actor or musician in private life.

One day Miss Fogerty announced that I was now proficient enough to be tested in the hall itself. Having deposited me on the platform she vanished, to reappear in one of the distant boxes. It was a gloomy December afternoon, and the heavily-shrouded roof admitted very little daylight. An absurd sense of shyness came over me as I stood there, though what there was to feel shy about I don't know. In bell-like tones Miss Fogerty commanded me to say *Everyone Sang*. 'I can't hear you,' she warned, when I was half-way through the first stanza. So I started again, resolved to speak out loud and bold. When, to the best of my ability, I had resonantly informed the vast twilight of the vacant auditorium that 'the song was wordless, the singing will never be done', I lowered my eyes and discovered that Miss Fogerty was not my only listener. Immediately below the brass rails of the platform four charwomen, on hands and knees, gazed at me with upturned faces and suspended brushes. I felt a bit foolish; but they eyed me apathetically and resumed their floor-cleaning. Meanwhile Miss Fogerty had reappeared in a less remote box with 'Quite good. Now say *Aftermath*'. So I asked the charwomen whether they had forgotten the war yet, duly reciting my way to the last line, where I urged them to 'Look up and swear by the green of the spring that you'll *never* forget!' But they had ceased to bother about me, and my exhortation caused no further interruption of their work.

XVIII

'Is it worth while beginning this note-book with a description of the first-class cabin where I've spent the last forty-eight hours? I like it—this creaking, heaving, vibrating, white, polished box. I like it—not only for itself, but because the man who booked the other berth in it has been so infinitely obliging as to remain on land. And what a relief it is to be among people to whom one need not speak! I haven't shared a single idea with anyone since I left London early on Sunday morning. My thoughts feel white and shiny like the walls of this cabin. I don't want to go on deck and gulp the Atlantic air. I prefer the detachment of lying in bed, reading Trelawny's *Records of Shelley and Byron* by the discreet sunshine of my electric light. In fact I'm living in a kind of cold-storage or vacuum. Existence in England abandoned, the whole thing shrivels and fades like a film on a screen. And America is a blank wall, because I can't visualize it, and don't want to.'

The date was January 21st, and I was going to New York by the Dutch liner *Rotterdam*. For the next three days I wrote nothing, owing to very rough weather during which I remained recumbent, imbibing brandy and milk. On January 25th I was able to note that the coast of Newfoundland had been hazily visible that morning, and that the last week had cleared things up in my head. 'Events of the past year assume a sort of perspective. I haven't experienced this sense of mental seclusion since I was in hospital in the autumn of 1918.' But one of the ' events of the past year' had been a bad dentist who had filled a hollow tooth without bothering to extract the dead nerve, and my last two days on the boat were tyrannized by a raging toothache which came on quite suddenly, and was worse than ever when I went ashore.

'*Hotel Seville. January 28th*, 9.30 *p.m.* Got off the boat this afternoon about three. Met by one of J. B. Pond's people, who brought me to this hotel in a very old taxi through streets inches deep in snow slush. My watch refuses to go, my luggage hasn't yet arrived from the docks, and the hotel is a rather depressing one. I have eaten a nasty dinner and been interviewed for two newspapers. One of the reporters asked me—did I think that the war had had a humanizing effect on the world?—was I related to 'Sir Francis Sassoon?' had I much hope for the future of the world? —did I write much of my poetry in the trenches? This was what he called hog-hauling a story out of me. I told him about my tooth. He became humane and advised me to plug it with tooth-ache wax, and directed me to a drug-store, after being mystified when I called it a chemist's shop. Plugging has made the pain more acute.' After writing this, I telephoned in desperation to Mrs. Thomas Lamont, to whom Masefield had given me an intro-duction. Never-failing in kindness to visiting English poets, she marvellously arranged for me to go to her dentist early next day. Meanwhile I spent the night in a tropical temperature. The radi-ators in my room were full on; I didn't know how to turn them off; and I distrusted the climate of New York so much that I was afraid to open a window!

In the morning, when my tooth had been skilfully quieted down, I presented myself at the Pond Lyceum Bureau to obtain information about my two months' lecture tour. At our previous meetings Pond had been rather reserved in manner. He was now even more so. He received me with the same unassuming friend-liness, but I saw at once that he was uneasy about something. The reason for this was soon revealed. By the terms of our agreement he had guaranteed me a minimum of twenty-five lectures at a hundred dollars each, also paying my steamer fares and travelling expenses. It was, therefore, a complete surprise when he glumly announced that only two engagements had been booked for me in February, and none at all in March. He attributed this to the exceptional influx of British authors that winter, adding that the reaction against the war had already set in. All the usual clubs and colleges had been circularized with the folder-advertisement which he now handed me, but it seemed that the services of 'England's Young Soldier-Poet' weren't in demand. He did not tell me that, about a week before, he had actually cabled to me, urging can-cellation of my tour. I had come by an earlier boat than he had expected. The cable was posted on to me, and I only received it when I had been in America three weeks.

By all this I was less perturbed than might be imagined. Pond

made it clear that the only solution was for me to get what engagements I could by my own endeavours. This put me on my
mettle, and I walked out of the Lyceum Bureau resolved to show
the clubs and colleges that I was worth listening to, however much
they might disagree with my views on the war which they were
ceasing to be interested in. Yet it seemed possible that those charwomen at the Albert Hall had been an omen of transatlantic
inattentiveness to my crusade. Anyhow, whether I liked it or not,
I had got to speak this evening at the Annual Dinner of the Poetry
Society of America, and Pond had warned me that much
depended on my making a favourable impression there. But I had
no chance to prepare a speech, since I spent half the afternoon
being interviewed, and photographed by magnesium lights, in my
hotel bedroom. After that Pond called for me in a taxi to take me
to a reception at the National Arts Club. The taxi also contained
Mr. and Mrs. W. B. Yeats. It was the first time I had beheld the
author of *The Land of Heart's Desire*, and I did so with awed
respectfulness. The National Arts were personified by a crowd of
enthusiastic ladies, among whom he maintained a statuesque and
remotely gracious demeanour, aided by his commanding inches
and eye-glasses with a black ribbon. Clinging to a cup of tea, I did
my ineffectual best to imitate him, incapable even of asking
myself whether this was an appropriate kick-off to my career as a
minor prophet denouncing war.

While hurriedly dressing for the dinner I told myself that I
must be calm and collected. But my brain felt all to pieces after
such an exhausting day, following on a sleepless night. Luckily I
had provided myself with some made-up white ties which looked
as if they'd been tied quite naturally. This was just the sort of
emergency I'd foreseen when instructing my tailor to have them
contrived. The trouble-saving tie now made me feel less verti-
ginous about that unprepared speech of mine. Buckling it at the
back, I remembered how the tailor, when fitting on my new
dress-suit, had proudly remarked, 'In that coat you could go anywhere, sir!' This trivial thought somehow pulled me together.

Sitting at the speakers' table at the Astor Hotel, I overlooked
an arena containing about 250 people. I was placed between
Charles Hanson Towne, the genial editor of *M'Clure's Magazine*,

and a granddaughter of Nathaniel Hawthorne. The banquet
lasted four and a half hours, so I was given full opportunity to
become accustomed to my surroundings, for I had been sitting
there nearly three hours before being called upon to speak. Pro-
hibition was, of course, a noteworthy element in the proceedings.
I have often wondered what my speech would have been like if
champagne had been flowing freely. As it was, the absence of
alcohol effectively banished hilarity. The President of the Society
led off with a longish oration in which he referred to the parliament of the poets and ended by saying that it was 'now time to
unloose the horde of words'. The next three speakers took the hint
by being long-winded and diffuse. One of them was the Japanese
writer Noguchi, who read an elaborate lecture in colourless tones,
thereby producing an inevitably flat effect. All this was to my
advantage. I rose to my feet resolved that, whatever happened, I
would avoid verbosity and be natural. Conscious of my youthful
appearance and of being, probably, the youngest man in the
room, I presented myself as a modest, naïve sort of person, anxious
to be friendly. Beginning in a style of slangy simplicity which
went down well and evoked appreciative laughter, I worked up to
a befitting but still boyish seriousness which declared my faith in
poetry and poets. For what I actually said I have only the following newspaper report. 'Mr. Sassoon, who arrived in New York
from Europe recently, said he came with a toothache and would
leave with a heartache. Asked by interviewers for his first impression of New York, he had replied, "As I rode through the streets
in a taxicab I kept saying to myself, Oh hell! where's the nearest
dentist?" Mr. Sassoon said that if he should be asked to vote for the
Prime Minister of living English poets he would cast his vote for a
man whom most Americans probably knew only as a prose writer,
Thomas Hardy. He read three of his own poems and gave a fourth
—*Everyone Sang*—in response to applause.'

Of the three speakers who filled up the final hour of the
unalcoholic evening, the first was local and unlively, the second
embarrassingly jocular, and both went on much too long. The
third was Yeats, who began by saying, 'It is late, and I will be
brief' in a manner which courteously implied that 'the horde of
words' had been unloosed excessively. Dignified and authorita-

tive, he commented on the difference between the subjective poetry of his generation and the objectivity of mine. It was a beautiful performance, which should have been heard earlier in the evening. After that a number of poets came up and shook hands with me, among them Edwin Arlington Robinson, the veteran Edwin Markham, and a young lady named Edna St. Vincent Millay, who has since become celebrated. I could only smile upon them in a dazed way, deeply relieved at having got through my performance creditably. Pond, while taking me back to my hotel, was most encouraging. He told me I had 'made a great little hit' which would do me no end of good. My after-thoughts, as confided to my diary, were that I didn't know how I was going to get through three months of this sort of thing, and that I felt as if my soul had been undressed in public. At the moment this was quite true, for the day had been a terrifically tiring one. Nevertheless, while making my 'great little hit' at the Astor Hotel I had thoroughly enjoyed the feeling of putting my poems over on the audience. It was all very well for me to complain about undressing my soul in public; but both then and thereafter I was aware of the somewhat insidious allurement of doing it.

Two days later I received the following gracious letter from the Poetry Society's President (who was editor of a magazine called *Current Opinion*):

Dear Mr. Sassoon,

I want to thank you for your presence and your speech at the dinner. You and Yeats were the salvation of the evening. The amount of facetiousness and frivolity developed was a disappointment to most of us and I fear it may have given you a false impression of our American poets who, as a rule, take their art and themselves seriously. Your talk was full of charm and made every one of your auditors a friend. I think America will take to you quickly and heartily.

Cordially,
EDWARD J. WHEELER.

I also received one from C. H. Towne, asking me to send poems to *M'Clure's Magazine*, and ending: 'I predict the greatest success for you in America. You made a tremendous impression last evening.' When I showed these to Pond he seemed surprised that I did not realize that the concluding sentences of each had been written so that he might quote them in advertising me. On my reminding him that they were private letters, he replied that in the lecturing business there was no such thing as a private letter.

*   *   *

During the next week my campaign of making myself known was in full swing. I was interviewed for a lot of newspapers and magazines, and went to a continuous series of lunches and dinners where I met many well-known literary people. I also went to the opera, and heard Mr. de Valera make a speech at a League of Nations debate. In one of my lucid moments I remarked to my diary that I was leading a sort of cinematograph existence. 'I visualize myself walking rapidly about as people do in films. No-one else seems to smoke a pipe. To-day I went into a shop and bought some pipe cleaners, and at once felt more my natural self. Most of the people I meet have to be judged by their possible usefulness in getting me paid engagements, which is rather unpleasant and doesn't suit me at all.'

My first 'commentative reading' is described as follows: '*February 6th*. To-day began with a hustle; the streets deep in snow, and myself sure I should miss the train. When I heard a negro going along the corridor shouting "North Philadelphia—First stop", it suddenly seemed strange that I should be on my way to a girls' college in America to spout my war poems. However I did arrive, and the college—Bryn Mawr—is an extremely good one, and I am sitting in a beautiful little white bedroom listening to the wind in the trees and reconsidering the evening's events. More than 300 girls were in the lecture hall. Their bright-coloured dresses made quite a flower-garden effect. After the introductory remarks, which I'd memorized, I read twenty war poems; a fairly tough programme, but they never stirred, except for a sort of rustle of released breath after each poem. (One young lady came up afterwards and asked why I hadn't read *Suicide in Trenches*!) They insisted on more, so I read some of my pleasantly

179

lyrical ones. It is appalling—the amount of poetry one can read in an hour! At a reception afterwards I shook hands with most of them, and they asked simple, engaging questions and were very nice. It is queer—the things one does in front of an audience. Half-way through the war poems I felt that the tension was becoming too acute, so I said, "I can't help feeling that that old gentleman with the whiskers is looking at me all the time". The old gentleman was a full-length portrait of the founder of the college, which hung at the far end of the hall. It spoilt the cumulative effect of my carefully-planned sequence; but I think the emotional strain is too much for a sensitive audience.'

The 'introductory remarks' referred to had been laboriously composed before I left England. They explained the purpose of my war poems and my reasons for reading them in public. But at Bryn Mawr the three typewritten pages never came to life. They sounded didactic and unspontaneous. At all my subsequent readings I spoke from a few rough notes and relied on naturalness for the character of my 'comments'. My pauses, while wondering what to say next, were a positive asset in my repertoire. At the end of one reading a lady came up to the platform to tell me how much my magnetic silences had meant to her.

XIX

After the first few days I had moved to a small flat in West 44th Street. Compared with the hotel, Westover Court seemed almost homely. Up three flights of stairs, with no 'elevator', my nocturnal outlook was dominated by the Putnam Building, above which blazed the electric sign of Wrigley's Spearmint Gum. Flanked by two peacocks whose tails were cascades of quivering colour, about a square acre of advertising space contained the caption, 'Don't argue but stick it in your face'. To be living in the reverberant glitter of Broadway and Theatreland was at any rate an acclimatizing experience, I thought, while walking home at night among the crowds who shuffled among heaped snow which looked artificial, as though pretending to be sugar. Meanwhile I had lunched with the editor of *Vanity Fair*, Frank Crowninshield, at the Coffee House Club, and he had offered what seemed to me the enormous sum of a hundred dollars for an article on War Poetry. This had to be delivered within four days, and it surprises me that I was able to get it done under the distracting conditions of my social engagements. What surprises me still more is that *Vanity Fair* agreed to print a second article on 'Thomas Hardy as Poet'. The first one was sprightly enough to give satisfaction. Its successor, very properly, lacked the breezy and intimate tone required by a magazine whose guiding principle was literary chicness. Some of the lines quoted must have mystified many readers. Well might they ask why they should be expected to divert their momentary minds with such queryings as

> *Has some vast Imbecility,*
>   *Mighty to build and blend,*
>   *But impotent to tend,*
> *Framed us in jest, and left us now to hazardry?*

Anyhow, I refrained from telling them that Hardy had wondered 'if Man's consciousness was a mistake of God's'. And I promised Crowninshield that I would send him something really amusing next time—a promise which was fulfilled a few months later in the form of a deplorably facetious spoof interview with myself, a preposterous parody of Robert Nichols' presentment of me as a dynamic personality.

During those first weeks in New York I was unavoidably victimized by my numerous letters of introduction. This sounds an ungracious way of putting it; but the fact was that my career as a visiting candidate for celebrity would have been quite complicated enough without these additional obligations. Feeling that I must make use of them, I incurred much more than I was equal to. An overwhelming invasion of telephone messages and invitations accumulated until compliance was reduced to desperation. To an elderly quietist like myself, the whole thing appears absurdly unprofitable. Ten years ago I might have described it all with gusto. My foremost feeling now is that it must have been terribly tiring. And I am grumpily aware of the irony, to put it no stronger, of my position. I had come out as a crusader for the belief that wars must not be allowed to impede human progress; and here I was, just a nine-days wonder. President Wilson once remarked that 'Peace is the healing and elevating influence of the world'. Neither his views nor mine have made much progress. Anyhow, in the middle of February the Sunday edition of the *New York Tribune* contained a long article about me with a 'banner headline'—'Lilting Poet. Back from War. Speaks in Trumpet Tones'. For the moment I felt that this was fame, and I no mean trumpeter. I did not remind myself that by Monday morning the newspaper would be 'with Yesterday's Sev'n Thousand Years', or connect the publicity which Louis Untermeyer, indefatigable anthologist of English poets, had been allowed to give me, with the favourable effect I had made on one of the *Tribune* editors when lunching with him at the Harvard Club.

Untermeyer's enthusiasm for modern poetry was centralized in a voluble and exuberant personality which sometimes left me a bit dizzy. His receptivity was prodigious, though at that period of his career he was prone to disregard all poets who weren't under fifty and still alive. For him, poetry was an exciting affair which had only recently been invented. He was refreshingly buoyant, and his smart-minded immaturity was preferable to pedantry. With the Untermeyers I felt more at home than anywhere else in New York. I spent several evenings at their 'apartment', and heard some splendid playing by that intellectual pianist Richard Buhlig. It was there that I met two of the most prominent American poets, Robert Frost and Vachel Lindsay. While talking to Frost I felt—as one usually does with original writers—that he was just as good as his poems. The essence of them was in him, gravely humorous and obliquely commentative. When picturing the puritan monochrome of the New England landscape, Frost somehow reminds me of Crabbe, though his masterly technique and subtlety of thought have a flexibility and variety of which Crabbe's prosaic eighteenth-century mind was incapable. But, like Crabbe's, his style has the homespun strength of sobriety. It is a unique voice, uttering wisdom with studied and supple casualness. Often most full of meditative meaning in what he leaves half unsaid, his poems are rich in single memorable plain statements, such as 'the groundwork of all faith is human woe', and 'I had a lover's quarrel with the world'. It is a philosophy of inexpectance and assentive renunciation. There is much in nature against us, he remarks, but

> *Take nature altogether since time began,*
> *Including human nature, in peace and war,*
> *And it must be a little more in favour of man.*

That is about as far as he allows himself to go. Vachel Lindsay, on the other hand, was consistently unreserved and declamatory. Whereas Frost's verse has the inwardness of a man talking quite naturally to himself, Lindsay wrote as an evangelist, accompanied, as it were, by banners and brass bands, in an intoxication of colour and elocutionary emotion. I heard him recite *The Daniel Jazz* and *General William Booth Enters into Heaven*, those irresistibly effective syncopated incantations. But when talking to him, though his individuality was vigorous and unaffected, I felt that his poetry was a *tour de force*, and more of a dithyrambic exhibition than (as with Frost) an integral expression of his inner self.

* * *

Sydney Cockerell had given me an introduction to Miss Belle Greene, of the Pierpont Morgan Library. This resulted in occasional hours of quietude, otherwise unobtainable. My visits to the library were an escape from the flurry and precipitancy of over-

engaged days. Silence was there, and the serenity of those im-
perishable memorials of genius which could put a spell on my
spirit and make the meretricious glitter and daemonian din of
'Broadway and the 'Forties' seem remote and unreal. Miss
Greene herself, apart from those abilities which qualified her for the
immensely responsible post of curator, was a woman of large
humanity, humour, and commonsense. She could enlighten me
about most of the people I had been meeting, thereby making me
feel less lost and undirected. And, to my gratitude and delight,
she and her assistant, Miss Thurston, allowed me to take out anything I wanted and then left me to absorb it in solitude. The little
manuscript room was a sound-proof sanctuary from the clamorous
mutability of the modern world. I can remember sitting there one
afternoon with my eyes on a folio page of faded brown writing.

> *This light and darkness in our chaos join'd,*
> *What shall divide?—the God within the mind.*

An odd rhyme-ending, I thought; and then remembered that, in
those days, joined was pronounced *jined*. For a moment, time dissolved; the millionaire museum was transmuted to immateriality.
For I was staring at the original manuscript of Pope's *Essay on
Man*. Whispering the words, I found them applicable to my own
temporarily disordered existence, in which the God within the
mind was being obliterated. It was a relief to be reminded of one's
own unimportance. The shelves around me were filled with
literary everlastingness in its primal visibility. The room was a
sort of ante-chamber to Parnassus. I wasn't so foolish as to fancy
that the ghosts of the immortals were localizing themselves
among the pages across which their pens had travelled; but the
atmosphere of association with them affected me strongly. I had
been looking at an album of Keats relics. There was a lock of
his blonde, silky hair, and his last scribbled message to Fanny
Brawne. 'The passport came this morning—I shall not be ill
long—Farewell.' For the first time since I left England there
were tears in my eyes. The nearness of heart-broken Keats on
that scrap of paper was a more vivid reality than all the Poetry
Societies of America. In the presence of such things my heart
cried out for the living word, and I became conscious of the

fatuity of my undertakings for the Pond Lyceum Bureau. The living word. . . . What had it felt like, to be my true poetic self? I had left that inmost self in England. He was probably pottering about at Weirleigh, an invisible presence in the little room where *Everyone Sang* had been written.

∗   ∗   ∗

Foremost among the New York friends of Robert Nichols to whom he had commended me were Mrs. Winthrop Chanler and her brother-in-law John Jay Chapman. During February I went several times to the Chanlers' house. Cultivated and charmingly friendly, they took me to concerts, and studiously avoided the subject of my war poetry, which was evidently regarded by them with orthodox disapproval. Robert had specially urged me to get on good terms with Mr. Chapman, whom he described as 'a tremendous stimulator'. A few days after my arrival I was introduced to him at the Coffee House Club. He said little, and I must have thought him unimpressive, for my diary merely referred to him as 'rather a nice old thing'. About a week later, however, my opinion of him improved. 'Dined with J. J. Chapman and his wife. No-one else there. A delightful homely couple, quite first-rate. They made me feel uneducated but encouraged! J.J.C. only sees the heroic side of war, probably because his eldest son was killed fighting for France as an airman. They talked about William James, whom they knew well.'

Mr. Chapman was a bull-necked, stockily built man, with a beard, short bristly hair, small scrutinizing eyes, and ears growing close to his head. It was a kindly but uncompromising face. His only peculiarity was that he had lost his left hand, and wore a hook. When a young man, having struck someone in an outburst of anger, he had put his hand in the fire as an act of expiation. I had been told this story by Robert, and it was the only clue I had to his character. Even then, the hook seemed part of his personality; as I think of him now, I am unable to dissociate it from the fanatical element in his nature. One afternoon, not long after the dinner, he asked me to come and see him at the Century Club. There was, he wrote, something he wanted to talk seriously to me about. Having no notion what this could be, I was completely taken by surprise when he embarked on a solemn warning and remonstrance against my error in trying to spread anti-war propaganda. He asserted that I was brain-sick, had nothing new to say about war, and that my war poems were a pathological exhibit. He insisted on 'the spiritual benefits which a righteous war brings to humanity', and maintained that he would have liked the war to have lasted three times as long as far as the U.S.A. was concerned in active participation. The situation created was thus a strange and almost ludicrous one. Robert Nichols, after going about America reciting my poems and making me well known, had introduced me to his best friend there. That friend was now dogmatically demanding that I should withdraw from my lecture tour! Flabbergasted—and somewhat affronted by being called a pathological exhibit—I returned to Westover Court and wrote in my diary: 'He is a dear old man, but I can't accept his point of view. He said that the art of life is, largely, learning how to do nothing. This may be true at his time of life; but I didn't come to New York for that purpose, as I know to my cost!' Anyhow I was too busy to bother about it, though I can remember relating the incident to Rivers, who was in New York at the time, on his way to deliver a series of lectures at Johns Hopkins University in Baltimore. He cautioned me against arguing with such people, adding that I should find my views being automatically applauded by those who agreed with them and opposed by the unconvinceables who were past praying for. Only among the open-minded minority would my evidence be of any significant value. Meanwhile I got successfully through my second reading, which was an inconspicuous one, at a women's club about thirty miles from New York.

My next appearance, on February 24th, had been arranged by Miss Thurston, of the Morgan Library. I was to address an influential audience as the guest of her club, the Cosmopolitan. She warned me that a fair proportion of them would be antagonistic, so I outlined a speech which combined a defiant challenge to the anti-pacifists with what I considered an artful admixture of impartiality. I therefore went to the club well primed up; but the preliminaries were exacting for a highly strung and unpractised speaker. I was entertained at a large dinner party. About half the guests were people who had shown friendliness to me and my opinions. The other half gave me an uncomfortable suspicion that they were out for my blood. There was something in the polite way they eyed me which suggested that they hoped to assist at a fiasco.

At nine o'clock, having been allowed barely time to swallow my cup of coffee, I was led to the platform, wondering how the hell they expected me to collect my ideas for what was practically an extempore speech on a crucial occasion. I had been sitting next to a sister of the soldier poet Alan Seager. Reserved and seemingly sympathetic, she had told me that a good many ex-officers would be in the audience. There was an atmosphere of lively expectation, and the large room was crowded to capacity. Now it so happened that the president of the club was Mrs. J. J. Chapman, upon whom had therefore devolved the duty of introducing me. This she performed in a quiet, gracious, and non-committal manner; but it seemed queer that she, of all people, should be doing it. I have preserved the notes for my speech, which lasted about forty minutes, and still strikes me as a very decent, unrhetorical presentation of my evidence against war. It was a ramblingly descriptive, anecdotal account of life in the infantry. I laid stress on those elements in war service which brought out men's finest qualities of cheerfulness and endurance, but expressed a conviction that the indictment of war was to be found in the exploitation and betrayal of those qualities. For the common soldier, the glory of war was an expediently invented falsehood. And I said that no one who had been in a shell-shock hospital, as I had, could be entirely reasonable about the 'uplifting effects' of war on the individual. It was a genuine attempt to balance the good and bad elements, but I made it provocative by the poems which I read as illustrations. These were interpolated at points calculated to startle complacency. My diary described the speech as follows. 'Spoke in a halting, conversational way at first, diffident and persuasive. Told a few stories which made them laugh, while giving outline of an infantry private's existence. When they had got to feel at their ease with me, suddenly read *Suicide in Trenches*. Described heroism of front-line padres. Then read *They*. Worked up to climax with *Attack*, *Lamentations*, and *Memorial Tablet*, as contrast to 'joy of battle', ennobling effects of war, etc. (Someone hissed the line 'Such men have lost all patriotic feeling'.) Finished with *Aftermath* and *Everyone Sang*. There was very loud applause, and a feeling of excitement. Chapman then hopped up on to the platform and let fly at me in an extraordinary emotional explosion, pacing to and fro wagging his hook. Poor Mrs. Chapman and I sat there not knowing which way to look. He said my stuff wasn't poetry; that I was in an abnormal state of mind; and that if I were to be believed we must discard as worthless all the heroism of the past, including Thermopylae. There was some hissing when he finished, and not much clapping. After waiting to see if anyone else wanted to get up and make trouble for me, I said that I had only offered my evidence of the humanity and inhumanity of war as I had seen it, and that I believed we must find a substitute for it as a creator of heroism. I was very sorry to be in public disagreement with Mr. Chapman, and could only say in conclusion that I still thought him a very nice man. (Magnanimous gesture, combined with modest youthful charm; but I really meant it, and was fearfully embarrassed by the scene he had created.) The result, of course, was that my popularity increased, and people crowded round being nice to me.' *February 25th.* 'Very tired, after being awake all night with a splitting headache. Alone all day except for an hour at the dentist's and ditto at the Morgan Library, where I looked at the manuscript of *Diana of the Crossways*. Miss Greene showed me the lock of Keats' hair again, and told me that she'd been obliged to remonstrate with Mr. Pierpont Morgan, who had taken to giving away *single hairs* to distinguished visitors!' I had received a note from Miss Thurston in which she apologized for 'the unfortunate episode of this evening, and for having asked you to a place where your work was the subject of criticism. Your perfect attitude in return has won you hosts of friends, and I hope the strength of their support will help you to let the memory of an unhappy moment fade away.' She had been much upset, and it was to reassure her that I went to the library. Next day the following letter from Chapman arrived.

My dear Sassoon,

Sorry to miss you this morning. It was a suffering occasion last night. I think I suffered as much as you did. If you *will* do it why you must: and I suppose the universe will not be wrecked by you or by my trying to stop you. As for the wrecking of a ladies' club or two it's not of the smallest consequence. But you can get out of the way of people who want to exploit you, and your dogma or message, or whatever it is. I say you *can* avoid them. The pro-Germans will try it politically, and the women will do it emotionally. They'll love you—but O my, there's nothing in it, except wayward motherliness (I don't see how the universe stands the women in it). Well, good luck and let me hear from you. Nature's stronger than mental aberration at your age.

Yours sincerely always,
JOHN JAY CHAPMAN.

Since the episode has been considered worth mentioning in his biography, I may as well reproduce the account given. 'Chapman had sought in vain to dissuade him from carrying his gospel of disillusion and war-weariness to American youth. This gospel was the burden of Sassoon's message to the women of the Cosmopolitan Club. It was more than Chapman, on fire with the heroisms of war, could stand. When Sassoon stopped speaking, Chapman, urged by ladies who shared his indignation, mounted the rostrum, and asked what would become of the world if the philosophies of fear and self-pity were to prevail, what Washington would have thought of a young man who went about after Valley Forge preaching "no more bleeding footsteps in the snow". Some of Chapman's best friends joined in hissing him, and there were outraged departures from the room—even as there were those who stood with Chapman in the whole affair. Afterwards he commended the Cosmopolitan Club as a place where people could hiss if they wanted to. At the time, he wrote to his son at Grenoble in these terms: "Well, the poet Sassoon made such a speech and read such poems about the nature of war, and the war, and how the men were sacrificed, and didn't know what they were fighting for, and committed suicide in the trenches, and were in an abnormal condition of excitement when they went over the top, with hits at every good influence in the war, church, patriotism— in fact the most painful talk I ever heard—that I had to call him down. The audience was surprised and grieved at my denunciation, and thought it very ungentlemanly. But really, you know——" That was not quite the end of it. A letter from Mrs. Chapman to the sons in Europe tells that their father called on Sassoon on the day after their encounter, and, finding him out, left a card. "Of course if he had seen him he would have removed the few remaining hairs on his scalp. But the card had just the friendly affectionate expression, lying on Sassoon's hall-table, that represented Papa's true impulse in leaving it." More than that, Chapman wrote later in the day to Sassoon, warning him against allowing himself to be exploited.'

Long afterwards, Robert Nichols told me that Chapman was pained and surprised because I ignored his conciliatory gesture. He couldn't understand why it was that I avoided seeing him again. I have regretted it myself, for he was a lovable though extravagantly contentious character, with spiritual and intellectual powers which amounted to genius. In attacking me, he was, of course, merely defending his romantic idea of the heroic aspects of war. But it was with the purpose of revealing the realities of front-line soldiering to people of his mentality that I had come to America. The 'friendly and affectionate expression' of Papa's card on my hall-table didn't affect the central situation, which was that a rabidly indignant old gentleman had publicly denounced the satire and sincerity of my war poems. He may or may not have been reasonable in describing my philosophy as one of 'fear and self-pity'. But, had he known more about me, he might have understood that I had lived through all the phases of emotional self-sacrifice, and had been a good soldier even after I had become disillusioned about the war. Chapman was fifty-eight when the incident occurred. Now that I am that age myself, I can fully understand his insistence on courage as the best attribute of all. Even then I was prepared to affirm that war lifts some men above themselves in gallantry, fortitude, and self-sacrifice. But I am not, like Chapman, a combative character, and am therefore unable to believe that individual acts of bravery justify us in creating orgies of homicidal calamity. War may be a biological necessity; it may also be indirectly productive of beneficial results. But militarism is a science which depends on the exploitation of human gullibility. Thomas Hobbes wrote, about three hundred years ago, that force and fraud are in war the two cardinal virtues. Within the limits of my understanding I agree with him.

XX

On March 10th I was in Philadelphia to speak at a meeting of the Women's International League for Peace and Freedom (an appellation which looks almost ironical when put on paper in 1945). The meeting was a rather imposing affair, organized in aid of Hoover's Famine Committee in Europe. I stayed at the Rittenhouse Club, which afforded me my first experience of traditional America, for its atmosphere was quietly exclusive and ripely flavorous. Rambling and unmodernized, the club gave me a delightful feeling of mid-Victorian comfort. It was like an elderly gentleman whose clothes are odd, old-fashioned, and distinguished. Looked after by a discreet old servant, I rejoiced in the recognizableness of my surroundings, of which I seemed to be almost the only occupant. Through the kindness of Mrs. Winthrop Chanler, I was there as the guest of Owen Wister, an author of whom I knew nothing except that he was eminent and had written a book called *The Pentecost of Calamity*. He was away from Philadelphia, which I didn't regret, since he was a friend of J. J. Chapman, and I suspected that his attitude towards my 'gospel of disillusion and war-weariness' would be similar to Chapman's. Had I met him, I shouldn't even have known that he was a grandson of Fanny Kemble, a circumstance which I now consider exciting. She had lived in America until he was eighteen, and he had been thirty-three when she died in London—she whose theatrical triumphs had been witnessed by Sir Walter Scott, who had been an admired associate of Samuel Rogers, Macaulay, and Longfellow, and the favourite correspondent of Edward FitzGerald in his later years. For my 1920 self it would have been an opportunity wasted. Had I talked to Owen Wister in the pleasant old library of his club, it would have been with no sense of the historic literary past. I should merely have unburdened myself of momentary immaturities, and there could have been none of that 'memorable and admirable discourse' referred to by Henry James in a letter to Wister after he had visited Lamb House in 1909. And by the way I have discovered, in his *American*

Siegfried's Journey, 1916–1920

Scene, a comment on the Rittenhouse Club. Staying there in 1905, he mentions 'the large friendliness, the ordered charm and perfect peace of the club, housing me with that *whole* protection the bestowal of which on occasion is the finest grace of the hospitality of American clubs.'

I have laid some stress on my inaptitude for making the acquaintance of Owen Wister because it serves to illustrate my behaviour to the 'correct', Europeanized people I encountered in America. It amuses me now, when I remember how many of them asked whether I had known Henry James, and how unresponsively I replied that I hadn't. They, of course, had, and were all-beautifully equipped for a cosy discussion about *The Ambassadors, The Golden Bowl,* and the rest of the Jacobean game which I had yet to learn and delight in. There was, for instance, Mrs. Cadwalader Jones, a lady of high quality, sister-in-law to Edith Wharton, through whom she, too, had become 'a great friend of dear Mr. Henry James'. I was presented to her in a Pullman car, when returning to New York after giving my 'commentative reading' to the Elizabethan Club at Yale, and I must snobbishly add that she was travelling with the wife of ex-President Taft, to whom I was also introduced. Captivated by the lively refinement and intelligence of Mrs. Cadwalader Jones, I realized that this was an occasion which would be socially advantageous if I availed myself of her invitation to come and have another talk with her. But somehow or other we never met again, though she asked me, a couple of months later, to stay at her house on the Maine coast, where I should, no doubt, have had a delightful time, 'mixing in the selectest circles'. This evasive behaviour was largely caused by the misgiving I have always felt about being 'collected' by fashionable folks in the manner so acutely described by Henry James in *The Death of the Lion.* 'Mrs. Cadwalader' was a person to whom I took an immediate liking, and obviously 'a great lady'. Unfortunately I was doing my best not to be a gentleman—not a socially-exploited gentleman anyhow. Also I had observed, when among people whose political opinions were less revolutionary than mine, a tendency to treat me as an object for sympathy on account of my 'having had such a nerve-racking time in the trenches'. This I resented, regarding it as their method of eluding my unpalatable revelation of a war which they preferred to think of in noble phrases, Relief Organizations, and, perhaps, economic consequences. Whereupon the present writer intervenes with his prudent proviso against unfair generalizations about people who, for all he knows, were wiser and more humane than he, and in any case only acting in accordance with their lights. But I must return to the Rittenhouse Club—or rather to the Bellevue-Stratford Hotel, where, according to my diary, 'I addressed about three hundred in a sort of ballroom. Made a hit by saying "Good luck" when sipping glass of water for the first time. Very cheap effect! Read a group of non-war poems. Then, after a short speech by one of "Fight the Famine" Committee, read war poems and talked extempore. Reading went well, although the slow pace I go at, to ensure being heard and understood, rather spoils the poems. Ended with Hardy's sonnet "Often when warring for he wist not what". Shook hands with a lot of them afterwards, including a conscientious objector (with a bigoted face, not spiritual) and a dear old lady who exclaimed in sepulchral tones, "I feel as if I had been at the funeral of the world!" Another old lady said she didn't altogether agree, but knew Thomas Hardy.'

On my way to Princeton University next morning I noted that the *Philadelphia Public Ledger* had a headline 'Poet Favours Ruthless War', reporting me as having said that 'the so-called German atrocities were not atrocities at all—they were simply part of that terrible thing called war. The only way to fight a successful war was by brutal efficiency'. What surprises me now is that I had the temerity to express any opinions at all about a phenomenon which is, apparently, as uncontrollable as an earthquake. But I was a booby-trapped idealist, and 'young men', as Francis Bacon wrote, 'stir more than they can quiet, fly to the end without consideration of the means'. If I were asked to make a speech about war now, it would consist of a couple of sentences. 'The only effective answer that a poet can make to barbarism is poetry, for the only answer to death is the life of the spirit. Explosives cannot destroy the immaterial or dumbfound the utterance of inspiration.'

At the present time nobody needs disillusioning about war. The

G 193

danger seems to be that they accept it in a fatalistic way and that future generations may regard its recurrences as inevitable. My old lady at the Bellevue-Stratford Hotel was more prophetic than she knew. If she had lived long enough she would have been present, if not at 'the funeral of the world', at the obsequies of all frustrated leagues for peace and freedom.

*   *   *

I must explain that my lecture tour had by now become entirely dependent on my ability to obtain engagements by my own exertions. Early in March it had transpired that the Pond Bureau was on the verge of bankruptcy. This had been brought about by the failure of Maeterlinck to speak intelligible English, which had resulted in the cancellation of his tour with a huge loss of money to his agent. I was always on the best of terms with Pond, who treated me well. But all he could do was to tell me to collect my earnings independently and pick up what engagements I could as I went along. Like Sir Walter Scott, I love to be particular, so I will provide the details of my 'lecture season' in the form of a batting average.

Appearances	Times unpaid	Total	Most for a lecture	Average
26	2	2,180	200	90.83

As I had been at a disadvantage from the outset owing to the glut of British lecturers earlier in the winter, this might have been worse.

On March 18th I left New York for Chicago. I can remember the train crossing a wide river of broken ice and stopping at Albany, a town which would now tempt me to explore it—though not very hopefully—as a pilgrim in quest of Henry James's youthful background. But I was unaware of Albany's importance in his early history, or of those alembicated recoveries of it which loom from his vista'd perceptions of the past, so brooded-on, so restlessly and reflectively analysed by his exquisite sensibilities. I was merely on my way to Rochester, where I was due to address, that very evening, the Associate Alumnae of Vassar College. My diary briefly records that I was 'dead tired after the four-hundred-mile

journey and the strain of the past weeks, but carried the reading
through with a sort of desperate gaiety'. Feeble-mindedly resorting to my press-cutting album, I find a couple of columns headed
'Youthful Poet Entrances with Unusual Verse. Proves to be
Short-haired Regular Fellow.' The reporter described the large
audience as 'frankly won by the clean-cut young Englishman,
who looked a very likeable chap, the sort who might take a flier in
oil stocks and know the batting average of most of the big leaguers.
He did not talk much, but said what he did with a disingenuous
lack of practice which made it doubly pleasant'.

In 1945 I find some difficulty in believing that it was really me
who went to Chicago all by himself, with nothing awaiting him
there except a single Pond engagement at a girls' school. 'Chicago!'
I exclaim. 'How can it be possible—when I go nowhere now, from
one year's end to another?' Anyhow, I took leave of Rochester late
on the following night, in a snowstorm, and after waiting two
hours for the train. 'Lumbered through Chicago in a bus', says my
diary, 'and came straight out here'. 'Out here' was Ferry Hall
School, at Lake Forest, about thirty miles from the city. My diary,
I must confess, has a way of supplying details which would otherwise have been beyond recovery. Ferry Hall School is one of them.
'Gave my show to about 150 in the school chapel. Good place for
speaking. Poems went well. Voice improving. Miss Tremaine, the
principal, is a very fine woman.' Memory can add nothing to this
report. Fine though she was, Miss Tremaine is, for me, only preserved from oblivion by that scribble. Like much else in my lecture
tour, she and I were 'ships that pass in the night, and speak each
other in passing'. I had forgotten her as completely as the Cam-
berwell Beauty butterfly which I observed while walking by the
waters of Lake Michigan next morning, and duly made a note of.
Nor can I remember how it came about that for the next eight
days I stayed with the Horace Martins, whose house was only a
few minutes' walk from the school. Possibly I had the admirable
Miss Tremaine to thank for those days, which were much the
most peaceful I had experienced since arriving in the States.
Quiet, elderly, and graciously considerate, they lived in a low
rambling wooden house surrounded by trees. Mr. Martin was a
retired lawyer, and an immense reader of English books, which he

refused to acquire in their American editions. In my bedroom I found all the London literary journals, five weeks old, but none the less palatable for that. The Martins seemed to realize that I needed a rest. They made no attempt to entertain me, merely putting me in touch with a few people in Chicago who could arrange for me to give readings. Meanwhile I felt that the fewer the readings were the better I should like them. I preferred to remain where I was, conversing with Horace Martin about his favourite authors, of whom Henry James (whose invisible presence seems often to be at my elbow) was not one. On my second night in this haven of refuge I recorded that I had seen a full-blown Aurora Borealis for the first time in my life, and that it was much more impressive than the advertisement of Wrigley's Gum which gratuitously irradiated the windows of my flat in New York. My first expedition to Chicago was with a letter of introduction to John Alden Carpenter, the distinguished composer, an entirely delightful person who afterwards made song settings of several poems of mine. It so happened that there was a Casals recital that afternoon, to which he took me. I had never heard Casals before, and made the following note: 'His face while playing unaccompanied Bach—eyes closed, and a sort of luminous appearance, serene and saint-like. When he stops he is once again a small, rather cruel-looking man in a black coat, throwing frigid little bows at an audience which he seems to be despising.'

Two or three days later I was rung up by Carl Sandburg, and went to see him at the office of the *Chicago Daily News*, where he was labour editor. The Whitmanesque poet of the Middle West was then not much over forty, but might have been more. Experience was deeply graven on his face, and his eyes were philosophical of things endured and done. Sitting in that dingy little newspaper room, with an old grey hat on his head, smoking a large companionable pipe, he appeared to have discarded inessential concerns and found his formula for arriving at the root of the matter. Here was a man who thought before he spoke (his voice was deep, and slow but undrawling) and had studied the natural history of humankind with the observation of a trained reporter and the compassion of an imaginative mind. Like Robert Frost, he struck me as being a deeply serious humorist, though more rugged and moulded on a bigger scale. One thinks of Frost as leaning on a gate, looking into an orchard in the dusk of a rainy day. A meadow is enough for him when musing on imponderables and the minutiae of nature, seeking a synthesis between eternity and the ephemeral. His poetic ancestry goes back to the early civilization of New England. Generations of maturing are behind his persuasive soliloquies. Sandburg watches a bronze evening sky above the gloaming prairie; the cloud mountains are like great memories. Or he confronts what he has called 'the sunset sonata that comes to the cities, when the skyscrapers throw their tall lengths of walls into black bastions on the red west'. He turns his emotions into manifestoes for the multiform America that is, and is to be. These molten and prolific prose statements have the rhythmic vitality of song. One feels that no other method could have encompassed such amplitudinous material. His shorter pieces are rich in ironic vernacular humour, vignettes and apophthegms acutely observed and strongly felt. Compared with Frost's, his poetry has the quality of vivid poster work. For Frost excels in delicate line and subdued almost achromatic tones.

I spent a long and unforgettable afternoon with Sandburg, during which he showed me what he could of the polyglot raw material of Chicago, indicating its teeming rudimentariness with a sort of laconic affection. No-one understood it better than he, or has word-painted it with such vital realism and originality. Standing on the roof of a huge building (I think it was the headquarters of the Amalgamated Clothing Workers of America) we stared across the city and its canyon-like streets and façades. A stormy sunset transfigured Michigan Avenue, colouring the drifted clouds of factory smoke. I remarked that it seemed funny to think of me coming to tell Chicago that war doesn't pay. 'I guess you just done what the good Lord told you to do,' he replied with a slow smile. 'Maybe a few of them'll believe you. But they can't know unless they've been there themselves. Bullets, bombs, bayonets, gas, are nothing more than words to them.'

The moment when he said that now seems to have been the central point of my time in America. No-one else had put it to me like that. The conjunction of the man and the vast sunset-transfigured city causes that moment to return with the insistence of indelible experience. Disproportionate to the context of my narration, the memory makes me unwilling to go droning on about that lecture tour. I want to continue talking about Sandburg, a reperusal of whose writings has put me in an argumentative mood. Sandburg has defined poetry as 'a series of explanations of life, fading off into horizons too swift for explanations'. In other words he is mainly concerned with the momentariness of life and his perceptions of its sensuous effect on him. Such poetry is, undisguisedly, improvisation; its spontaneity is largely conditional on not pausing to consider coherency. Selection has to be experimental and instinctive. The writer is attempting to intercept life while it is in motion. Hence the rejection of metrical stability, and the consequent sacrifice of incisiveness and intensity. An objection to this loose impressionism is that it resembles the provisional scenario or preliminary ingredients of expression rather than the finished work of art. Poetry is the result of a process, partly subconscious. Superficial demonstrations of what the poetic impulse feels like are unsatisfactory; it is doubtful whether durability can be imposed on the transitory and the evanescent. Vitally evocative poetry is the essence of innumerable apprehensions of experience. But one must admit that, in the long run, those apprehensions don't provide much to write home about. My own belief is that none of us have many things to say which are inherently memorable. Those few things are a condensation of our simplified humanity, and most of them can be traced back to childhood. They belong to what a living poet has called 'the mighty motherhood of sense', and should be used with economy and discretion. Meanwhile I mistrust random improvisings, even when performed by the pioneering genius and bright vocabulary of a Sandburg. 'Explanations of life' should be evolved and stated once and for all, not incontinently ejaculated in blissful immunity from the restrictions of versecraft. For this 'poetry of the immediate present', invented, of course, by Whitman, is a medium which has deliberately abrogated finality of form. It has been rather nebulously described, by D. H. Lawrence, as 'the rapid momentaneous association of things which meet and pass on the forever incalculable journey of creation; everything left in its own fluid relationship with the rest of things.' Let us leave it at that. Being old enough to know my own mind, I prefer the controlled tranquillity of Collins' *Ode to Evening* to 'the seething poetry of the incarnate Now', which not infrequently emerges as over-elaborate hybridized prose.

*   *   *

On the evening of March 30th I arrived in Toronto, after twenty-three hours in the train, which was five hours late. Dishevelled and greatly overdue, I went straight to a big dinner party which was being given for me by Vincent Massey, who, by his high intelligence and wealth has done so much to foster the arts in Toronto. I was staying with Professor Pelham Edgar, a charmingly friendly but rather fatiguingly talkative man, who was in a flutter of excitemeut about my performance, which would be the central ingredient of a 'Benefit' for the poet Bliss Carman. I had casually assumed that I should be giving the usual reading to a moderate-sized audience, so I was horrified when Pelham Edgar told me that I was expected to lecture, for not less than half an hour, on contemporary English poets, in addition to reading my war poems. He had taken it for granted that I had some such lecture prepared. So after receiving a couple of newspaper men, being motored all round the town, and conspicuously entertained to luncheon at the Art and Letters Club, I retired to my bedroom with the prospect of delivering, to about twelve hundred people, within a few hours, an as yet unwritten lecture. Overtired as I was, the desperate situation seemed irretrievable. At this juncture, however, a helping hand arrived in the shape of my friend 'Toronto' Prewett, who had returned to his native place for a time after studying English literature at Oxford during 1919. I explained the plight I was in, and between us we vamped up a superficial conspectus of living British bards—Toronto's providential collaboration converting what had previously appeared an inevitable catastrophe into a light-hearted *tour de force*. I went to the Convocation Hall rather queasily sustained by his assurance that I should 'get away with it' more successfully by being bright and chatty than if I had composed a serious academic discourse. Fortunately for me, the audience was indulgent, and my impu-

dently unconsidered remarks were accepted as 'Toronto' had predicted. As usual, my war poems proved themselves extremely
effective. One of the newspapers compared me to 'an avenging
angel through whom the voice of slaughtered youth was speaking'. This was rather how I had seen myself, for I was becoming a
conscious performer, enjoying the sense of playing on the emotions of my hearers, though aware of a dangerous allurement
towards histrionic artifice.

On April 2nd I was back in Chicago, where I spent the next
fortnight as the guest of Mrs. Kellog Fairbank, experiencing a
good deal more than I could digest. My hostess was a person of
limitless vitality, large-hearted, and strongly democratic in her
political activities, which were, at that period, concentrated on
supporting the Presidential candidature of Mr. McAdoo. Magnificently good-natured, she appeared to have made up her mind to
present me with the freedom of Chicago and all that it contained.
There were moments when I should have liked a little less of it.
I dined with an opulent railroad director, lunched with a millionaire meat-packer (who asked me whether I was acquainted with
the King). I was shown over the stockyards, went to several
orchestral concerts, and the circus, and inspected two large lying-
in hospitals. I also had the privilege of being introduced to Jane
Addams, the notable social reformer, but it was a case of 'We met,
'twas in a Crowd'.

In the Fairbank household nothing ever stood still, least of all
the family motor-car, which afforded Mrs. Fairbank an outlet for
her breath-taking spurts of energy, whether she was rushing me
off to an evening party or bustling me forty miles along bumpy
roads to get a glimpse of the steel industry district at Gary. On
Easter Sunday I noted that I had 'met Raymond Robins at lunch.
He has been to Russia, and talked a lot about Lenin. This evening,
went to a party in a smart white and gilt apartment several stories
up. Children, cracker-pulling, and charades; everyone making a
deafening cackle. Had a flare-up with an old gentleman who compared Socialists to smallpox microbes, but refused to argue when
I said I liked Socialists. Rode with Mrs. Fairbank yesterday along
the Lake Drive, a regular watering-place tittup, on a capering
chestnut hack, wearing ridiculous borrowed gaiters.'

Siegfried's Journey, 1916–1920

During my last week in Chicago I 'done what the good Lord told me to do' four times. My main performance was under the patronage of the National Council of Jewish Women. On this occasion a large and finely serious audience stimulated me to a minor-prophet-like peroration about the martyrdom of the common soldier. Judging by my notes, my eloquence must have been somewhat inflated. That tendency to indulge in theatrical oratory was growing on me. Anyhow, the effect was beyond what I'd aimed at, for someone went into hysterics at the back of the hall. I also gave a reading at the Arts Club, to what my diary audaciously described as 'a crowd of dilettante prattlers'. A couple of appearances at ladies' clubs completed my campaign to impress anti-war convictions on a city of over two million inhabitants, speaking almost every language under the sun.

*   *   *

It was unfortunate that half my lecture engagements were crowded into the three weeks after April 7th. In consequence my nerves became overstrained, and there were times when I went on to the platform wondering whether I should get through my performance at all. On the way back from Chicago I spoke to about five hundred students in the Physics Lecture Hall at Cornell University. Three days later I gave a commentative recital from the stage of the Greenwich Village Theatre, which Pond had hired for my 'only public appearance in New York'. Columbia University and Vassar College followed in quick succession. My next effort, at the Free Synagogue, in Carnegie Hall, seems worth describing in detail. On that Sunday morning, I found myself sitting between two Rabbis, facing a congregation of more than two thousand. Behind the platform there was a heavy curtain with apertures in it, through which the cantors sang the service in magnificent voices. Rather floridly introduced by Rabbi Wise as 'our friend and teacher', I stepped to the lectern to read a selection of my poems, which was all that I had been asked to do. What happened then was entirely unpremeditated by me. The congregation looked prosperous and complacent. They antagonized me, and I decided that the Free Synagogue ought to be approaching its

Siegfried's Journey, 1916–1920

Maker in a less materialistic frame of mind. I myself was only there as a topical 'turn'. Rightly or wrongly, the service seemed to be an example of misplaced enterprisingness, though designed to make the Jewish ritual 'a living and up-to-date actuality'. Also I was in a state of suppressed irritability, and therefore liable to do something unexpected. Anyhow, rendered confident by the admirable acoustics of Carnegie Hall, I surprised myself by delivering a denunciatory address. The gist of it was that my hearers knew nothing about war, and would do well to remind themselves of its realities. It was as though some angry prophet in my remote ancestry had taken control of me. My recollection is that I spoke with stern and dispassionate ferocity. That may be only my imagination, but it was certainly my intention to do so. What the congregation made of it I do not know, but when I quitted the lectern, after reading some of my most scarifying poems with unfaltering intensity, the expression of Rabbi Wise's fine face suggested that I had lowered my popularity by several pegs, and, if still a teacher, was no longer a friend. Everyone then settled down to a long and elaborately-prepared sermon by the visiting Rabbi, whose proficient oratory worked up a prodigious peroration in which he indicated a series of significant events in history, concluding each one with 'the Jew was there'. Skilfully modulating his voice towards the culminating pronouncement, he finally informed us that, when the Last Trump sounded above the blood-red dawn of the Day of Judgement, the Jew would—as we had all anticipated—be there. Let me add that if, on that long-awaited and much-needed occasion, all the best of them are lined up, civilized humanity will be well represented, and the Recording Angel will have no cause for complaint.

In the evening I provided an entertainment at the MacDowell Club which proved so unadmonitory and whimsical that a lady came up afterwards to tell me that she would never again say that Englishmen have no sense of humour. On the following day I betook myself to Boston for my two final readings. The first was at Wellesley College, where my audience of young ladies was as charmingly appreciative as it had been at Vassar. After that I had to screw myself up to address the Poetry Club at the Harvard Union. Being by now thoroughly overtired, I wasn't at all looking forward to this occasion, especially as I had been told that there would be some strong militarist feeling to contend with. I was staying with Harold Laski, the most gifted of the *New Republic* group of writers who had done so much to help and encourage me. He was then at the height of his amazing youthful vitality, and eager to introduce me to the most interesting people in Cambridge. But I was too fatigued to profit by what should have been one of my most stimulating weeks in America. Anyhow, after allowing me a day in bed, he deposited me on the platform at the Harvard Union, and I managed to create a sufficiently favourable impression, though I gave the audience an uncompromising demonstration of my point of view. That no opposition became evident may have been due to the presiding presence of Miss Amy Lowell, who was mainly responsible for my being there at all. Although by no means in agreement with my opinions, she was a generous admirer of my work, and had written to tell me that I was the one man whom the Harvard undergraduates wanted to hear. After the meeting we spent a memorable evening in her beautiful library. Listening to her and Laski, I felt almost non-existent as a talker. They were a remarkably contrasted couple—he, small, boyishly brilliant, provocative in argument, and essentially generous and idealistic; she, stout and masculine, jocularly downright and dogmatic, smoking a long Manila cigar, and completely confident that 'Imagism' was the poetry of the future. At that time she was working on her monumental Life of Keats. She showed me her copy of his 1817 *Poems*, inscribed by him to Fanny Brawne (*F.B. from J.K.*). Thus ended my diminutive attempt to make known to Americans an interpretation of the war as seen by the fighting men. My belief that it was not altogether ineffective is based on the fairly numerous letters I received from soldiers who had been on the Western Front. They, at any rate, were grateful for what one of them called my great and caustic truths. And let it be remembered that the soldiers of the 1914–18 War were, time and again, the victims of what now seems to have been amateurish mismanagement and incompetence. It was at their expense that England taught herself how to wage modern warfare. Against this I made my individual protest. But I must now admit that it was just as well that she *did* learn!

XXI

After coming back from Boston at the beginning of May, I moved into a better set of rooms in Westover Court, hired a grand piano, and bought a straw hat. This signified an alteration in my plans. I had intended returning to England early in June, but had done nothing about booking my passage. I now discovered that all the liners to Europe were full-up until the middle of August. My original programme would have taken me to Washington and several other distant places where I had been asked to lecture. I had even thought of going to San Francisco for the Presidential Election—heaven knows why! Having realized that these activities would be the allies of a nervous breakdown, I now, with profound relief, cancelled everything and retired into private life. The piano, therefore, indicated a resolve to seek mental seclusion, while the straw hat symbolized an inclination to loaf about New York as an idle observer with a blank engagement-book. I was indeed feeling spiritually used up. For three months most of my days had been crowded to capacity with appointments, of which, it seemed, the only restful ones had been with my dentist, whom I had visited nineteen times. Staring at a carved eagle on the cornice of a lofty building with my mouth conscientiously agape, I had anyhow spent nineteen hours of compulsory quiescence. To my dentist the mouth that uttered war poems was merely an object for expert investigation.

I had only one friend in New York with whom I could really feel—and behave—like my ordinary self. It is true that this friend insistently regarded me as extraordinary, and had his own humorous views on what I ought to be like when behaving naturally. But in sympathetic and practical helpfulness he was unfailing. I have often wondered how it was that Providence, notoriously neglectful of inexperienced young men arriving alone in New York, should have come to my assistance by arranging that my nearest neighbour in Westover Court should be Sam Behrman, who was then working for the *New York Times* and doing odd jobs in journalism, and is now—I rejoice to say—S. N. Behrman, one of America's most conspicuous playwrights. During my first few days at Westover Court I knew of him only as a rather too diligently clacking typewriter in an adjoining flat. Tired and irritable, I probably resented the noise as a bit of a nuisance. If so, it was the only time Sam Behrman has been anything except a blessing to me.

Recalling him as he was when he introduced himself, I am confronted with a much slimmer version of the prosperous dramatist of to-day, whose face has amplified to magisterial benevolence, and whose demeanour has acquired philosophical composure. The years have made that face a map of kindliness and temperate sagacity. At six-and-twenty it was irrepressibly alert with the enthusiasms and acute inquiries of an actively discovering intelligence. His spectacles gleamed with lively intentions and his movements had a darting rapidity. He was, in fact, an able little Harvard graduate, and I assumed that his interest in me was mainly journalistic. His typewriter would clack out a vivacious article about me, and thereafter I should lose touch with him. No assumption could have been more mistaken. His purpose, as I realized almost at once, was to be useful. From the first I felt that I could confide in him, and from the first he did much to steer me through the perplexities by which I was beset. I had begun to dread the letters and telephone messages that awaited me every time I returned to my bare and dreary flat. Once I had gained the co-operation of Sam, I could carry them into his little room, with its untidy accumulation of books and papers and its pleasant atmosphere of work in progress. Greeted by his beaming countenance, I could fling myself into an arm-chair, light my pipe, and watch him run through my correspondence, which he illuminated with respectful or satirical comments. It wasn't possible for him to mitigate my surfeit of social liabilities, but he helped me to differentiate between the people who mattered and those whom I could safely disregard.

Above all, I could sit back and share his amusement at what he called my praeternatural popularity. When I complained of the redundance of Americans who wanted to meet me, he remarked that when I signed my contract with Pond I had been under a strange misapprehension. 'You evidently relied on him to protect you against publicity. I must warn you that he is not an organizer of anonymity. Pond has quite a prejudice against invisible celebrities!' This quizzical way of talking epitomized his conception of my character. He preferred to regard me as a quaintly trustful person on whom life was playing a series of practical jokes. Delighting in my supposed simplicity and unworldliness, he would warn me that unless I took care I should corrupt the immaculate atmosphere of Broadway by my Satanic subtlety and depravity. This had the inevitable effect of making me behave very much as he expected me to do. The personality evoked by him was an exaggerated rendering of my natural self when stimulated by someone sympathetic and intelligent. While with him, I became so voluble and engrossed in what I was saying that my limbs were liable to conduct themselves absent-mindedly. My movements were uncontrolled and precipitate; I fell over things, forgot what I was about, and continually fulfilled his idea of me as a begetter of absurd situations. Frequently, when I had done something which amused him, he spoke of me in the third person. For instance, after I had been in New York about a month, he discovered that I had not been to my publisher's office. 'He hasn't yet called on his publisher. Another example of his deeply-organized business instinct!'

Anyhow, the conjunction of Sam and myself created episodes which I could only call typical; they did not happen when I was with other people. There was one in a taxi-cab which has since become a cherished anecdote of his. One afternoon we were on our way through snow-shovelled streets to a Theatre Guild performance of Tolstoy's 'Power of Darkness', for Sam was eager to interest me in the technique of play-writing, of which I was totally ignorant. The taxi was ramshackle and rattlesome, and so small that when my legs were extended there was considerable pressure on the framework behind the driver. This leg extension was a mistake; it caused a comprehensive crack across the glass. The driver, a nimble and gnome-like little man, must have seen the crack reflected in his wind-screen. Instantly pulling up with a jerk, he jumped out, put his head in at the window, and shouted, 'Twenty dollars!' In the brisk exchange of repartee which ensued, Sam explained that I wasn't accustomed to travelling in midget taxi-cabs, and that my legs were subject to spasms of reflex action. After advising me to leave my legs at home next time, the driver agreed to accept ten dollars.

*   *   *

While writing these American chapters I have often indulged in comparisons between the crude experience and the proportions in which it emerges in the perspective of matured remembering. The experience, of course, was unreeled in an indiscriminative process of making what one could of it. Sam Behrman, therefore, was only visible among much else that must have seemed likely to be more memorably significant afterwards. Most of the people I was meeting were in some way successful or well known, while he had yet to prove his ability. To those who got a glimpse of him in my company, he was merely 'that little chap who goes about with Sassoon'. He himself would have been the last to foresee that he would ultimately become the main human fact of my visit to the United States. It would have been the same, even if he had remained an obscure journalist. For it is because of what he then was that I now find him superseding everyone else. At the same time I tell myself 'how like life it is'—the spectacle of my former unconsciousness, not only that he was a man with a notable career before him, but that he would mean so much to me in subsequent years.

In a previous passage I have suggested that highly-culti-vated New York society somehow failed to attract me. Those large polite luncheons and distinguished dinners, where I was among people of scarcely perceptible American accent, had brought me a sense of sterility. I much preferred to be sitting in the Algonquin Restaurant with Sam. There was little to be gained from conver-sing with ladies who knew all the latest inside information from the British Embassy at Washington, and bored me with superficial opinions about novels, plays, and pianists. From Sam in his shirt-sleeves, tapping out a column of publicity for an illiterate impres-ario who controlled half a dozen theatres, I got a feeling that I was in touch with the reality of New York. And the men he intro-duced me to—mostly writers and actors—were obviously doing something besides discussing second-hand ideas and the dispositions of their acquaintances.

Anyhow, as already indicated, my return from Boston was attended by a strong inclination to avoid high-class hospitalities and relieve my overtaxed nerves by playing the piano and strolling about the streets in a straw hat. It was at Sam's instigation that I moved to a larger flat; and when I helplessly remarked that if only I had a piano I should feel quite myself again, he picked up the telephone, and within twenty-four hours a magnificent instrument from Steinway's was being hoisted up the stairs. He was also responsible for a first experiment in story-writing which occupied me at that time. Without his conviction that I was capable of producing prose works I should never have attempted this. Encouraged by his ardent assumption that it would be a masterpiece, I began it with the deluded excitement of one who had never studied problems of construction and had yet to learn the difference between creative outline and completed manuscript. My chief character was a young English pianist who never quite came to life, and would have done better to have given his narrative in the first person. But I had resolved to cultivate a strenuous detachment from my subject matter. The scene was laid in New York, so I had plenty of material around me to choose from. Employing what I considered an effective constructive device, I began and ended the story with the pianist playing Bach's *Chromatic Fantasia*. This was intended to symbolize his spiritual pilgrimage, and Sam thought it a splendid idea. 'There are moments in the lives of men,' it began, 'when they are conscious only of the spirit within them, when that spirit, pausing on its journey, stands isolated between the known and the unknown, powerless to discern what shall be, yet serene in reconciliation with all that it has endured.' I then sailed on with 'In the dusk of a New York winter afternoon a young Englishman was playing the *Chromatic Fantasia* of Bach,' and so on. . . . In less high-flown language, the pianist was unaware of the emotional complications which awaited him when he arrived in America for his concert tour. The story described them. Looking at it now, I am surprised to see how easily I picked up the knack of fiction-writing. But as an attempt at a tragic love story it was a failure. Too emphasized and

explanatory, it was much overwritten and often slickly smart. I
only find it tolerable where it revives memories of the Broadway
background and epitomizes the collaborative quality of my companionship with Sam, who appeared as a subsidiary character and
whose influence pervaded the performance throughout.

At that period his critical judgement was as immature as my
own. As a literary adviser he was liable to lapses into magazine
mentality. Yet the seriousness with which he treated my story has
now become a touching recollection; and the ineffectual thing itself
is interwoven with the texture of our times together. I see myself
at the end of an evening's work, tilting my chair back from the
table on which the scribbled sheets are scattered. An uncurtained
window is open, and beyond the huddle of roofs an immense
moving-picture sign spells out the names of cinema stars, letter by
letter. (One of them, I remember, was Mary Miles Minter, whom
I freely associated with Mint Gum.) Listening to the familiar
drone and clatter of the unsleeping city, I am visualizing myself
as an unknown literary genius at the outset of his career. His name
will never be advertised in electric letters nine feet high; but
some day, perhaps, Westover Court will achieve discreet distinction as the location of his earliest endeavours as a novelist. (I am
told that it has been pulled down and that the site is now occupied
by the Paramount Building.) I go to the piano and play a few bars
of the *Chromatic Fantasia*, to which I frequently resort as an aid
to composition. Then Sam's nimble figure appears in the doorway,
and he tells me to 'stop those fumbled fugues' and come out for a
club sandwich at the Claridge. This was a crowded, cheerful
restaurant which gave me a comfortable feeling of emancipation
from intellectual responsibilities as a lecture tourist. It was, in
fact, a place frequented by people who might conceivably have
read the works of that expert and diverting author O. Henry, but
were unlikely to have heard of Henry James.

At the Claridge occurred one of those incidents which Sam considered characteristic of me. Sitting at a table on a narrow balcony
above the arena of the restaurant, we had finished and paid for our
supper, but were carrying on an animated discussion which was
causing me to perform unconscious operations with my legs. My
feet were on the ledge of the balcony, thereby exercising pressure

against a heavy box of floral decorations. When the box toppled off the ledge I had time to observe that it had just missed a large party of smoked salmon and lager beer consumers below. Sam snatched up his hat and hurried me away before the creator of the crash had been identified. When we were safely out on the sidewalk he remarked that my legs would end by getting him arrested.

XXII

Often, while reconstructing my transatlantic experiences, I have wished that I could more photographically remember what it all looked like. But when I think of Fifth Avenue the only visual response I get is the doorway of a famous photographer who exhibited my likeness to the passers-by for several weeks. (Wondering whether it did my reputation any good, I sometimes stopped to inspect my features; but I never observed anyone else doing so.) Even the outside of Westover Court refuses to reveal itself, though I have a hazy recollection of a few discouraged trees at the entrance. It seems that I must have been too much preoccupied for my sensory apparatus to absorb impressions. I can remember watching a terrific thunderstorm which lit up the roofscapes with daylight distinctness, but my nasal imagination fails to recover a single United States smell. And, as everyone knows, for bringing the past to life there is nothing better than a good smell, whether it be pungent or aromatic.

By the end of April I had ceased to bother about keeping a diary, so I am now a mere vehicle for the capricious revelations of an unaided memory which prefers not to take the situation too seriously. Entreating it to recover something important, I receive nothing in return except frivolities. For instance, I see myself sitting in the Untermeyers' flat on a very sultry June night. I have been invited to meet Amy Lowell. She is reading us her latest and longest Imagist poem. She does it with lively expressiveness, but it continues almost an hour. I fall asleep. Fortunately she attributes my closed eyelids to mental concentration. After that my irresponsible collaborator persistently incites me to give an account of my first game of golf in America. As the game ended in a somewhat unusual way, I feel justified in doing so.

Well, I was staying with John MacCurdy, an eminent psychopathologist, to whom I had been introduced by Rivers, though not—as J. J. Chapman might have assumed—as an object for professional investigation. MacCurdy had a delightful house about thirty miles from New York. We had motored out there,

and after an excellent but lazifying lunch he suggested the aforesaid game of golf. I warned him that, although my handicap
had once been six, I was completely out of practice. He assured me
that I should soon run into form, but I was feeling muzzy-headed
after my late nights at Westover Court, and it seemed unlikely
that my ball would run into anything at all except the rough. A
set of unfamiliar implements didn't improve my chances of success. My psychologist friend, by the way, was the most deliberate
golfer I have ever played with. His waggles were numerous, and
he performed each shot twice over, once with an imaginary ball
and then with the real one. His handicap was twelve, but his
monumentally serious attitude to the game has, possibly, brought
it a well-deserved reduction since that blazing hot afternoon on
the links of the Westchester County Club. Standing on the first
tee, I was glad to observe that the fairway, though bordered by a
jungle of unmown grass, was a wide one. Not wide enough for me,
however. Seldom can that course have been the scene of such
lunatic slicings, suicidal hooks, and excruciating toppings by a
visiting Englishman. On my way towards the first green, when
wielding a heavy iron among the wild flowers, I missed the globe
altogether. At the next attempt I struck it just far enough for it to
be undiscoverable. After that—apart from losing every hole—the
main feature of my game was losing balls. MacCurdy was well
supplied with new ones, but before we were half-way round he
was shaking the old ones from the base of his bag, and soon afterwards we had run out of ammunition. Except for the one he was
playing with, I had lost them all. We therefore returned to the
club-house. I happen to remember that on our way back he tactfully drew my attention to a Scarlet Tanager which was sitting in
a cherry-tree. It must be added that in our subsequent matches
my play improved, and once or twice I managed to defeat him.
But after that farcical first encounter he might well have decided
that I was too expensive a partner to be persevered with. Mac-
Curdy, however, was not only an optimist but an extremely
generous one.

★   ★   ★

It was at the end of the first week in July, when New York had become oppressively hot and I was wondering how to get away from it, that I received an invitation to stay with a man I had met but once and talked to for less than ten minutes. He was an elderly bachelor named Edward Warren, who had introduced himself at the end of my Wellesley College reading and had then suggested that he would be glad to see me any time I cared to come to his house near Portland, Maine. Several other agreeable people had offered me indefinite hospitality, and, like the rest of them, Mr. Warren disappeared from my mind until, more than two months later, he renewed the invitation. 'You can stay as long as you like and there will be no-one here but me,' he wrote. I was hesitating whether to make the three-hundred-mile journey when I remembered that he had told me he had known Robbie Ross quite well. It was probably this which settled the question, for there was a sort of freemasonry about having known Robbie. After a night in the train, I was met at the station by Warren with an old-fashioned horse carriage. While we drove along from Portland it already seemed as though I were having a proper holiday and had arrived at the end of a journey which had begun when I left England. On our way out of the town we had called at two or three shops to pick up hampers of provisions. There was something about this which I found comforting. People in New York didn't take their fish home under the back seat of a wagonette. Warren, in his loose linen jacket and wide-brimmed sun-hat, looked quite a provincial character, though in reality he had travelled all over Europe and was an honorary fellow of Corpus, Oxford.

The landscape, though it hadn't the cosy charm of our home counties, gave me a sense of being in a nice unenterprising neighbourhood where plain-minded families preferred to read the news once a week in the local paper. I was making the much-needed discovery that even in America life could be leisurely, that flies could buzz around a horse's ears as it clip-clopped along a dusty summer lane, and that washing could be hung out in the untidy orchards of low-roofed homesteads where dogs barked at passers-by from their barrels. When a chicken ran across the road, it looked oddly unrelated to the bird of similar species which Sam and I had consumed on the previous evening in the roof-garden restaurant of the Astor Hotel. Rumbling along in the wagonette, I contemplated a scene of human habitualness where the hours went their rounds with sensible deliberation and the forces of nature knew nothing about office routine and quick lunches obtained by putting fifty cents into a slot machine. In fact I was really in the country, and the flavour of it was wonderfully reviving.

Meanwhile I was listening with half my mind to Warren, who had begun a conversation which continued, with intervals for rest and recuperation, during the next four weeks. It was a sort of one-sided Platonic dialogue, for he discoursed unhurryingly in pages and paragraphs, and my unobtrusive responses seldom led to anything like a debate. It was obvious that what he wanted was the company of a younger man who would listen while he ventilated his literary and philosophic speculations. There were, of course, interludes of pleasant talk about people and unserious subjects, but on the whole his mind revolved on an immaterial plane, and I felt that I was learning quite a lot from him. He had wide and varied knowledge and finely cultivated taste, and had used much of his wealth in the service of the arts. Among other things, he was a famous authority on ancient Greek vases, and had acquired a superb collection of them for the Boston Museum. He was an excellent classical scholar, and spent much of his time studying Greek and Latin authors. Sensitive and sympathetic, there was nothing pedantic about him. Though a little long-winded, he was never tiring or tedious. The effect of all this was highly beneficial to me. It was an escape from the crowded exigencies and ephemeralities of the previous months. We had now reached Fewacres, and the provisions were being handed out to a servant. Once again I must confess to a defective memory, for I am unable to remember anything about Warren's servants except that their services were inconspicuous and efficient. The house was a moderate-sized one, and I don't think there were more than two of them. My host was a superfine organizer of luxurious simplicity. The perfect country food happened without any fuss. The only occasion on which he became eloquent on the subject was when we had blueberry pie for the first time. This was a new experience for me, so he was particularly anxious that I should appreciate its merits.

Siegfried's Journey, 1916–1920

In other ways the amenities of Fewacres showed how good
Warren was at devising a serenely civilized existence. The charm
of this philosopher's retreat was that it seemed to have been set in
its half-wild surroundings as naturally as a farmstead. The landscape was its garden, and the darkness of distant woods its boun-
dary. And the weather, creating an illusion that Warren had it,
too, under control, was worthy of the land of the Lotus Eaters.
'At this time of year', he remarked, 'the whole country is as
habitable as a room.' Conforming to his admirable habits, I
achieved the rapid recovery of physical fitness with which youth is
so miraculously endowed. The mental composure that accompanied it was to some extent promoted by Warren's resolute disregard of my war-poet personality. Not one word did he utter
about my lecture tour or its concomitant circumstances. He was
an intellectual autocrat, and my performances didn't interest him.
Every morning his mind was occupied with Plato, Lucretius, and
Dante. After lunch he usually had something to say about Shelley
and Wordsworth. And after dinner he liked to sit in a long chair
and watch the sunset sky. High thinking was the order of the day,
and I was immune from the anti-militarist vocation which had
involved me in such inordinate arguments and explanations. No
longer a self-conscious young man with a message, I listened to his
reflections on what he had been deriving from Plutarch and
Pindar, or drew him out about his New England ancestors, his
travels in Europe, and such pages of his youthful history as he felt
moved to relate. It was evident that he enjoyed my company and
was giving me the best of his mind. He had the temperament
which excels in intimacy with the young and finds fullest reward
from gaining their confidence. Though thirty years older than I,
and essentially a grave, grey-haired man of learning, he could
make me feel that I was with a person of my own age. He was
rather touchingly gratified when I addressed him with light-
hearted levity.

Considered in retrospect, the Fewacres episode affords me
special satisfaction because I believe it to have been memorably
delightful to Warren, in whose face I read signs that life had
not always been a happy experience for him. And I have learnt
(if I may be permitted a moment's moralizing) that for such

215

interludes of fortuitous felicity one must be deeply grateful. Mutability and misfortune cannot undo them. In the abysm of time they are gifts of fortune. Youth accepts them as its due, not realizing their value until long afterwards. But when they visit those who, like Warren, are worn and weary, a few weeks of unclouded happiness, enlivened by the discovery of a freshly unfolding friendship, are—well—let us say salutary, and moralize no more.

The word salutary reminds me that I have yet to explain the process by which I so quickly transformed myself from a jaded Westover Court story-writer to a specimen of sunburnt health. For this the Fewacres routine of up early and early to bed was primarily responsible. But what did me most good of all was the old white mare to whom I was introduced on my first morning. A relation of Warren's had sent her from Boston for the summer months, and she was leading a rather neglected existence, as he had given up riding. She was a gentle, aristocratic creature, and I thoroughly enjoyed grooming and making much of her. Every day, before the midday sun became too hot to be pleasant, I rode out, exploring the country 'with the slow motion of a summer cloud'. I am one of those people on whose minds riding produces a profoundly serenifying effect. The old mare smoothed me out wonderfully. In fact I am inclined to think that she was more to my liking than anything else I encountered in America. Anyhow, she was an antidote to what had disagreed with my constitution while fulfilling my half-frustrated contract with the Pond Bureau. Also she provided me with an active occupation during the long mornings while Warren was absorbed in Hellenic research. Not for me the well-thumbed lexicon or the difficult delight of Aristotle's Ethics. What I wanted was to be bronzed and brainless, to acquire the exquisite sensation of the after-effect of profuse perspiration, and to see the old mare improving in her coat as a result of my vigorous applications of the body-brush.

Another outlet for my energy was the river, which was less than a mile away across the fields. Compared with English ones, it was an unsophisticated river, lonely, swift-flowing, and somewhat besnagged by submerged trees. I went there after tea, when Warren had returned to his textual annotations, though now and again he would accompany me on an expedition in the canoe. I am not a strong or confident swimmer, and have often wished that I were. Here, I thought, was an opportunity to improve myself. After a few days I began to feel on better terms with the water, and decided to test myself by swimming to the other side. The river was only about a hundred yards wide, but the current was strong, and I had some difficulty in getting across. I had resolved to make for a point exactly opposite, where a tree was leaning half into the water. As I approached it I became breathless and aware of losing my nerve. At this moment one of my legs got entangled in a snag. (Those legs again, Sam would have exclaimed had he been watching me.) After sinking once I extricated myself and floundered wildly to the overhanging bank. When I had regained self-possession I gazed gloomily at the canoe and asked myself how I was going to get back to it again. Why, O why, had I risked my life in this deceitful New England river? Why hadn't Warren warned me that it was dangerous? (He told me afterwards that it had an evil reputation for drownings.) Then a bright idea dawned on me. I had exhausted myself by contending with the current. All I had to do was to drift with the stream. By this method I made a comparatively easy return journey. But my subsequent bathes were unventuresome and even pusillanimous. I felt that I could never be fond of that river again, charming though it looked with the evening sunlight blazing on its broad reaches as I paddled up its unfrequented, foliage-reflecting alleys with the water chuckling under the canoe.

XXIII

The last of my lecture tour press-cuttings is headed 'Great Liner Off Amid Scenes of Pre-War Enthusiasm'. The reporter described how 'floral wreaths of all sizes, boxes of flowers, telegrams, and other manifestations of good will, poured upon the ship through the morning hours for the 1,100 cabin passengers'. It must not, however, be supposed that any of the enthusiasm was expended on my own departure, which was as inconspicuous as I could have wished. I was merely seen off by Sam. Neither of us felt at all jolly about it, for the chances seemed to be against our ever meeting again. I had no expectation of revisiting New York (an assumption which has so far proved correct) and it appeared improbable that he would ever come to England. Somehow I couldn't foresee Sam as a successful writer. I felt that his abilities would be exploited and the winnings of his work appropriated by others (an assumption which has been falsified in spite of his incurably disinterested character). Anyhow, the lively scenes which we witnessed from an upper deck of the *Imperator* were almost entirely due to the presence among the passengers of a party of film stars. Steam launches cruised around the liner, containing vociferous devotees of the celebrities, who were acknowledging manifestations of good will by waving samples of the floral tributes which had been showered on them. When I asked Sam how much of it was spontaneous he replied that it was a hundred-per-cent spontaneous gesture of publicity organization. He added that by cultivating the acquaintance of the human species I could make a profound study of mental vacuity. (Since then he has made that investigation for himself as an eminent scenario writer at Hollywood.) When he went ashore I was consoled by the presence of Ben Huebsch, with whom I shared a cabin. For some years he had been a highly discerning publisher of good literature in America. I had found him one of the most likeable men I had met there, an opinion which has since been constantly confirmed.

There is much to be said for simplifying one's life. When

standing on the deck of the *Imperator* with Sam Behrman and
Ben Huebsch, I was between the two men who have, from then
till now, been my closest friends in America. Lack of enterprise
may account for this, but the fact remains that I have found them
fully adequate for my requirements. This affords me a sense of
thrifty satisfaction which is probably one of the clues to my
temperament. Meanwhile the *Imperator*, making a first voyage
since being allocated to the Cunard Company by the inter-allied
Governments who had confiscated her from the Germans, pro-
gressed in an unhurrying way, taking eight days to reach Southampton. I was feeling so healthy and full of pent-up energy that
when all the passengers were below having lunch or dinner I
used to run round the upper deck jumping the white railings like
a hurdle-racer, and on one occasion I startled Ben by swarming
quite a long way up a mast. Though only a few years senior to me,
his calmly judicious and benevolent personality somehow
prompted me to extravagantly juvenile behaviour. I enjoyed
making him wonder what monkey tricks I should indulge in next.
I can see his face now, with the large spectacles and expression of
humorous anxiety, when I looked triumphantly down from the
slippery mast which I was embracing.

I suppose that most people, while travelling on a large well-
behaved boat, are luxuriously detached from ordinary existence.
To this obvious sensation I surrendered unconditionally, well
supported by the weather, which was calm and cloudless. For the
time being there was no need to bother about anything. The
Atlantic was an interval between my seven months' absence from
England and a future which, when contemplated at all, persistently remained indefinite. Alone in my cabin in the cool of the
evening, I did sometimes wonder what I was going to do with
myself, for I had become doubtful of my aptitude for political
activities, and Sam's instigations towards story-writing had ceased
to stimulate me. All I really wanted was to go on being a poet, and
one couldn't make that into a whole-time occupation.

Mischa Elman's cabin was quite close to mine, and I often heard
him playing, envying him the continuity of his career. The
memory of those evening hours has a strange serenity: the drone
and thud of the turbines, the pad and patter of feet on the deck

above, the smell of new paint, the lapping of waves on the side of the ship, the sunset seen through my porthole; and Elman practising the Bach *Chaconne*. It must be that eloquent violin which has brought the scene back to me with such singular intensity, imbued by the vague physical richness and expectancy of youth. Memorable because those moments were set to music; and remembered as though I were watching in a convex mirror the tiny reflection of someone else—someone who could not foresee that he would one day have outlived the faculty of setting his meditations to music, someone whose future was predictable only as an unrestricted exploration of multitudinous emotions, and whose stock of self-knowledge was altogether negligible. Far removed indeed from the fireside autobiographer who with ever-pausing pen retraces the trivialities of twenty-five years ago from the period of chaotic decivilization towards which the *Imperator* was conveying him. In one of those pen pauses he asks what has happened to the opening chords of the Bach *Chaconne*, which could formerly announce that all was well with humanity as he understood it. In strength and simplicity the statement remains unassailable. But all it has to offer now is belief in a thousand years of reconstruction. And what earthly use is that to him? He wonders what his obsolete self would say if some prophetic presence came into the cabin and warned him that he would one day commemorate the next twenty-five years with a quotation from Ecclesiastes: *The heart of the sons of men is full of evil, and madness is in their hearts while they live, and after that they go to the dead.*

Ecclesiastes, however, was writing well over two thousand years ago, with an all-embracing pessimism as to the value of existence which I do not share. My quotation is a generalization on the state of things brought about by the Second World War. And if I could make my obsolete self listen to me, I would tell him to stick to his trust that somehow good will be the final goal of ill. For despair is death, and belief in life is the essence of it. And I would tell him, though he would secretly decide that I was merely maundering, that when approaching the grand climacteric one of his compensations would be a realization of the unassuming littleness of life in relation to the stately progress of the centuries. Why this should have become a consolation to me I am unable to explain. It is a feeling I get when reading the letters of a well-loved author. Turning a page, I find that he is writing a year later, and the sense of foreshortened action somehow comforts me. Nothing much had happened in those twelve months. Time had just gone gently on. Dullness and disappointment and disquietude have been wiped off the calendar as though they had never been there. One's own cycle of experience will be like that when seen in perspective. Nothing of any significance during long periods, though one may be interested in remembering what the weather was like. This is probably a symptom of growing old and unenterprising; but it also means a sensible acceptance of life in its true dimensions. Judged in proportion to universal human attitudes, our personal existence is no more than a solitary gesture—a repetition of immemorial behaviour. Once in his lifetime, perhaps, a man may be the instrument through which something constructive emerges, whether he be the genius giving birth to an original idea or the anonymous mortal who makes the most of an opportunity which will never recur. It is for the anonymous ones that I have my special feeling. I like to think of them remembering the one time when they were involved in something unusual or important— when, probably without knowing it at the time, they, as it were, wrote their single masterpiece, never to perform anything comparable again. Then they were fully alive, living above themselves, and discovering powers they hadn't been aware of. For a moment they stood in the transfiguring light of dramatic experience. And nothing ever happened to them afterwards. They were submerged by human uneventfulness. It is only since I got into my late fifties that I have realized these great tracts of insignificance in people's lives. My younger self scornfully rejected the phrase 'getting through life' as reprehensible. That I now accept it with an equanimity which amounts almost to affection is my way of indicating the contrast between our states of mind. The idea of oblivion attracts me; I want, after life's fitful fever, to sleep well.

*   *   *

Leaving my little bit of philosophizing to look after itself, I must now return to the promenade deck, where the film stars, in accordance with their custom, are consuming champagne in the middle of the morning and behaving with what may be described as an eminent exhibitional aloofness. The constellation consisted of four young women and one young man, in whom the selective acumen of the moving-picture-makers had discovered the qualities required for world-wide popularity. They were quite ordinary silly people, receiving enormous salaries for doing as they were told and making faces. Their fame was ephemeral; and their undistinguished style of speech accounted for the fact that, when film performers began to be heard as well as seen, these bright particular stars ceased to shine. Meanwhile they occupied the Imperial Suite of the liner, and their proceedings afforded continuous entertainment to the curiosity of their fellow passengers. Their associates were a trio of film company promoters or directors, from whose features one inferred that business transactions with them would be to one's disadvantage. I didn't at all like their looks, and to that aversion my cognizance of them would have been restricted but for a nightly event wherein they were prominent participators. This was a selling sweepstake on the mileage of the ship's run for each twenty-four hours. People bought tickets, and those which weren't blanks were auctioned. Ben and I used to get a lot of amusement from watching the affair, which had been taken charge of by the aforesaid financial experts, who sat at the end of a long table with the over-dressed actresses grouped around them in effective attitudes. In what they considered an ingratiating manner, these gentlemen addressed the meeting as though it were a large family gathering, indulging in sprightly gesticulation and badinage when inviting bids. The holder of the successful ticket usually received more than a hundred pounds. I cannot remember the technicalities of the gamble, but there must have been something behind it which invited criticism of the methods adopted. Towards the end of the voyage there were increasing signs of dissatisfaction from a rival party led by a dark-haired man and woman of dashing demeanour who might or might not have belonged to the class which lives by its wits. They resented the sweep being made into a private enterprise, and the tension was increased when, by an inopportune coincidence, one of the film people drew the winning number. On the penultimate evening

feeling ran so high that the lady leapt on to the table and in ringing soprano tones appealed for fair play, openly accusing the
auctioneers of being a couple of crooks. This vivid and dramatic
gesture naturally brought matters to a head. Instinctively revert-
ing to type, the assistant auctioneer, towards whom I felt a special
antipathy, grabbed a bottle by the neck. In the general confusion
which ensued there must have been the makings of a mêlée, for,
on the pretext of acting helpfully, I made a bee line for the bottle
grabber and soon had the satisfaction of sitting on his chest. I happen to remember that his collar came off, so I must have made
quite a thorough job of it. The ship's officers then intervened; the
protagonists were conducted to their cabins, and the selling sweep
for the day was declared null and void.

*   *   *

It needs no pointing out that there is an essential disparity
between being alive and memoirizing it long afterwards. But the
recorder of his vanished self must also bear this in mind, that his
passage through time was a confused experiment, and that
external circumstances had yet to become static and solidly discernible. An eminent Victorian has told us that we read the past
by the light of the present; concerning our means of interpreting
the present he said nothing, so I infer that he found it unreadable.
I myself am inclined to compare the living present to a jig-saw
puzzle loose in its box. Not until afterwards can we fit the pieces
together and make a coherent picture out of them. While writing
this book I have often been conscious of this process. In relation to
his surroundings my younger self seemed to be watching a play
performed in a language of which he couldn't understand more
than an occasional word. His apprehensions of the contemporary
scene were blinkered, out of focus, and amorphous as the imagery
of a dream. I have felt that throughout the journey described in
this book he was like someone driving a motor-car on a foggy
night, only able to see a few yards ahead of him. Nevertheless I
have contrived to reconstruct an outline which represents everything as though it had been arranged for him beforehand. I have
aimed at unity of effect, even when it entailed making him
appear somewhat stupider than he actually was, and have thus

created an illusion that the traveller was controlling his circumstances instead of being helplessly entangled in them. I can only suggest that somebody with more metaphysical ability than I can command should investigate this discrepancy between the art of autobiography and the rudimentariness of reality. Can it be that the immediacy of our existence amounts to little more than animality, and that our ordered understanding of it is only assembled through afterthought and retrospection? But I am overstraining my limited intelligence, and must extricate myself from these abstrusities.

Anyhow, in concluding this account of my impercipient past I am able to recover one authentic glimpse which shows that I was to some extent aware of the conjuncture I had reached in my career. On the day after his return from America the subject of this autobiography was walking slowly across Trafalgar Square. It was a Saturday afternoon, hot and brassy-skied. Not many people were about; the fountains were playing; he stopped to lean on one of the parapets. Lulled by the splash of the water, he asked himself what it was that he had come back to. His lecture-tour self was on the other side of the Atlantic, self-conscious and elated with success, a *tour de force* personality whose histrionic tendencies needed suppressing. No interviewers had awaited 'England's Young Soldier-Poet' when he arrived at Southampton. That object of public interest had ceased to exist. Dining at the Reform Club, he had felt as though he had never been away. It seemed probable that interest in war poets was on the wane. He felt a vague craving for reclusiveness and obscurity. Meanwhile almost everyone he knew in London was away from it, and Trafalgar Square had a vacant, out-of-season look. 'What, *you* back again? I didn't know you'd been away!' it appeared to be saying. In a moment of clairvoyance he realized that he had come to the end of the journey on which he had set out when he enlisted in the army six years before. And, though he wasn't clearly conscious of it, time has since proved that there was nothing for him to do but begin all over again. To that occupation let us leave him. Picturing him in the clear afternoon light, in his New York straw hat, with the National Gallery in the background, I can almost believe that I have been looking at a faded photograph.